Green lines
u & dil.   370.942/3

P £2.00

D0275135

FOUR HUNDRED YEARS OF
ENGLISH EDUCATION

Historians undertake to arrange sequences—called stories, or histories—assuming in silence a relation of cause and effect. These assumptions, hidden in the depths of dusty libraries, have been astounding but commonly unconscious and child-like; so much so, that if any captious critic were to drag them to light, historians would probably reply, with one voice, that they had never supposed themselves required to know what they were talking about.

The Education of Henry Adams, (1918) 382

FOUR HUNDRED
YEARS OF ENGLISH
EDUCATION

BY

W. H. G. ARMYTAGE

Professor of Education, University of Sheffield

UNIVERSITY OF OXFORD
DEPARTMENT OF EDUCATIONAL STUDIES
15, NORHAM GARDENS, OXFORD. OX2 6PY

SECOND EDITION

CAMBRIDGE
AT THE UNIVERSITY PRESS
1970

Published by the Syndics of the Cambridge University Press
Bentley House, 200 Euston Road, London, N.W.1
American Branch: 32 East 57th Street, New York, N.Y. 10022

First edition © Cambridge University Press 1964
This edition © Cambridge University Press 1970

Library of Congress Catalog Card Number: 78-85709

Standard Book Numbers:
521 07596 3 clothbound
521 09583 2 paperback

First published   1964
Reprinted   1965
Second Edition   1970

First printed at the Villafield Press, Bishopbriggs, Glasgow
Reprinted by photolithography in Great Britain
by Bookprint Limited, Crawley, Sussex

CONTENTS

CONTENTS

PREFACE TO THE FIRST EDITION

'What has the history of education always been?' asked Oswald in H. G. Wells' *Joan and Peter* (1918). 'A series of little teaching chaps trying to follow up and *fix* the fluctuating boundaries of communities . . . like an insufficient supply of upholsterers trying to overtake and tack down a carpet that was blowing away in front of a gale.' The winds of change were often not as forceful as he implied, nor have the teachers been quite as helpless. For Wells, and the traditionalists whom he opposed, tended to quote history at each other, and by so doing they evaded rather than illuminated the problems of growth and adaptation. Such special pleading often prevails where histories of education are centred round certain institutions or educational thinkers, relegating the influence of national policy, religious conviction and economic needs to the periphery. As a result little attention is paid to the way in which these affect schools and colleges, and indeed to the way in which schools and colleges affect each other.

Such attention is often impeded by the time lag between what is intended and what happens. Thus the effects of the Fisher Education Act (passed at the same time as *Joan and Peter* was published) have only just exhausted their impact, whilst the plans outlined in the last chapter of this book will have only really worked themselves out at the beginning of the next millennium —unless a millennium is ushered in before that time. This book sketches the historical determinants of English educational endeavour over the last four hundred years, and its development around certain recognisable turning points, in order that the student may acquire insight as well as information. Yet information has not been ignored, and to indicate where more can be obtained, bibliographical notes linked (at times perhaps too closely) with each chapter, are given. They do not include references to *Hansard* for, where necessary, the text gives day and month and year. Nor are full references given to various Royal Commissions or Select Committees, for which readers are advised to consult P. and G. Ford, *A Guide to Parliamentary Papers* (1953), *Hansard's Catalogue and Breviate of Parliamentary Papers 1696–1834* (1953), *Select List of British Parliamentary Papers 1833–1899* (1953), *A Breviate of Parliamentary Papers 1900–1916* (1957), *1917–1939* (1951) and *1940–1954* (1961). Similar statistical help can be found in B. R. Mitchell and P. Deane, *Abstract of British Historical Statistics* (1962).

Other bibliographical assistance can be found in the *British Journal of Educational Studies*: on educational periodicals by Asher Tropp (VI (1958), 151–155); on the history of English grammar schools by W. E. Tate (I (1953), 164–175; II (1954), 67–81, 145–165); on the history of science teaching in England by J. F. Kerr (VII (1959), 149–160); on the history of teacher training in England and Wales by N. R. Tempest (IX (1961), 57–66); and on the history of education in the British Army by T. A. Bowyer-Bower (IV (1956), 71–77). Moreover the Library Association issued in 1961 a *British Education Index* covering published work from 1954 to 1958, and another it is hoped will follow, whilst the National Foundation for Educational Research have published, under the editorship of Mrs. A. M. Blackwell, *A List of Researches in Education presented for higher degrees in the Universities of the United Kingdom and the Irish Republic 1918–1948* (1950); *A Second List . . . 1949–51* (1952), *Supplement I, 1952–53* (1954) and *Supplement II, 1954–55* (1956) and *Supplement III, 1956–57* (1958).

W. H. G. A.

PREFACE TO THE SECOND EDITION

A new final chapter, dealing with events since 1963, has been added, encompassing the Plowden, Dainton, Latey and Swann Reports and their implications.

W. H. G. A.

I

THE POLITICS OF PROTESTANTISM
1563–1603

I

At a dinner in Windsor Castle on 10 December 1563, some of Queen Elizabeth's principal officers of state discussed the news that some schoolboys had recently run away from Eton. Queen Elizabeth's former tutor, Roger Ascham, who was also present, observed that 'young children were sooner allured by love than driven by beating to attain good learning'. He sustained his point of view so well that Sir Richard Sackville, the Treasurer of the Exchequer persuaded him to expand his thoughts into a book. This Ascham did, but unfortunately died two years before it was published in 1570.[1]

Before the Windsor diners loomed a nightmare struggle with Catholic Europe: a nightmare which, with ideological mutations, most of their successors have had to face. To keep England Protestant, no instruments were more effective than its schools, and no subjects in these schools more illuminating than the 'holy languages', Latin, Greek and Hebrew. Some of them had either been, or were influenced by, exiles under Queen Mary. These exiles had returned to force the pace of their fellow countrymen in religion and politics. Many exiles were country gentry, who in various continental towns had improvised 'universities'—as at Strasbourg under Peter Martyr. 'They left,' as a modern writer has it, 'as a faction and returned as a party,'—aware of continental Protestant practice, with experience of living in a non-episcopal society. They were endowed with the virtues of a 'godly' life, based on 'godly learning'.[2] Such slogans they could further disseminate by a vigorous press, which inveighed against Romish survivals, like vestments, in the Elizabethan church.

One of the Marian exiles, John Foxe, published in 1563 the first English edition of his *The Acts and Monuments of Matters happening in the Church.* This anecdotal treasury for Protestants, popularly known as Foxe's Book of Martyrs, was bought by many clergymen for their churches where it was chained to the lectern and sifted for sermons. Almost all Puritan households turned to it as the standard authority for church history. To Catholics, Foxe's 'Golden Legend' was an affront, especially since in the prefacing calendar, martyrs took the places of saints. It went through nine editions before 1641 and three abridgements before 1615.

The Church of England also acquired, in the year 1563, two other powerful weapons: the Thirty-nine Articles and the Oath of Supremacy. The Thirty-nine Articles settled a controversy that had, with intermissions, been raging since 1536, when the Ten Articles were issued.[1] Since then, the Bishops' Book (1537), the Six Articles (1539) and the King's Book (1543) had tried in vain to provide a doctrinal formula. The Oath, imposed by 5 Eliz. c. 1 on 'all schoolmasters and public and private teachers of children', ensured that they recognised the supremacy of the Queen in church matters before receiving their episcopal licences to teach.[2] And, as an additional insurance, archdeacons and bishops were, annually and triennially respectively, to make visitations to ensure that 'lewd schoolmasters' were not 'corrupting religion'.

II

As the most important figure at the dinner, Sir William Cecil, Queen Elizabeth's principal Secretary of State, was especially interested in education. In 1561 he had entered upon what was to be a 37-year Mastership of the Court of Wards: a very superior kind of magistrate's court to manage noble children. At Cecil House in the Strand he set up what has been called 'the best school for statesmen in Elizabethan England, perhaps in all Europe'.[3] The education of the 'Queen's Wards', as these sprigs of the nobility were called, excited the sea-captain Sir Humphrey

Gilbert, Raleigh's step-brother, to send Cecil a scheme whereby they might be taught mathematics, geography, physics and surgery as well as moral philosophy, Greek, Latin, Hebrew, logic and rhetoric, as well as 'Spanish, Italian, French and High Dutch'. Gilbert proposed that their teachers might employ their leisure translating foreign works of science and scholarship, conducting experiments (and delivering an annual report on them), or 'setting forth some new bookes in printe, according to their several professions'. 'By erecting this Achademie,' Gilbert argued, 'there shal be hereafter, in effecte, no gentleman within this Realme but good for some what, Whereas now the most parte of them are good for nothing.'[1]

Cecil's interest in education was not so much doctrinaire (after all, he had stayed in office under the Catholic Queen Mary from 1553 to 1558), as political. His great opponent, Robert Dudley (created Earl of Leicester in 1564), had already exhibited a desire to marry the Queen even at the expense of involving England in continental entanglements. So, as time went on, Cecil not only built up a secret police, but devised a suitable version of events which was ordered to be taught in schools. One of his instruments was Christopher Ocland, a schoolmaster, whose account of the troubles antecedent in Elizabeth's accession, *Anglorum Praelia* (1580), was ordered to be used in grammar schools.

Cecil valued schoolmasters and used Thomas Ashton, who had refashioned Shrewsbury into the largest school at the close of the century, on confidential errands to Ireland. He was also kind to the Puritan Robert Browne, who taught in London without a licence and who took, with Robert Harrison, the first steps to separate from the Church of England. Browne's kinship with Cecil saved him from immediate arrest.[2]

III

The Papists fought back. That sharp maintainer of the old religion William Allen, after circulating in disguise during the years 1562–1565 exhorting the Catholics of Lancashire, Norfolk and Oxford not to conform, opened a seminary at Douai in 1568 to provide a substitute for the schools they could no longer enter. From Douai well over 400 secular priests poured into England, with Fathers Persons and Campion the vanguard of a new offensive launched in 1580 and 1581 to win back England to the fold. In the latter year, 23 Eliz. c. 1 made it high treason for anyone to reconcile or be reconciled with the Catholic faith and imposed a year's imprisonment on any schoolmaster who should absent himself from the parish church on Sundays or holy days. Keepers of private tutors were fined £10 a month, and informers on them promised a third share of the booty. Four years later, in 1585, 27 Eliz. c. 2 imposed the stigma of treason on any student at a continental seminary unless he returned to England within six months and took the oath of supremacy within seven days of landing.

The situation was perilous. The Catholic Mary Queen of Scots was imprisoned in England, Elizabeth herself was under sentence of excommunication, and in 1588, after Mary's execution, Philip II of Spain, attempted, unsuccessfully, to enforce the sentence. The Armada's failure only intensified the efforts of the seminarists. English colleges at Valladolid (1589) and Seville (1592) were established and so further restrictions were imposed in 1593 by 35 Eliz. c. 2 which forbade 'popish recusants' to move five miles beyond the compass of their homes without an episcopal or justice's licence.[1]

To prevent Irish students going abroad and being 'infected with Popery and other ill qualities,' and so becoming 'evil subjects' a College of the Holy and Undivided Trinity was chartered in Dublin in 1592. It had been mooted by the first Protestant Archbishop in 1536 and by Cecil himself in 1563. But whether, in describing it as 'The Mother of a University' the Crown intended further colleges to be founded is obscure. The first Provost reinforced the intention of the founders by telling the leading citizens of Dublin that from henceforth they need not hazard their children abroad 'for the acquiring of foreign accomplishments.' The hazard in the Elizabethan ages was very real, since Popery and treason were then synonymous.[2]

4

IV

Cecil had other agents too, in his policy of securing the Protestant succession. The attorney of the Court of Wards was Robert Nowell,[1] one of whose brothers, Alexander, Dean of St Paul's, wrote the 'Small Catechism' now virtually embodied in the Book of Common Prayer, whilst another, Lawrence, an enthusiastic map maker, proposed in 1563 that maps should be made of all counties, a task subsequently undertaken by Christopher Saxton in 1579.

It was Alexander Nowell who, in a sermon before Elizabeth's second parliament in 1563, suggested that the revenues of one abbey in each shire should be set aside for the encouragement of scholars. The Speaker of the House also complained of the 'want of good schoolmasters' remarking 'the tree of knowledge groweth downwards, not upwards'. Bills to remedy this had been introduced in 1549 (twice) and 1553 (twice), but so far nothing of substance had been done.

The tree of knowledge was, however, being watered by the fount of private charity, tapped by pulpit orators like Alexander Nowell. *Certaine sermons appointed by the Queen's Majesty* (1563) and *The second tome of homelys* (1563) stressed the 'stewardship' of riches by directing attention to the needs of the poor. These convinced Protestant merchants, especially in London, that poverty bred ignorance and Popery.

They had been generous in the century before Queen Elizabeth's accession, but (taking account of the price rise) they were even more generous in the century that followed. No less than 109 endowed schools and 49 unendowed schools were founded all over England by London merchants alone. In London itself, the generous provision made for St. Paul's School in 1512 by the Mercers' Company was emulated by others, so that fourteen schools were established which afforded an education 'probably the best (then) available in the Western world'.[2] These fourteen schools catered for five to seven per cent of the male population of the metropolis.[1] And, to supplement them, another fifteen grammar schools were founded in Middlesex.

Similar educational insurance against Popery was also manifest in all but six of the English counties. In Lancashire, Cheshire, Shropshire, Staffordshire and Herefordshire they established another 44 grammar schools. Another 72 grammar schools, with four in Wales, two in Scotland and one in Calais, gave the impressive total of 153 foundations established by them between the years 1480 and 1660. 'Perhaps even more truly than the great Queen,' a recent American historian has written, 'these enlightened and responsible London merchants were responsible for winning the west for Protestantism, and for giving to the region the social and cultural institutions required for life in the modern world.'[2]

In addition London merchants strengthened 141 existing foundations in the provinces—more than half of which had been established by local generosity. They provided 57·7% of the total endowments given by the rest of England. The extent of their generosity was such that they have been called 'in a true sense the founders of the endowed schools of England,' who made 'freely and readily available new channels for ability and ambition across the whole terrain of the society'.[3]

Similar donations by Protestants in Bristol, Buckinghamshire, Hampshire, Kent, Lancashire, London, Norfolk, Somerset, Worcestershire, and Yorkshire, brought the total up to 542 schools. Indeed in these ten counties, there was an endowed grammar school for each 6,000 of the population. No boy lived more than twelve miles from a grammar school where he could obtain a free education.[4]

This flow of charity increased in Elizabeth's reign. Thirty-two schools were founded, among them Rugby (1567), Bedford (1565) and Aldenham (1599), which amply repaid the total of £32,530 expended on them. These schools took boys between the ages of 6 and 8 and kept them until they were fit to enter Oxford or Cambridge at the age of 14 to 16. And by 1600 every boy, even in the remotest part of the country, could find such a school in his own neighbourhood competent to do this.

These charities received massive protection in 1601 as a result of the Statute of Charitable Uses (43 Eliz. c. 4). This Act marks the emergence of the secular charitable trust. Previous trusts for prayers or 'superstitious' purposes had been outlawed in the time of Henry VIII. Now, services like education, care of the sick and the maintenance of highways and bridges could grow under this Act. For, if abused, the Act empowered the Chancellor to appoint a commission to inquire into their use. In interpretation of the Act, the courts developed the principle of *cy près* (as near as possible), to ensure that whatever the ambiguity, the charity should remain for public use rather than private enjoyment. For the next 287 years the procedure it laid down remained standard, whilst its preamble is still valuable today.[1]

V

As the grammar schools multiplied, increasing numbers of boys proceeded to the universities, helping them rapidly to recover from the bewildering changes of the previous twenty years. Cecil himself became Chancellor of Cambridge in 1559, and Lord Leicester of Oxford in 1564, by which year the number of residents at Cambridge increased to 1,267; those at Oxford being rather less than two-thirds of this. Young dons abounded; according to H. C. Porter there never can have been a period at Cambridge when there were so many of them.[2] These young Cambridge dons added their voices to those of the Marian exiles outside protesting against vestigial Romish practices in the Reformed Church. Some of them, like Thomas Cartwright, the Lady Margaret Professor of Divinity, went further and aimed at eliminating the entire episcopal system, and setting up in its place an austere Genevan regime, with elected pastors and governing by elders. For this Cartwright lost his chair in 1570.[3] Embryo forms of these minuscule theocracies arose amongst them, as the *classis.* Here were the germs of Presbyterianism and within ten years from the Windsor dinner, the word 'Puritan' was being used to describe the activities of these young theocrats.

After Cartwright's expulsion in 1570, the freer spirits of the universities, whose piety had been moulded by him or by his successors, Laurence Chaderton or William Perkins, scorned the institutional security of a living, preferring instead to be mendicant preachers. These preaching ministers, descanting on the Geneva Bible of 1560, grew in number. When homilies were issued to be read from the pulpit, they took to the press with such vigour that from being an adjunct to the pulpit it became an autonomous educational medium. Two fresh Cambridge nurseries of these 'lecturers' were created in 1584 when one of the Windsor diners, Sir Walter Mildmay, built Emmanuel College Cambridge on the site of a dissolved Dominican House, a foundation sustained by gifts from London merchant princes like Henry Billingsley and Sir Wolstan Dixie; and Sir Philip Sidney's aunt, the Countess of Sussex built another, Sidney Sussex College, on the estate of the Grey Friars.[1]

The ageing Queen in 1593 appointed Thomas Nevile to the Mastership of Trinity (founded by her father 47 years before). Nevile ruthlessly removed rows of houses and old buildings to build his magnificent great court, and enriched its library by taking many fine books from Canterbury Cathedral.

One of the last acts of the Great Queen was to accord to the universities the right to send representatives to Parliament, a right petitioned for by Cambridge since 1566 and Oxford since 1570. Whether they feared for their own corporate security (accorded them under the Crown in Parliament in 1571), or whether the Puritan faction wanted a political base from which to resist restraints, the universities did not rely on graduate members of Parliament (36 in 1563, 106 in 1593), to represent their point of view. They retained their right to send members until 1948.[2]

The spirit of the Elizabethan universities, especially of Cambridge, was to find expression in the institution of the American colonies. Indeed, William Perkins, who died in 1602, exercised in the seventeenth century an influence almost as great as his great master Calvin and by 1610, his *Armilla Aurea* (1590) had reached fifteen editions. There the *classis* came into its own.[1]

VI

Anti-monastic, the Puritan code expressed itself in long diaries rather than auricular confessions, records of coming to grips with the world rather than running away from it. The parable of the talents was, to the preachers, a divine endorsement for labouring in one's vocation. So it was no accident that endowments for education spouted from an economy flexed by technological change. Here, too, 1563 marked an era: a patent for using water power to drain mines and crush ores was granted to Burchard Kranich (one of many such German miners in England at this time), whilst John Trew began his famous lateral cut beside the Exe which led to his pioneer pound lock; heralding a new technique of water transport in England. Mining, navigation, river improvement and the building of Elizabethan country houses stimulated mathematics. Robert Recorde, author of the outstanding English introduction to astronomy, *The Castle of Knowledge* (1556), wrote:

It is confessed amongeste all men, that knowe what learnyng meaneth, that besides the Mathematicalle artes, there is no unfallible Knowledge, excepte to bee borowed of them.[2]

Mathematical knowledge was fostered by the same shrewd patrons of universities. Thus Henry Billingsley, a haberdasher with interests in coal mines, who was later to become Lord Mayor of London and endow scholarships at Emmanuel and St John's Colleges Cambridge, published an English translation of Euclid in 1570 with a preface by Dr. John Dee.[3] This declared that mathematics would 'assist the common artificers' who with 'their owne Skill and experience already had, will be hable (by these good helpes and informations) to finde out, and devise, new workes, straunge Engines, and Instrumentes: for sundry purposes in the Common Wealth'. Another London haberdasher, Thomas Smith, took the lead in raising funds to endow a mathematical lectureship in London, the first lecture being given in his own house, and subsequent ones in the chapel of the Staplers' Company.[1]

Dee owned the largest scientific library in England at this time: some 4,000 volumes of medieval manuscripts and contemporary mathematical texts.[2] From 1560 to 1583 it was the scientific centre of Elizabethan England. Dee was a friend not only of Billingsley and Thomas Smith, but of most of the explorers as well: amongst his pupils were Thomas Digges, Muster-Master General to the English forces in the Netherlands, Sir Edward Dyer and Sir Philip Sidney—to whom he taught chemistry.[3]

Dee's greatest significance was his conception of what he called *Archemastrie*. As he defined it in the preface to Billingsley's Euclid:

The Archemaster steppeth in, and leadeth forth on, the *Experiences* by order of his doctrine *Experimentall*, to the chief and finall power of Naturall and Mathematicall Artes.

It was a great pity that his boundless optimism about the powers of *Archemastrie* led him to turn his efforts towards alchemy.

His apprehension of the experimental method should be set beside the way in which the common artificers responded to his work. Robert Norman, maker of mathematical instruments, said as much in his *Newe Attractive* (1581). So did Edward Worsop in his *Discouerie of Sundrie Errours committed by Landemeaters ignorant of Arithmetike and Geometrie* (1582).

Schoolmasters followed suit. Richard Mulcaster, the first headmaster of the Merchant Taylors' School in London from 1561–86, and later headmaster of St. Paul's from 1596–1608, argued in 1581 that the study of mathematics should begin as early as possible. He also proposed a separate mathematical college at the university and contemplated writing a book on the teaching of the subject.[4]

For just as some of the young Puritan dons wished to strip the

Church of Romish vestments, so others wished to strip Nature of the various masks that prevented the understanding of her ways. For new sciences were being generated by the constant marriage of theory and practice. Going up to Oxford in 1570 Richard Hakluyt acquired a passionate interest in maritime affairs and from there published his first book twelve years later. Others like William Barlow (whose knowledge of magnets is said to have antedated William Gilbert's by twenty years), Sir Henry Savile (who in 1621 endowed lectureships in geometry), Thomas Allen (the mathematician friend of John Dee the alchemist), his pupil Thomas Harriot (one of the geniuses of the age), Nathaniel Torporley, Sir John Davies (later surveyor of ordnance) and John Thornborowe (the chemist-bishop), warrant a recent American opinion that 'Elizabethan Oxford seems to have been in some respects more active in these matters than Cambridge'.[1] Cambridge men like Henry Briggs (of the logarithms), would have acknowledged this, for he wrote in 1619: 'I would very gladly have hope that Cambridge would follow apace as I have that Oxford will go further.'[2] But Cambridge was to produce four of the first six Savilian professors of geometry and astronomy at Oxford.

A third quasi-university took shape in England as a result of the generosity of a London merchant, Sir Thomas Gresham. In 1597 eighteen years after his death, Gresham College took shape near the Royal Exchange, offering lectures on astronomy and geometry to 'the greatest part of the inhabitants within the city who understand not the Latin tongue'. The first professor of geometry, Henry Briggs, drew up a table of logarithms, was an engineer and a helper of others, subsequently moving to Oxford as the Savilian professor of geometry.[3]

VII

The year 1563 also marked a decisive step to ensure stability in the economic field. To supply farming and ancillary crafts with the necessary manpower (for agrarian stability ensured a food supply as well as a stable social order), the Statute of Artificers (5 Eliz. c. 5) imposed upon some thirty crafts a seven-year period of apprenticeship. This made national what had hitherto been local practice, and the authority of the guilds was supplemented by rewarding informers with a share of the penalty imposed for breaches of the statute.[1]

These informers were embryo versions of modern inspectors. Men like Andrew Holmer in Devonshire and the aptly named John Leake of London were almost professionals. Though virtually exiled from Westminster after 1624, they lingered on as instruments of law enforcement until 1951. Had the legal machinery they invoked been really effective, the growth of industry would have been seriously restricted. That their effectiveness steadily declined was due to the growth of crafts where no capital or connection was required; and, where it was, to the merging of such crafts into the larger companies of late Elizabethan and early Stuart times. 'Tis good there should be informers in a commonwealth,' observed a contemporary, 'as in houses we keepe dogs to discover theeves.'[2]

A second great step in the welfare, as opposed to the warfare, state was taken in 1601 by the Elizabethan Poor Law (43 Eliz. c. 2), which remained for 233 years the basis of public provision for the poor. This conferred on churchwardens and overseers of the Act the power to apprentice pauper children between the ages of 5 and 14, until the age of 24 (in the case of men) and 21 (in the case of women). This power was subject to the consent of two Justices of the Peace. Though private charity humanised this system, it lingered on to provide in the following two centuries not only the personnel for the navy (after 1704), but cheap labour for the factories (until the Factory Acts of the nineteenth century).[3] Both this and the apprenticeship system of 1563 were supplemented by craft or trade schools run by town corporations. Such schools for nimble-witted clothiers, knitters and shoemakers established in, amongst other places, Lincoln and Leicester, were the real ancestors of our present technical schools.

VIII

These two statutes (and many another), added to the burdens of the Justices of the Peace, those unpaid administrators of the age. Apart from gratuitous admonition offered by such writers as Sir Thomas Elyot in *The Governour* (1531) and Sir Thomas Hoby in his translation of Castiglione's *The Courtier* (1561), such 'virtue and learning' as they acquired came, not so much from the universities, as from their attendance (if it can be so called), at the Inns of Court.

The Inns were closely connected with the Windsor diners. Gray's Inn, especially, was their family training centre. Here William Cecil's two sons and son-in-law, Sir Nicholas Bacon's five sons, Sir Francis Walsingham, his son-in-law, Sir Philip Sidney and Lord Howard of Effingham were all to be members. And members joined to dine with the great and influential, not to suffer the tedious ritual of 'moots,' 'readings' or 'lectures.' Wit and gallantry were more important than pedantry and bookishness. Like Mr Justice Shallow's contemporaries, many cadets were 'swingebucklers'.

'There are now more at the bar in one house,' said Christopher Hatton in 1588, 'than there were in all the Inns of Court when I was a young man.' The dramatists of the day capitalised on this by writing masques, revels and plays for them. Shakespeare knew Gray's Inn well for his *Comedy of Errors* was acted in their hall.[1]

As Lord Burghley's nephew, Francis Bacon, later remarked in his *De Augmentis*:

I am clearly, in favour of a collegiate education for boys and young men; nor in private houses, nor merely with schoolmasters. For in colleges there is greater emulation of the youth among themselves.

Preoccupation with precedent and the importance of facts set in their proper historical context were fostered by attendance at the Inns. Men like Edmund Plowden, Sir Simonds d'Ewes and Sir

Christopher Hatton were to garner wisdom from the past, whilst John Selden and Francis Bacon were to make history by writing it.[1] Bacon was to make history in another context too, for in a masque he wrote for the festivities planned by Gray's Inn at the end of 1594, he depicted a Prince taking advice from various councillors, one of whom urged him to found 'a most perfect and general library,' a 'spacious and wonderful garden,' 'a goodly huge cabinet' and a still house or laboratory furnished with 'mills, instruments, furnaces and vessels, as may be a palace fit for a philosopher's stone'. This advice Bacon was powerfully to amplify in the following century, offering a message that the country gentry were to find more profitable than dinners at the Inns. He was but two years old when Sir William Cecil and his fellow-officers of state had nonchalantly discussed the absconding Eton schoolboys. Now he was to be himself a great officer of state, but there was to be nothing nonchalant about his plans for the advancement of learning, which he first published in 1605.

II

SUITS FOR SCIENCE

1603–1660

I

The sharp rise in endowments under the Stuarts is best symbolised by that of Thomas Sutton. As Master and Surveyor of Ordnance in the north of England he made a fortune from exploiting the Durham coalfield and gave £130,000 of it to establish an almshouse and school in the old property of the Charterhouse. His heirs contested this, enlisting Sir Francis Bacon to argue that the proposal would disturb the balance of recruitment for farming, and if charitably bestowed, the money should really go to the universities.

This last was an argument more in Bacon's line. For he was a believer in the redemptive potential of science. As he later argued, mankind could recover what it lost by the Fall if it could but unlock nature's secrets. God could thereby be magnified in the elucidation of his works. As endowments showered down on grammar schools and universities, Bacon considered what foundation could best serve the end he had in view, the advancement of 'the arts'. Such 'new arts, endowments, and commodities for the bettering of man's life' could in his opinion, only be won by 'kindling a light in nature,' through experiment. He despaired of existing colleges, where knowledge was 'as it were imprisoned in the writings of certain authors, from whom if any man dissent, he is straightway arraigned as a turbulent person or innovator'.

So he asked King James to finance a good encyclopaedia, and in an appendix to his proposal, sketched an institution in which it could be compiled. The sketch for this institution was issued by his secretary Dr Rawley as the *New Atlantis*.

Here, in the guise of Solomon's House, Bacon sketched a

gargantuan research establishment, a series of conservatories, laboratories, engines, gardens, anatomy theatres, sound houses and furnaces where, by experiment, man could enlarge the bounds of his empire 'to the effecting of all things possible'. Experiment, in the *New Atlantis*, was a hierarchical operation. Abstracts, brought from abroad by the Merchants of Light were to pass to Depredators to collect in books, then to Mystery Men to tabulate, and then to Pioneers to try new experiments. The results of these new experiments were to be passed to Compilers to reorganise knowledge in the light of the results, then to Dowry men to elucidate things of 'use and practice for man's life'. Then higher officials still, called Lamps, were, after many 'conferences,' to direct more searching experiments, to be carried out by three Inoculators. Finally, three Interpreters of Nature were to draw out 'axioms and aphorisms'.

If Bacon's injunctions had been heeded, Britain might have escaped the Great Rebellion.[1]

II

Bacon was not so much rapping at a locked door as beckoning in the vestibule behind one already open. His contemporaries, William Gilbert of Colchester, who had derived great stimulus from the navigators for his work on magnetism, and William Harvey, by using the analogy of the pump to explain the heart's role in the circulation of the blood, showed what the craftsman could contribute. Moreover, an increasing desire to discover 'natural magic' by institutional research had been stirring men's minds. 'Secrets,' and 'engines of perpetual motion' had been offered to Queen Elizabeth by Edmund Jentil, who tried to get out of gaol by offering to reveal 'a device whereby a vessell of burden may easlye and safely be guided both against winde and tide'. Ralph Rabbands had also offered her 'the rarest engine that ever was invented for sea service' that would 'passe upon the seas and ryvers without oars and sayle, against wynde and tyde, swifter than any that ever hath been seene,' together with 'flying fyres' and 'firy chariotts'. Rabbands proposed in 1574 that an academy or college should be established at public expense where 'ingenious, politic and learned men and apt artificers' could work. Henry Marshall proffered 'an engine which shal breake the aray of anye battell being ready to joyne'. In 1603 a book of inventions was dedicated to James I: one being a machine which would 'convey the voice for a thousand paces without showing any one near you were talking'.[1]

Groups of like-minded scientists were also no new thing, and were already in being not only in England but in Italy, France, Germany and Denmark. Even in prison the Earl of Northumberland and Sir Walter Raleigh maintained their own laboratories and contacts with mathematicians like Thomas Harriot. Shakespeare may possibly have satirised this 'School of Night' in *Love's Labour's Lost*.[2] For when Raleigh was imprisoned in the Tower in 1603, Harriot joined the 'Wizard' Earl of Northumberland, with Robert Hues, another intrepid voyager who had accompanied Thomas Cavendish round the world. Another group had foregathered round Sir Hugh Middleton, the builder of the New River in London. It began on 15 October, 1613, as a society of free candid enquiry where religion and politics were banned and a century later became the Robin Hood Society.

Several moves were made to institutionalise such groups. In 1617 Edmund Bolton secured the support of King James I for an Academe Royal of letters and science at Windsor, and by 1624 he actually had 84 working members or 'essentials' appointed, one of whom was Sir Tobie Matthew, a friend and correspondent of Francis Bacon, and an ardent Papist, who wished to see the Catholic Hierarchy re-established. The death of the Duke of Buckingham, however, put an end to Bolton's scheme.[3] A second scheme, proposed by Sir Francis Kynaston in 1635 envisaged a Musaeum Minervae, in Bedford Street, Covent Garden, where a knowledge of medicine, music, astronomy, geometry, languages and fencing could be acquired. But the universities and shortage of money killed this.[4]

III

King James himself was preoccupied with his own grand design: a college in Chelsea, where learned divines could hammer out a truly Erastian theology. Hammering was the operative verb, for one of the fellows exuberantly proclaimed that he would 'loosen the Pope from his chair were he fastened thereto by a tenpenny nail'. A collection from all the churches in the kingdom was set on foot to build and maintain it, a futile gesture as the cost almost swallowed up the amount collected. Begun in 1609, Chelsea College was a virtual white elephant from the start, but it was to figure in many subsequent schemes for educational reform.[1]

Meanwhile, the grammar schools were producing an educated laity, who demanded sermons rather than surplices, and were prepared to pay lecturers to deliver them.[2] This suited many of the young graduates from the universities who were being produced in numbers greater than the Church could find places for.[3] Ordinary churchmen, as James I reluctantly acknowledged in 1616, were despised by 'people of all degree from the highest to the lowest'. So the Puritan lecturers had much to complain of: pluralism co-existing with poverty in the Church, and sale of offices in the state.[4]

If the novice lecturers were 'initiated' at the universities, their practical training ground was St Antolin's in Bude Row, London, where daily lectures were given by them, to which citizens were summoned at 6 a.m. by an hour-long ringing of the bells. These lectures, founded in 1559, became after 1617 a spiritual staff college for the Puritans. Another occupant of a London living, to which parishioners enjoyed the right of presentment— All Hallows Broad Street—Richard Stork, suggested that a society should be formed to buy up presentations, advowsons and lay impropriations. The idea, mooted since 1612, was adopted and developed in the year of his death, 1626, when four merchants, four lawyers and four clergymen joined together to do so. They called themselves the Feoffees for Impropriations and they also took over the management of the St Antolin lectures as a training centre. The Feoffees for Impropriations could now side-step episcopal restrictions, using the revenues to sustain not only lecturers but schoolmasters of their own choice. By 1630 they were so successful that the Royal Chaplain, Peter Heylin, foresaw that 'they would have more dependencies than all the prelates in the kingdom'. So in 1633, Laud, who had brought Oxford to heel, ordered them to dissolve and meet no more, yielding their purchases to nominees of the crown.

But the ingenuity of the Feoffees was not exhausted. Two of them were members of the Dorchester Company, two of the New England Company and four of the Massachusetts Bay Company: all having, as their object, the founding of a Godly Commonwealth in the American Colonies. Laud's dissolution of the Feoffees led some to emigrate. Others who remained, harboured justifiable grievances.[1]

In the case of schoolmasters, a simple solution presented itself: the private school. These now began to take shape in the Puritan purlieus of London, like Rotherhithe, where Thomas Gataker started a school in 1611 with Thomas Young, a tutor to Milton, as one of his assistants. Another Puritan divine who opened a private school, at Aldermanbury, about 1619, was Hezekiah Woodward. In *Of the Child's Portion* (1640) Woodward advised parents 'Nothing comes into the understanding in a natural way but through the senses . . . Make the child not a hearer only but a *party in the business . . . Speaking wholly is lost labour*'. His realistic attitude to education owed as much to Bacon as to the Presbyterians, whom he later deserted to become an independent. Non-puritan private schools existed too: one of the most successful being that in Goldsmith's Alley, London, opened by Thomas Farnaby, who voyaged with Drake, was a friend of Ben Johnson and died in 1647.[2]

An 'academy for the mute' was recommended by John Bulmer in *Philocophus or the Deafe and Dumbe Man's Friend* (1654). He proposed to teach them the visible language of signs and gestures, reading of the lips, and the enjoyment of music through the teeth. In an earlier treatise, *Chirologia* (1644) he had discoursed on the 'language of the hand' giving types of 'chirograms' to illustrate his meanings.

IV

At this stage a fresh stream of inspiration came from abroad, not this time from Geneva but from Elbing, in North Germany in the person of Samuel Hartlib who was a Baconian first and Puritan second and opened a school at Chichester, leaving it in 1630 for Duke's Place, Holborn, where, for the next 30 years, he maintained a one-man intelligence agency, not only for England but at times for Europe too. He fused religious and scientific aims, wanting, like Bacon, to discover 'the best experiments of industrial practices in husbandry and manufactures . . . tending to the good of this nation'. 'He setteth more men aworke, both within and without Great Britain than perhaps any man did of his rank and position,' wrote his friend John Dury, who for his part worked for 'ecclesiastical peace'. Both admired the Moravian exile, Jan Amos Comenius, who urged that children should be taught on realistic lines. Hartlib published his books in 1637 and 1639.

The Puritans took Hartlib seriously. John Williams, Bishop of Lincoln, placed him in charge of his 'academy of young noblemen at Buckden in 1632,'[1] whilst other bishops like Ussher (Armagh), Davenant (Salisbury), Hall (Exeter) and Morton (Durham), and politicians like John Pym and John Selden listened to his suggestion that Dury and Comenius should be invited to England in 1641 to establish a version of the New Atlantis in the form of an academy to produce universal books and a universal language and to stimulate universal schools. Significantly, one of the buildings suggested to house this enterprise was the unfinished Chelsea College.[2]

Comenius' arrival in 1641 marked the flash-point in the

juncture of Baconism and Puritanism in England.[1] In the month before the invitation was issued, the Commons had confiscated the lands of deans and chapters to devote them to 'learning and piety'. Comenius hoped they would finance 'the plans of the great Verulam respecting the opening somewhere of a universal college wholly devoted to the advancement of the sciences'. He thought that 'men will say we are drunken and dreaming,' but comforted himself by concluding 'the answer is to make men drunk'. Heady draughts were prepared by Hartlib for his bookish Puritan allies in the form of a prospectus which brought the *New Atlantis* up to date: *A Description of the Famous Kingdom of Macaria*. Through an Office of Address, Hartlib argued (a kind of central clearing house of discoveries), England could multiply its resources to become a Macaria, with schools, colleges, a national health service, a system of highways and bridges, and a trained clergy: all sustained by a tax on fortunes. The next step forward in the Reformation leading to the Kingdom of the Saints was to be obligingly supplied by applying the Comenian version of Bacon's ideas.

But Pym was more interested in a Puritania than a Macaria. When he and his party carried the Grand Remonstrance in Parliament on 22 November 1641 by eleven votes, they crystallised the issues around which the Civil War was to be fought. Clause 187 announced their intention to reform the universities. The House of Commons then resolved that they intended to confiscate the lands of deans and chapters to promote learning.

When the Irish Catholics revolted, Pym quarrelled with Hartlib's other patron, Williams (now Archbishop of York), and turned his attention to fighting the King. So Comenius, wooed by the Swedes, left England on 21 June 1642.

V

Failure to establish the Comenian 'universal college' was but one of a series of attempts that had been made in England since 1603 to establish universities. Ripon (1604),[2] Carlisle (1617),[3]

Manchester (1640),[1] and York (1640),[2] had all, in various ways, been aborted.

Now, with Hartlib busy as the Civil War broke out, further schemes went forward. He really earned Dury's tribute as 'the boss of the wheel, supporting the axle tree of the chariot of Israel'. John Milton proposed that academies should be set up in every city to serve 'at once as both school and university' for some 150 to 200 students between the ages of twelve and twenty-one. In the Dedication of his *Tractate on Education* (1644), he described Hartlib as 'a person sent hither by some good providence from a far country to be the occasion and incitement of great good to this island'. By 1647 Hartlib himself was recommending that a university should be founded in London, and that Gresham College should be remodelled so as to foster the study of the scientific principles of trades.[3] This excited William Petty to amplify it in a pamphlet addressed to Hartlib in 1648 proposing the shortening of apprenticeships and the establishing of a college of 'tradesmen' and a college of 'science'.[4]

Such proposals snowballed, pouring in thick and fast in the hectic post-war ferment of 1649: for pansophic colleges in each country town (made by George Snell); for state supported teachers' colleges (by Dr Bathurst); for a college of husbandry at Fulham (Cressy Dymock); for an academy for women (Adolphus Speed); for an academy at Bethnal Green (Balthazar Gerbier); and for one in London (Hugh l'Amy and Peter Le Pruvost).[5]

Young men caught the enthusiasm. The 22-year-old Robert Boyle was treated to some of Hartlib's suggestions that Vauxhall should become a depot for models and philosophical apparatus where 'artists and mechanics' could freely resort for 'experiments' and 'trials of profitable inventions'.[6]

All cathedral and collegiate chapters were dissolved on 30 April 1649. So Durham petitioned, as York had again done two years earlier, for a university. The matter was referred to the committee dealing with sequestered lands. Voices, increasingly strong, were raised in complaint against the 'monopoly of means of learning' exercised by Oxford and Cambridge 'as if,' wrote

Dury, 'without the formalities and constitutions of old settled in them, there could be no truth of learning'.[1] When it seemed that the universities were to be spared the fate of the cathedral chapters, John Hall, a 22-year-old Durham man, asked Parliament:

Where have we anything to do with Chemistry, which hath snatcht the Keyes of Nature from the other sects of philosophy by her multiplied experiences? Where have we constant reading upon either quick or dead *anatomies*, or occular demonstrations of herbes? Where any manuall demonstrations of Mathematical theorems or instruments? Where a promotion of their experiences, which if right carried on, would multiply even to astonishment? Where an examination of all the old tenets? Review of the old experiments and traditions which gull so many *junior* beliefs, and serve for nothing else but for idle priests, to make their sermons more gaudy?[2]

More schools and especially more universities 'one at least at every great town in the nation' and in all of them 'competent maintenance of learned men,'[3] were proposed by William Dell, master of a Cambridge college, whilst from Wales, Dr John Ellis suggested Ludlow as the site of a Welsh University.[4] So much talk of reform and of increasing the spirituality of the universities roused the latent conservatism of their former graduates. Cromwell, as the instrument of this conservative reaction, took over. As a quasi-monarch (and in the opinions of many historians he might have been given the crown had he lived longer), he did establish a Baconian type of university at Durham under Ezreel Tonge, an enthusiast for 'the whole design of founding a College of Sciences with several schools and a library,' as one of the four tutors.[5] Another foundation at Shrewsbury was promoted by Richard Baxter, the great divine, during the years 1646 to 1656, but, though his scheme excited the interest of one of Cromwell's major-generals. it failed through lack of money.[6]

VI

Baconian-Comenian ideas took root, however, in the convention, by another refugee, Theodore Haak, of an 'Invisible College' of professors at Gresham College. They began to meet in the rooms of Samuel Foster with Hartlib and Haak acting as secretaries. Dury's son-in-law, Henry Oldenburgh, another German Protestant, was to succeed them. Amongst the members were the 'back-room boys' of the Parliamentary army like Jonathan Goddard (Cromwell's personal physician), John Wallis (the cipher-cracker), William Petty (the surveyor of conquered Ireland) and Cromwell's own brother-in-law, John Wilkins.[1]

These meetings were concerned, according to Wallis, with 'what hath been called *The New Philosophy*, which from the times of Galileo in Florence, and Sir Francis Bacon in England, hath been much cultivated in Italy, France, Germany and other parts abroad, as well as with us in England.' In other words they met to report on experiments and the state of natural science, and they excluded theology and state affairs from their agenda.[2]

After Wilkins' arrival at Wadham in 1648 a group sprang up there too. For Wilkins was, in Hartlib's opinion, 'a very ingeniose man, and had a very mechanical head. He was much for trying experiments and his head ran much upon the perpetual motion.' It included other friends of Hartlib's, like William Petty, whose 'flying thoughts' were put on paper at that time and Dr. Bathurst, the proposer of State supported teachers' colleges. When Wilkins moved to Cambridge as master of Trinity in 1659, a third group sprang up there, leaving the Oxford group to enjoy the hospitality of Robert Boyle, who equipped a laboratory where Peter Stahl lectured. Boyle even suggested that the government might establish the New Atlantis in Ireland at a cost of some £12,000.

VII

These groups survived Cromwell, when more institutional innovations like Durham College were dissolved. For when they were ejected from Oxford they regrouped round Gresham College, under the patronage of Charles II, who was, from his own exile, not uninterested in chemistry. Petty was knighted and Wilkins elevated to a bishopric, whilst other members of these Baconian 'cells' formed a society under royal patronage known as the Royal Society of London.

The occasion of its foundation was a discussion after one of Christopher Wren's lectures on astronomy at Gresham College. Its first 'curator of experiments' was Robert Hooke, appointed in November 1662, a believer in the role of the natural philosopher as a charitable man. A specialist in mechanics, he also anticipated the modern theory of combustion in chemistry, and was a botanist and zoologist of distinction.[1]

The Royal Society refused to be involved in either theology or politics. It had to, to survive. For as one of the early fellows, Bishop Sprat, remarked, it was not proper for 'experimenters' to teach young men since 'it would not only devour too much of their time, but it would go near to make them a little more magisterial in philosophy than became them'. Its example was contagious, for as Sprat remarked, the dispersal of the 'Genius of Experimenting' was such that 'all places and corners are now busie and warm about this work'. The Restoration might close universities and schools to all but Anglicans, but the spirit of Bacon and Comenius was lively and active. Just as in 1649 John Hall had seen that it was better to grave *things* in the mindes of children, than *wordes*,' so Sprat envisaged an education which would 'excel the *Methodical*' by applying 'the Eyes and the hands of children, to see, and touch all the several kinds of *sensible things*'.[2]

Perhaps the symbol of what was happening was provided by

Christopher Wren. His earliest architectural venture was a transparent three-storied beehive for Samuel Hartlib; his greatest, the rebuilding of London after the Great Fire.

III

THE NATIONAL RELIGION VERSUS NATIONAL NEEDS

1660-1732

I

Restored to power in 1660, the Royalists tried to make the Anglican Church truly national by uprooting the Dissenters from their public offices (by the Corporation Act of 1661), and from their church livings (by the Act of Uniformity of 1662), by alienating their congregations (by the Conventicle Act of 1664) and depriving them of the privilege even of preaching in corporate towns (by the Five Mile Act of 1665).[1]

Known as the Clarendon Code, these acts produced a diaspora. Over 2,000 clergymen refused to conform, preferring to leave their livings and take to the remote country places where they could teach and preach. It was not too hard for such ministers to make a living if they could help by applying themselves to the betterment of their communities. Thus Adam Martindale, when deprived of his living in 1662, began to teach mathematics at Warrington, and for the next 24 years made dials for miners, surveyed land, and wrote books—activities which earned him the protection of Lord Delamer.

In addition, some of them established 'academies' to train ministers—some 23 being recorded up to 1690. The first to do so was probably John Bryan, an ejected minister of Coventry who organised an academy at his home in 1663. Soon it became customary for ministers to invite trainees and instruct them in a broader curriculum, which included science. Charles Morton, for instance, a former student at Wadham College in the days of the embryo Royal Society, opened an academy at Newington Green in 1675 where students formed a council, teaching was conducted

27

in the vernacular and a five-year curriculum was planned. Morton objected to the 'securing of the key of knowledge and tying it fast to some men's girdles, or making it too hot or heavy for others to touch'. When his success led to the inevitable episcopal enquiries, he emigrated to America, where as Vice-President of Harvard he has been credited with the same pioneer scientific spirit as he displayed in England.[1] The most distinguished pupil at Newington Green was Daniel Defoe, the eighteenth-century H. G. Wells. His *Essay on Projects* (1697) suggests insurance companies, asylums, military colleges, academies and high schools for the education of women.[2]

By 1689 Independents and Presbyterians established a common fund to support such academies, and the Congregationalists followed suit in 1695. From these spores grew larger academies, in places like Sheffield, Bridgnorth, Bridgwater, Bolton, Bristol, Exeter, Findern, Gloucester, Saffron Walden, Stratford-on-Avon, Hungerford, Ipswich, Lyme Regis, Manchester, Newport Pagnell, Northampton, Tiverton, Tewkesbury, Warrington and Whitehaven. At Sheffield, Christ's College Attercliffe was founded in 1689 as a successor to a more fugitive academy at Rathmell. Amongst its pupils were a professor of mathematics at Cambridge (Nicholas Sanderson), a Lord Chancellor of Ireland (John Bowes) an Archbishop of Canterbury (Thomas Secker), and the most popular Nonconformist divine in London (Thomas Bradbury). The most successful old boy was the most unfilial: Secker said: 'only the old philosophy of the schools was taught there; and that neither ably nor diligently. The morals also of many of the young men were bad. On the whole, I spent my time there idly and ill.'

Schoolmasters had also to subscribe to a declaration of loyalty and to obtain a licence from the bishop of the diocese. Many refused to do this, some, like the headmasters of Eton, Shrewsbury, Bedford Grammar School, and King's School Canterbury for reasons Puritan, others like the headmasters of Merchant Taylors', and Magdalen College School, for reasons Catholic. Like some of the ejected clergy, about 150 of them started private schools of their own, yet even in this they were not secure, for the government prohibited Dissenters from teaching in any public or private school under penalty of a £40 fine. The Archbishop of Canterbury followed this up in 1665 with a letter to his bishops asking for information of all teachers in their dioceses, especially as to whether they frequented 'the public prayers of the church, and cause their scholars to do the same; and whether they appear well affected to the government of his majesty and the doctrine and discipline of the Church of England'. The Archbishop's campaign was renewed seven years later when he demanded that all non-subscribing teachers should be proceeded against 'by the most effectual remedies that may be'. In the main, they were left unmolested by the authorities, though sometimes, when feeling against them ran high, they had to go into hiding. Isaac Girling, for instance, was warned by the local bishop that he was to be prosecuted.

Nonconformist academies were regarded with great suspicion by churchmen. The author of the dedication of the second part of Clarendon's *History*, in 1704, described them as existing 'contrary to law, supported by large contributions,' and accused them of breeding up youth 'in principles directly contrary to monarchical and episcopal government'.

To the extravagant Dr Sacheverell, they were 'Seminaries wherein . . . all the hellish principles of fanaticism and anarchy are openly professed and taught to corrupt and debauch the youth of the nation'. The campaign against them reached a climax of repression in the Schism Act of 1714 which was mercifully repealed soon after the accession of the House of Hanover.

II

Over against the Clarendon Code must be set the Navigation Acts, another corpus of legislation designed to buttress an English institution; in this case English shipping. An 'English ship' was defined by the Navigation Act of 1660 as one commanded by an

English captain with a crew three-quarters English. An even more exact definition by a further Act of 1662 was that it had to be 'built in England.' Only such English ships could, according to an earlier Navigation Act of 1651, carry imports from Asia, Africa and America. 'It is the want of Mathematical Learning in School that makes us so weak at sea, and so deficient in manual Trades, yea and this learning to be so little known and studied in the Universities' lamented John Newton in 1677.[1] He was in a position to know, for he had established a mathematical school at Ross in Herefordshire ten years earlier and wrote good text-books.

'The safety of men's lives and estates' on the sea led Samuel Pepys to establish in 1677 a special lieutenant's examination for naval officers. As a result, a number of coastal schools like Dartmouth Grammar School in 1679 took up mathematics. Later, in 1702, navigation instructors began to be appointed on ships.

The shortage of mathematics teachers was such that a mathematical side was established by Charles II at Christ's Hospital for boys coming from the grammar classes at the age of fourteen and a half. The first master, John Leake, was appointed in 1673, but he was unsatisfactory. His successor, Peter Perkins, a former private mathematics master, a Fellow of the Royal Society, died within three years of appointment. The third master, Dr Robert Hood, engaged an usher to do the teaching. Both the fourth and fifth resigned, one because he was a profligate, the other because of the high standard of the Trinity House examiners, and it was not until 1709, when James Hodgson, Flamsteed's nephew by marriage, took over, that the post was held for any length of time.

Christ's Hospital mathematical school influenced other schools. One pupil, Thomas Crosby, opened a mathematical academy at Southwark in 1710 which lasted for 40 years. Another, James Jurin, went on to teach at Newcastle Grammar School from 1709 to 1715 before becoming secretary of the Royal Society. Two others were appointed by Peter the Great to teach navigation at the newly established Moscow School of Navigation and Mathematics in 1701. After eight years of teaching one of these was killed by robbers, and the other was transferred to St Petersburg in 1715 as Professor of Navigation in the new naval academy there.[1]

Other English schools were founded to specialise in mathematics. At Rochester Sir Joseph Williamson, President of the Royal Society, founded one in 1709 where 'the mathematics and all other things which may fit and encourage boys to teach for the Sea Service' should be taught: its first master, John Colson, later Professor of Mathematics at Cambridge was one of the Fellows of the Royal Society who recommended the Board of Longitude to assist John Harrison to complete his third clock. Joseph Neale (ob. 1710) founded a similar school in Fleet Street, London in 1715, and Richard Churcher, a retired East India Company servant, a third at Petersfield. Men like John Arbuthnot cited the example of France where professors of the subject visited the French sea-coast towns four times a week.[2]

Mathematics was such an important ingredient of national strength that when the Schism Act was drafted in 1714 to curb the dissenting academies, special exemptions were made in cases where 'any part of mathematics relating to navigation, or any mechanical art' was taught. The Tory leader in the Commons, Bromley, actually offered to abandon the Bill if in its place the Whigs would accept another disfranchising Dissenters.

III

Industry too was becoming more important to the nation. At the Restoration, or soon after, Britain was using two million tons of coal annually: five times as much as the rest of the world.[3] Winning this coal elicited engineering techniques and scientific calculations that still further fostered the study of mathematics, geology and chemistry, together with the making of 'dials' and other instruments for surveying.

Surveyors were especially active in London after the Great Fire and were kept active by the enclosure movement. Engineers busy improving river navigation were winning their professional status. All needed trigonometry, and to help them teachers of the subject appeared such as Adam Martindale (1623–86) in Cheshire and South Lancashire; Gilbert Clarke (1627–97?) in South Lincolnshire and Northampton; John Taylor (1650–1701) and Thomas Golding (*fl.*-1660) at Norwich, and John Kendal (1676–1702) at Colchester. Often such men would migrate from place to place, like Abraham Sharp (1651–1742), a Yorkshireman who taught mathematics at Liverpool, helped the great John Flamsteed at the Royal Observatory in Greenwich, then taught for a time at Portsmouth, returning at length to Little Horton, near Bradford where he made sextants, sun-dials and telescopes; setting a tradition of exact calibration in South Yorkshire that was to be acknowledged by his successors.

Sometimes such teachers would work from their own houses, or go to a gentleman's house in the neighbourhood to explain the mysteries of surveying, trigonometry, or arithmetic essential to the 'dividing of enclosures'. Thus John Wing (1655?–1715), made himself useful in these ways in Rutland for nearly 30 years, and John Tipper (*fl.* 1699–1713), a schoolmaster at Bablake School, Coventry, visited 'gentlemen pupils' within eight or ten miles of Coventry to teach applied mathematics including navigation and dialling. Tipper began to issue one of the earliest popular mathematical journals with the singularly inapt title of *The Ladies Diary*. It was originally an almanac. For land drainage also surveying was important. In Lincolnshire, mathematics was taught by John Brampton at Sutton St Maries in 1701; in Essex by John Buchanan at Steeple Bumpstead in 1710; at Chersley by the Reverend Philip Cole in 1714.[1]

Sometimes a mathematical school was opposite to, and independent of the grammar school, as at Guildford in 1677–80. In others, as at Tiverton under John White, the local free school became a mathematical school. Most of them were listed by John Houghton in his *Collections for the Improvement of Husbandry and Trade* (1694).

Mathematical societies grew up. That founded in Manchester

in 1718 organised popular lectures, as did another at Newcastle. On the other hand, that founded in Spitalfields at the same time was an earlier version of a philosophical society of the type which was destined to take root in the north of England at the close of the century.[1]

From teaching mathematics many of these private teachers went on to become missioners of science generally. Thus John Harris (1667–1719) not only taught mathematics at his house in Amen Corner and in the Vestry room at St Olave's, he also got involved with the sea voyagers at the Marine Coffee House, publishing a *Collection* in 1705. He was aware of the continuous feedback between education and economic growth, and synthesised many articles from the *Philosophical Transactions* for his *Lexicon Technicum* (1709). This lexicon was recommended by the headmaster of Hull Grammar School to his pupils to help them elucidate technical terms in the *Spectator*.

Popular lectures in science caught on. By 1705 a 'course of experiments' began at the house of Francis Hauksbee in Giltspur Street and continued for six years in Wine Office Court off Fleet Street. By 1712 his namesake and nephew followed suit and by 1714 J. T. Desaguliers, another F.R.S., offered a course at Plough Court, Fetter Lane. Desaguliers' technical knowledge had acquired a quasi-religious flavour, for he brought to light the growth of the custom 'of admitting men into the *Society of Free-Masons*'. Freemasonry by Desaguliers' time had become openly deistic. It aimed at conserving and improving technical secrets gathered from all over the world. Its ideas were literally 'lodged' in the most technical of all activities, that of building. The Masonic mixture of mysticism and technical recipes made them worship God as the Great Architect.[2] To Desaguliers, Masonry was a practical and militant philosophy which adjusted the Newtonian world picture to Christianity. To him the Freemasons were the General Staff of the War against ignorance. Their constitutions of 1723 were written under his supervision:

Adam, our first parent, created after the image of God, the Great Architect of the Universe, must have had the Liberal Science, particularly Geometry, written on his Heart; for ever since the Fall we find the Principles of it in the Hearts of his offspring.

Desaguliers wrote an allegorical poem on *The Newtonian System of the World the Best Model of Government* (1728). Another popular lecturer and one time schoolmaster at Guildford and Chichester, Benjamin Martin, in his *Philosophia Brittanica* (1747), gave a similar popular exegesis of the Newtonian system, just as he had done for other popular scientific ideas ten years earlier in his *Bibliotheca Technologica*.

IV

The Newtonian world picture stems from Cambridge, where in 1663 Charles II allowed the chair of mathematics founded by Henry Lucas to be held by someone not in holy orders, college statutes notwithstanding, and ordered all undergraduates after their second year to attend his lectures. The second occupant of this chair, Isaac Newton, was elected because his predecessor and teacher Isaac Barrow recognised his ability and resigned in his favour.

In his *Principia* (1687) Newton gave a picture of the world as a vast machine, centred by the great geometer, God. Newtonian philosophy played in the eighteenth century the same role as Darwinism in the nineteenth. To Trinity College came Richard Bentley in 1700 as Master, who completed the process of making it the haven and home of physical science in England[1] by building for Roger Cotes, a follower of Newton and the Plumian Professor of Astronomy (a chair founded in 1704), the only observatory in Cambridge.[2] Cotes offered a course of lectures in experimental physics in 1707. Another of Newton's disciples, Robert Smith founded the prizes that still bear his name. Bentley also built a chemical laboratory east of Trinity Bowling Green, where the Italian Vigani could lecture to, amongst others, Abraham de la Pryme, William Stukeley and Stephen Hales. Even Newton had 'dabbled furiously' in chemistry.

A college of science was projected in London by Henry Howard and Christopher Wren in 1668, but owing to lack of funds it was never built there. The design, however, influenced the building, ten years later, of a museum at Oxford to house the twelve wagon-loads of specimens which Elias Ashmole gave the university in 1677.[1] Finished in 1683, the Ashmolean museum was the first of its kind in England.[2] Here Dr Plot lectured on chemistry (with demonstrations) three times a week.[3] Wren also left other traces of his work at Oxford by completing Christ Church buildings and crowning Tom Quadrangle with Bell Tower. Wren also built the theatre for Archbishop Sheldon, and the north block on the garden quadrangle of Trinity, whilst his pupil Hawksmoor built Queen's College, the Clarendon Building and the back quadrangle of All Souls.

The teaching of experimental philosophy (or Physics) at Oxford was proposed by Professor Gregory in 1700 and carried out by John Keill of Balliol and Theophilus Desaguliers until 1713.

Oxford's two newest colleges were, at their inception, in tune with the age. Worcester (1714) housed Dr John Wall, a student in the Ashmolean Chemical Laboratory who founded the Royal Porcelain Works at Worcester, while Hertford (1740) had, as Hart Hall, employed J. T. Desaguliers as a lecturer in experimental philosophy.[4]

Mathematics undoubtedly fostered the growth of private tutoring in the universities; and college tutors thankfully handed over to them the most laborious part of their work. At Cambridge, according to Rouse Ball, 'the whole instruction of the bulk of the more advanced students [in mathematics], passed into the hands of a few men who were independent both of the university and of the colleges'.[5] Such a one was Richard Laughton, one of the most influential teachers of the Newtonian theory of the universe to students.

The universities were in fact so independent of the government that determined attempts were made by Lord Macclesfield in 1718 to press the universities into the service of the state, and by the Reverend Humphrey Prideaux to make them more efficient bastions of Anglicanism. Among the 58 articles of reform which Prideaux was asked to submit to the Secretary of State were proposals for more rigorous examinations, a 'Drone Hall' for lazy university teachers, elections to fellowships and scholarships by merit, and the supervision of the university by a standing committee of twenty curators.

The one attempt which the government made to utilise the universities for political ends failed. In 1724 twenty king's scholarships were established at each university to train recruits for the foreign service, since the 'continual correspondence with foreign courts and agencies' required 'in a peculiar manner the knowledge of the modern or living languages both in speaking or writing, for which no provision hath yet been made in either of the Universities'. So chairs of modern history were set up by the Crown under which two teachers of modern languages were to work. Languages indeed loomed larger in the eyes of the advisers of the Crown in this matter than history. But the experiment failed: no organised civil service could take root as long as the system of patronage appointments was so strong. So the professorships of history and the lectureships in languages became sinecures. By the time that the historian Edward Gibbon and the educational writer Vicesimus Knox went up, nothing was known about the teaching of languages. Not until the bequest of Robert Taylor in 1788 was actually received in 1834 were steps taken to remedy this deficiency.[1]

v

As Bishop Sprat wrote in 1667 'the universal Disposition of this *Age* is bent upon a *rational Religion*'.[2] He was writing a justification of the seven-year-old Royal Society, to which several of his fellow bishops belonged, and which was essentially a Royalist body that had grown out of the meetings at Gresham College and at Oxford that took place during the commonwealth. Sprat and his fellow bishops argued that science gave a more intimate and sophisticated proof of a designing deity, and he urged the Church of England to 'persist, as it has begun, to encourage *Experiments*, which will be to our *Church* as the British Oak is to our *Empire*, an armament and defence to the soil wherein it is planted'.[1] If the Church were to oppose science, wrote Sprat, it would oppose the 'present *Inquiring Temper* of this *Age*'.[2]

As expounded by Sprat, the experimental method of the Royal Society had profound educational implications. In the first place, by publishing its *Philosophical Transactions* in English instead of Latin the Royal Society itself exerted a great influence on language. Plain and simple English was their style; what Sprat, their first historian, described as 'a close, naked, natural way of speaking; positive expression; clear senses; a native easiness, bringing all things as near the Mathematical plainnesse, as they can'.[3]

The Royal Society transcended sect. Puritan and Royalist, Nonconformist and Anglican could meet together on an uncommonly common plane. By 1719 John Eames, F.R.S., a theological tutor at the Fund Academy Moorfields (founded in 1701), was setting about the abridgement of the *Philosophical Transactions*. Later, he edited *The Knowledge of the Heavens and Earth made Easy* of his more famous friend, Isaac Watts, who not only wrote hymns but educational manuals as well.

Thirdly, the Royal Society gave an impetus to the teaching of handicapped children. John Wallis the mathematician was one of the first successfully to teach the deaf, and described his method in the *Philosophical Transactions* of 1680. These principles were to be followed by James Braidwood a century later.

Fourthly, the Royal Society gave powerful, if implicit, endorsement to the Comenian didactic. Thus Sprat asked whether 'it were not as profitable to apply the eyes, and the hands of Children, to see, and to touch all the several kinds of *sensible things*, as to oblige them to learn, and remember the difficult *Doctrines* of general *Arts*.'[4] This was yet further emphasised by another Fellow of the Royal Society, John Locke.

Son of a captain in the Parliamentary Army, Locke turned from Greek to medicine. Subsequent employment in public affairs coupled with experience as tutor to a noble family led him to develop ideas about education which he expanded in letters to his friend Edward Clarke of Chipley, for the benefit of Clarke's children. From these letters he quarried *Some Thoughts Concerning Education* (1693). He brought into educational writing the close observation of a fellow of the Royal Society; observation which extended to the hinterland of the range of man's intellectual powers.[1] He concluded that all knowledge comes from experience, via the senses; and that the purpose of education was not to 'perfect a learner in all or any one of the sciences, but to give his mind that freedom, that disposition, and those habits that may enable him to attain any post or knowledge he shall apply himself to'.

Locke insisted on the personal health and hygiene of children prescribing daily washing, little 'cockering or tenderness', no sweetmeats, early rising, and fruits of the right kind. Embodied in simple rules, these read: 'plenty of open air, exercise and sleep; plain diet, no wine or strong drink, and very little or no physic; not too warm and straight clothing; especially the head and feet kept cold, and the feet often used to cold water and exposed to wet.'

Subsequent writers built on this a theory of physical education. Francis Fuller, who cured himself of dyspepsia by exercise, wrote his *Medicina Gymnastica* (1704), which was running to its seventh edition by 1777. So too John Quincy caught up Lockeian ideas and incorporated them into his popular works on medical practice. Quincy was so affected by the mechanics of the human body that he declared: 'A human body as it comes under the Notices of a Physician, is merely a machine, and that whosoever goes any other way to enquire into its constitution abuses his faculties.'[2]

Locke made the study of the human mind respectable. Reading *Essay concerning Human Understanding* led Bolingbroke 'as it were, thro' a course of experimental philosophy. I am shewn myself; and in every instance there is an appeal to my own perceptions, and to the reflections I make on my own intellectual operations.'[3]

Subsequent schools of investigation into the extent of human knowledge were divided as to the powers of the human mind; some tended to exalt them, others to depreciate them. Both, however, showed that the study of man's own potential was now as legitimate as the study of his habitat. By 1730 Locke was recommended reading in the university.[1]

Though Locke did not believe that all men had equal intellectual capabilities ('there is a difference of degrees in men's understandings, apprehensions, and reasonings, to so great a latitude, that one may, without doing injury to mankind, affirm, that there is a greater distance between some men and others in this respect, than between some men and some beasts',[2]) yet he stressed what education could do. Describing the impressionable nature of the infant mind Locke compares it to 'an empty cabinet', 'a white paper devoid of any characters'—'a dark room',[3]—an uncised tablet on which the teacher could work.

Two other facets of Locke's inquiries influenced his generation: his defence of individual liberty and his belief that land should be the source of all taxation.

VI

The main English industry was agriculture. It provided the major economic and political rewards, it spelt stability in politics, it reinforced the mercantilist doctrine that food should be produced at home to preserve the balance of trade. It went with a general disparagement of the liberal arts, a disparagement encountered by Christopher Wase, organiser of what was the first enquiry into English grammar schools:

'There is an opinion commonly receiv'd,' he wrote, 'that the Scholars of England are overproportion'd to the preferments for letter'd persons,' and that those 'whom Nature or Fortune had determin'd to the Plough, the Oar, or other Handicrafts' were being diverted 'to the study of Liberal Arts.'

The increase of foundations, concluded Wase, was seen to be 'dangerous to Government'.[1] Though Wase tried to rebut the opinion by arguing that 'the more any Nation encreases in Wisdom, the more intrinsecal inforcements of Loyalty will they derive from the eternal Reason of that Law which enforms their obedience',[2] he was swimming against a tide of opinions forcefully expressed by Thomas Hobbes and widely diffused by Edward Chamberlayne.

'Never was anything so dearly bought, as these Western parts have bought the learning of the Greek and Latin tongues by reading of classical authors' Thomas Hobbes had asserted in 1651. 'Men from their childhood have gotten a habit (under false shew of Liberty) of favouring tumults; and of licentous controllers, with the effusion of so much blood': Hobbes' opinion was endorsed in these words by Edward Chamberlayne, in his *Angliae Notitiae or the Present State of England* (1669), a kind of almanac which ran to nearly twenty editions by the close of the century. Chamberlayne attributed the recent 'Sedition and Rebellion' to the tendency of country grammar schools to draw pupils from the lower classes.

To ascertain just what was the state of the grammar schools, Christopher Wase began, in 1671, a survey with a view to their defence. But after collecting material on 704 schools he was forced to abandon his enquiry because of the bishops who, according to John Aubrey, were 'unwilling to disoblige Gentlemen, who had gott the lands given to these Scholes into their hands and possession'.[3]

Edward Chamberlayne's son and successor as editor of the *Angliae Notitiae*, John Chamberlayne, became the first secretary of a society formed in 1699 to organise charity schools for 'those whom nature or failure had determined to the plough, the oar and other handicrafts'. This was the Society for the Promotion of Christian Knowledge, the most active, as it was to be the most long-lived, of the many ameliorative groups formed at this time. 'Next to inculcating Christianity itself,' opined its members, 'a greater service could not be done to the nation and the design of charity schools in general than to propagate a true judgement of the importance of agriculture in the nation.'[1]

VII

The prime mover of the S.P.C.K. was Thomas Bray, a passionate propagandist for Anglicanism abroad (which had led him to form the Society for the Propagation of the Gospel) and deeply concerned for its preservation at home. He was also, like many of his contemporaries, worried about the adequate enforcement of the laws against crime. He had no confidence in stricter J.P.s or in the many voluntary societies for the reformation of manners that sprang up at the time. The latter, indeed, roused hostility by cultivating the personal virtue of their members by corporate devotional exercises or arrogating to themselves the odious task of 'informing' (the only effective way of getting the J.P.s to act), on blasphemers, prostitutes and brothel keepers.[2]

Moral sentiments could be more effectively kindled, in Dr Bray's opinion, by establishing schools. In this he was influenced by the mystics of his day who tried to kindle the inner light by means of education. This belief, animating the Moravians and Swedenborgians later in the century, helped dissipate the stern view of the child as a vessel of original sin, and showed that heaven lay about children in their infancy.[3]

As a passionate catechist, Dr Bray was also perturbed by the very real Catholic revival of his youth, and the S.P.C.K. in one dimension at least was part of a strategic plan to set up 'little garrisons against Popery'.[4] For the Jesuits (who had been operating in the Savoy since the later years of Charles II) had founded a charity school under Andrew Poulton, prompting the Dissenter Arthur Shallet to establish another in direct opposition to it in Gravel Lane, Southwark.[5] More forceful than Dr Bray and his associates, the Government imposed a penalty of perpetual imprisonment on 'every Papist keeping school, educating or boarding youth for that purpose', after 25 March 1700. Informers were offered £100 if 'papist parents' were convicted of sending children or wards 'beyond the sea to be educated in papacy'. Moreover, Catholics who did not take the oaths of allegiance and supremacy at the age of eighteen were liable to forfeit their property.

Charity schools themselves were no novelty, nor were their allotropes, schools of industry.[1] Sir William Borlase had founded a Free School at St Martins, in 1628, to teach 24 boys and girls to knit, spin and make bone lace. Another was founded in 1642 at Lydbury North, Shropshire in an outhouse, where girls were instructed in the art of spinning wool and flax. Another was founded in 1670 by William Bower, a merchant of Bridlington, for 'the art of carding, knitting or spinning of wool'.

Mercantile writers had fanned this passion for productive efficiency. Andrew Yarenton, author of *Englands Improvement by Land and Sea* (1677, 1681), commended the spinning schools of Germany. Thomas Firmin published *Some Proposals for the Employment of the Poor* (1681) and followed it up by trying to run a self-supporting technical school. Four years later, in *Good order Established in Pennsylvania and New Jersey*, Thomas Budd, suggested a seven-year school where:

Boys could be taught and instructed in some Mystery or Trade as the making of Mathematical Instruments, Joynery, Turnery, The Making of Clocks and Watches, Weaving, Shoemaking or any other useful Trade or Mystery that the school is capable of teaching; and the Girls to be taught and instructed in the spinning of Flax and Wool, and Knitting of Gloves and Stockings, Sewing, and making of all sorts of useful Needle-Work, and the making of Straw Work, as Hats, Baskets etc., or any other useful Art or mystery that the school is capable of teaching.

John Bellers, the Quaker, issued *Proposals for raising a College of Industry* (1696), and in the same year the Board of Trade was established which received a report from John Locke in 1697 urging the establishment of working schools in every parish to which all children between 3 and 14 were to be sent.[2] At local level too, such ideas found increasing favour and in 1698 a workhouse school was founded in London where children were set to spin wool, knit stockings and cobble before being apprenticed at 12 or 14. The General Act (9 Geo. I. c. 7) for the Relief of the Poor in 1723 resulted in a number of workhouses appearing and with them charity schools. The spinning schools at Findon and Artleborough in Northamptonshire so impressed the S.P.C.K. that its secretary, Henry Newman, recommended them as models.

As a means of supplementing apprenticeship training, schools of industry were growing up before the S.P.C.K. was founded. Thomas Foley, a prosperous ironfounder, founded old Swinford Hospital in Stourbridge in 1677 so that boys who were 'objects of charity' might be 'taught by such masters as may bring them up in the fear of God and that when they shall be fit to be apprentices, care shall be taken to place them with such masters as may answer my great end, being the glory of God, and their real good'.[1]

VIII

The real novelty was the S.P.C.K. itself: the first national body in England to organise schools catering for children in the seven to eleven (and sometimes fourteen) age range. That the chief reading book, upon which all exercises were based, was the Bible, was wholly admirable. What was not was its exploitation as a divine endorsement of the 'great law of subordination'. For it was the cheapest, and most available and most stimulating text then available, as Dr Bray well knew. This is why he also busied himself with other societies for its more effective distribution, like the Society for the Propagation of the Gospel.

'Effectiveness' certainly characterised the work of the S.P.C.K. for in thirty-five years it helped form, or reform, over 1,500 schools,[2] whilst during the whole of the eighteenth century only 128 grammar schools were endowed. The methods by which the correspondents of the S.P.C.K. raised money for their schools were ingenious in the extreme.

Street lamps were farmed out in one London parish (St Paul's, Shadwell); court fines were shared in another (St Katherine's by the Tower); fees for the hiring of funeral pairs (at Water Orton, Warwick), or the proceeds of lottery tickets (Beverley) were obtained.[1] Perhaps the strangest method of augmenting the finances was that employed by the Sheffield Charity School at the close of the eighteenth century (and it was handsomely endowed): the collection and sale to gunpowder makers of the nitrous earth from the boys' lavatories.

One of the promoters of the S.P.C.K., Sir Humphrey Mackworth, an early industrialist, suggested that benefactors to the school should be incorporated. Often indeed, they availed themselves of the law and became joint stock companies. This provoked Daniel Defoe to write *Giving Alms No Charity*. There were of course more conventional methods of raising money: lay or clerical benefactions, corporations, colleges or livery companies, subscriptions, alms and collections (for which an annual charity sermon was preached and the children paraded). The S.P.C.K. also hoped that the sale of children's work would help.

The impact of charity schools can be detected in the comments of their critics. In 1728 they were accused of 'breeding up traitors' under teachers who were 'staunch Jacobites or furious High Churchmen'. More subtly, Bernard Mandeville, the Freud of his age, remarked that 'the more a shepherd and ploughman know of the world, the less fitted he'll be to go through the fatigue and hardship of it with cheerfulness and equanimity'.[2]

IX

Some members and masters of the S.P.C.K. rose above the terms of their briefs, and blazed, even if they could not follow up, eight new trails.

Most important was the example the society set of interdenominational co-operation in the establishment of schools. Up to the accession of Queen Anne, the S.P.C.K. provided an example of co-operation between Church and Dissent which was only broken with her accession. As the great Dissenter Isaac Watts explained in *An Essay on Charity Schools* (1728), this was because his co-religionists

found by sufficient experience, that the children were brought up in too many of these schools in principles of disaffection to the present government, in a bigoted zeal for the word Church, and with a violent enmity, and malicious spirit of persecution, against all whom they were taught to call presbyterians, though from many of their hands they received their bread and clothing. It was time then, for the dissenters to withdraw that charity which was so abused.

And though, after 1743, the S.P.C.K. became more and more a specifically Anglican agency and as such was run by clergymen, this should not obscure the excellent work done by the lay secretaries, Chamberlayne and his two successors Wanley[1] and Newman.[2]

Secondly, the S.P.C.K. linked school and life, for within fifteen years more than 20,000 children were in its schools, and another 10,000 had been apprenticed. The link was manifold, as poor children in the large towns were fed, clothed and registered by the local committees called into being by the S.P.C.K. Thirdly, in their activities, the S.P.C.K. really provided, in the words of a modern observer, a 'constant and affectionate surveillance' over the education of girls.[3] Fourthly, they worked to establish parochial libraries (some 139 up to 1768): an activity perhaps attributable to Dr Bray and Humphrey Wanley. These libraries, supplemental to the society's activity as an aggressive tract distributor, were reinforced by Act of Parliament in 1709. Fifthly the S.P.C.K., though ostensibly working through the framework of the church, coped with the problems of rural schools by secular methods and by 1703 had arranged for some London schoolmasters to act as teacher trainers.[4] By 1723 the S.P.C.K. was considering the erection of a 'Superior School for the raising of Schoolmasters and Schoolmistresses.'[5] The professional spirit was engendered too: a teachers' association was formed by Henry Dixon at Bath in 1712 to consult 'the best method of teaching their children',[1] whilst a 'Society of Schoolmasters' also took shape, which seems to have been vaguely recognised as an arbiter of professional morals (i.e. ensuring that members were loyal to the Hanoverian régime).[2] Sixthly, the 'quarterly exercises of Letters and Religion', organised to enable schools to elicit patronage, fostered the idea of examination as opposed to inspection.[3]

A seventh, if less tangible, advance made by the S.P.C.K. was that it grasped the need for simplifying existing methods of recovering charitable bequests for education. The Bill it promoted in 1712, though not successful, nevertheless pointed in a direction posterity would follow.

Perhaps the least appreciated role of the S.P.C.K. was in the field of educating adults. Correspondents were urged to form evening classes to teach adults to read. One of those who started an adult class was Samuel Wesley, the father of the great evangelist who formed a class of young farmers at Epworth.[4]

X

In a wider context than mere 'anticipations,' charity schools were based on a theory of education which evoked a violent reaction, of a kind also curiously modern. Their most astringent critic, Bernard Mandeville, wished specifically to diminish the number of petty schools and instead to erect 'at public charge' one or more first-class classical schools in each county which should be inspected twice a year. He also wanted to double the number of university chairs, especially in physics. His criticism and proposals were tacked on to a reissue in 1723 of *The Fable of the Bees: or, Private Vices, Publick Benefits* (originally published in 1714) as an *Essay on Charity and Charity Schools* and *A Search into the Nature of Society*. They caused an uproar. He ridiculed their promoters as 'diminutive patriots', 'appointers of schoolmasters' who obtained satisfaction from watching uniformed children processing to church:

The Rise then and Original of all the Bustle and Clamour [he wrote] that is made throughout the Kingdom on Behalf of Charity Schools, is chiefly built on Frailty and Human Passion.[1]

He continued:

Charity-Schools, and every thing else that promotes Idleness and keeps the Poor from Working, are more Accessory to the Growth of Villainy, than the want of Reading and Writing, or even the grossest Ignorance and Stupidity.[2]

His book was presented by the Grand Jury as a public nuisance, denounced by ministers and bishops and in France ordered to be burnt by the Crown hangman. For Mandeville proved that the existing ideals of society were unattainable and, in doing so, adumbrated the doctrines of free trade and utilitarianism:

'in the Choice of Things, Men must be determined by the Perception they have of Happiness; and no person can commit or set about an Action, which at that then present time seems not to be the best to him.'[3]

Good or evil actions, in Mandeville's world, would appear to be ones 'to the Hurt or Benefit that Society receives from them'.

Locke had denied that moral principles were innate, but Mandeville went much further and asserted that vices were. In this he carried forward the ideas of Thomas Hobbes by telling the story of a hive of industry which prospered through practising collectively what individually was condemned. Seizing on Hobbes' previous assertion that the mainspring of human action was selfishness, Mandeville extended his analogy to show just what disastrous consequences would ensue if (through divine intervention), private virtue did prevail and clear the hive of vice.

The curb to human selfishness was, for Hobbes, the establishment of a moral authority by a social compact, but to Mandeville this reward was the result of individual calculation as to the pleasure of being flattered by others, or the pleasure of imagining such flattery. The nature of this 'individual calculation' (itself stemming from Hobbes) was from now on to concern speculators on human motivation. The range of appetites was extended by David Hume to include a desire for pleasure in such things as benevolent actions. In his significantly named *Treatise of Human Nature, being an attempt to use the Experimental Method of Reasoning into Moral Subjects* (1739), 'Experimental' meant 'Newtonian', 'Moral Subjects' the humane sciences. He was the first to state his belief that the study of human nature was a science.[1] Even more important was his emphasis, in subsequent writings, on the stimulating effect of luxury on industry, an emphasis which was to undermine the purpose of charity schools: the inculcation of habits of industry.[2]

XI

For Hume held that the enforcement of endless toil would inhibit individuals and thought that they would more easily respond to variety. This variety was offered in abundance by the provincial press, which when the Printing Act lapsed in 1695 was able to emerge without fear of prosecution.[3] So in Norwich (1701), Bristol (1702), Exeter (1703), Shrewsbury (1704), Liverpool, Newcastle, Nottingham and Stamford (all in 1710) newspapers began to appear. There were 24 by 1723 and 130 by 1760. All exploited and expanded the literacy which charity schools had been founded to foster. Thus in 1712 the *Newcastle Courant* devoted two and a half pages to the scheme of Dr Jurin (Master of the Royal Free Grammar School) for 'a subscription course in mechanics', whilst the *Newcastle Journal* in 1739 promised its readers a weekly essay on useful subjects. Mathematical problems were also set. Indeed by 1747 the *Newcastle General Magazine* was even proposing to print extracts from the *Philosophical Transactions*. Above all, these papers (and others like them) enabled private schools to display themselves: advertisements for over 100 schools (mainly new) of various types appear in the columns of the *Northampton Mercury* alone, in the 40 years after 1720. Well might Dr Johnson, who as a young man contributed to a Birmingham newspaper some time after 1732, praise them as 'rivulets of intelligence which are continually trickling amongst us, which everyone may catch and of which everyone partakes'.[1]

IV

PRELUDE TO TAKE-OFF

1732–1790

I

The first and oldest pressure group of the dissenting laymen was formed in 1732 when Presbyterians, Baptists and Independents in London combined to form a standing committee to work for the repeal of the Corporation and Test Acts. In 'prudence and privacy,' these Dissenting Deputies lobbied ministers and M.P.s to 'remedy or prevent any inconvenience to the cause of civil and religious liberty'. Both in 1735 and 1739 they tried to secure the repeal of the Test Acts; though unsuccessful in this, they sustained a permanent brief for any injustices to their co-religionists. By attacking their disabilities piecemeal, they ultimately succeeded.[1]

Nor should the Dissenters' capacity to meet and defeat physical as well as political handicaps be overlooked, for both the blind and the deaf owe much to them. A tactile ciphering tablet on which the blind could perform and record arithmetical operations was made by Nicholas Sanderson, F.R.S., Lucasian Professor of Mathematics at Cambridge, a former pupil of the Nonconformist academy at Attercliffe, near Sheffield, and himself blind. His work was used rather unscrupulously by Diderot, in his *Lettres sur les aveugles* (1754), which also took cognisance of a series of psychological experiments on the blind that had been suggested to John Locke by William Molyneux,[2] performed by Cheselden[3] and discussed by Voltaire. Very anti-clerical, Diderot's book attributed to Sanderson sentiments which the sober Yorkshireman had not recorded elsewhere.[4]

The plight of the deaf and dumb eight-year-old daughter of a friend prompted Henry Baker, another Dissenter, to teach her, and in doing so he decided to devote himself to others similarly affected. By doing so he impressed Daniel Defoe, whose youngest daughter he ultimately married. Baker was a keen scientist as well: his microscopic work earned him election to the Royal Society in 1740 and fourteen years later he helped to found, and for a time acted as secretary of, the Society of Arts. Baker wrote a popular handbook on the microscope, in which he wrote: 'Every step we take serves to enlarge our Capacities, and give us still more noble and just Ideas of the Power, Wisdom, and Goodness of the Deity.'[1] The introduction of the Alpine strawberry and the rhubarb plant into England are the results of his correspondence with other scientists overseas.

The spirit was incarnate in Isaac Watts. Son of a Nonconformist schoolmaster and himself a tutor, Watts argued in his *The Improvement of the Mind*, that education could be carried on at any time, since the mind should be able to receive 'new and strange ideas upon just evidence without great surprise or aversion'.[2] Like Baker, he believed in the importance of observation:

> Sounds which address the Ear are lost and die
> In one short Hour, but that which strikes the Eye
> Lives long upon the Mind; the faithful Sight
> Engraves the Knowledge with a Beam of Light.[3]

Self-education was also fostered by the circulating libraries which began to spread at this time. One was established in 1728 by Morris Sendall, another in London in 1735 by Samuel Fancourt, who later went on to establish the Gentlemen's and Ladies' Growing and Circulating Library in 1746.[4] The coffee houses both in London and the provinces also offered books to their patrons.[5]

Reading, at least five hours daily, of 'the most useful books' was also the advice given by John Wesley to his preachers. Wesley converted a disused gun foundry in London to a Methodist chapel in 1739[6] and from now on his 'united society', organised in 'class meetings' and 'circuits,' and, after 1744, holding an annual conference, grew rapidly. Wesleyanism was a reading religion. 'Reading Christians will be knowing Christians,' said Wesley and he set the example by providing them with books which synthesised much current knowledge of science, like his own *Primitive Physic*.[1] From the Methodist Book Room in London (established in 1740), flowed a steady stream of such quasi-utilitarian books and pamphlets.[2]

A never-diminishing descant on the inequity of the Test and Corporation Acts led to the formation and reformation of associations composed of both Dissenters and Episcopalians in whose activities lie the germs of many later movements.[3]

II

The Dissenters' concern with the natural world was especially manifest in their academies.[4] Caleb Rotherham established one at Kendal in 1733, which had extensive scientific apparatus, and Rotherham himself was offering extramural instruction at Manchester ten years later. Admission to Philip Doddridge's academy at Daventry (opened in 1729) where English, rather than Latin was the medium of instruction, was not restricted to the potential ministers for whom he prescribed preaching practice in the surrounding villages. Students were taught shorthand and encouraged to specialise: 'an attempt to know and to do everything,' said Doddridge, 'will certainly be as unsuccessful, as it is extravagant'.[5] Natural science was taught by making experiments and descanting on their purpose. History, modern languages and theology were taught by the comparative method.

Doddridge influenced his successor Caleb Ashworth, and Ashworth taught Joseph Priestley, in whom the spirit of dissent found an archetype. A chemist (an interest which he valued as a valuable background to commercial geography), he particulary emphasised the value of history as 'anticipated experience'. In Priestley's hands history became the story of God realising himself in humanity, an endless activity of good men furthering His purpose by working for the happiness of posterity.[1] After corresponding with Hartley, he published an abridgement of his work in which he outlined the doctrine of the greatest happiness of the greatest number.[2] A second pupil of Daventry, Dr William Bull, was persuaded by the Anglican hymn writer, John Newton, to teach at his academy at Newport Pagnell in 1783. Newton's academy was supported by Methodists and later by the Clapham Sect. A later pupil of Daventry, Eliezer Cogan, urged the Nonconformists to establish classical schools, and suggested Anglican clergy should teach in them.[3] As part of their work in the growing industrial towns, the Dissenters founded academies of a lower order. The Northern Education Society (formed in 1756) established an Academy at Heckmondwike where Joseph Priestley's brother taught. Its success stimulated the foundation of three others at Northowram (1785), Idle (1795) and Rotherham (1795).[4] Similar activity among the Bristol Baptists led to the formation of an Education Society (in 1770). In 1776 a society for the propagation of the gospel in rural areas was formed, known as the Societas Evangelica—out of which grew the Hoxton Independent Academy in 1778.

'The Athens' of the Nonconformist north, however, was the academy at Warrington which opened with five students in a large brick building by the side of the Mersey in 1757. In two years it had twenty-seven. At first it admitted boys of fourteen or under, but by 1760 it began to take only those above this age.[5] Priestley's *Essay on a Course of Liberal Education for Civil and Active Life* (1765) indicates the breadth of its outlook, a breadth sustained by tutors like Dr John Aikin, John Reinhold Forster and William Enfield. The difficulty of sustaining discipline in it as a boarding establishment seems to have brought it to an end in 1783.

Many students also went from these academies to Scottish or continental universities (especially Leyden) and on their return applied their knowledge to local industries. Such a one was John Roebuck, the gun-founder and chemical engineer, a former pupil at Northampton before his university course at Edinburgh and

Leyden. Tutors, too, actively popularised science and its applications. The Reverend Abraham Rees, F.R.S., the Hebrew and Mathematics tutor at Hoxton and Hackney Academies, re-edited *Chambers's Encyclopaedia* in 1786 and between the years 1802 and 1820 produced a 45-volume *New Cyclopaedia*: a magnificently illustrated synthesis of science and technology up to that time.

But, compared to religion, the Nonconformists held that 'Classical learning, the belles lettres, mathematical science, and the whole encyclopaedia of human knowledge bear scarcely the proportion of the glow worm to the sun'.[1] Their religious outlook conditioned their stark psychological and political views on education. 'Train up a child in the way he should go,' ran the Biblical precept, 'and when he is old he will not depart from it.' Their Lockeian psychology held that God's laws could be indelibly imprinted on the clear warm wax tablet of a child's mind. Since all knowledge comes from experience, education, as anticipated experience, could do much to wipe out inequalities of status.[2] Such inequalities were against natural law, for, as Priestley argued, 'If any trust can be said to be of God and such as ought not to be relinquished at the command of man, it is that which we have of the education of our children.'

Dissenters fought (and were to fight), the state when it threatened to trespass on this most sacred acre. 'Education,' Priestley wrote in his *Essay on The First Principles of Government*, 'is a branch of Civil Liberty which ought by no means to be surrendered into the hands of the magistrate.'[3] The only role Priestley could envisage for the state was that of promoting liberty by abolishing the barriers to 'magistracy', like Test Acts, thereby recognising the common quest of all in the search for happiness. During the American War of Independence, the severity of the Test Acts was somewhat mitigated; in 1779 teachers were allowed to subscribe to a modified oath which ran: 'I do solemnly declare in the presence of Almighty God that I am a Christian and a Protestant, and, as such, that I believe that the Scriptures of the Old and New Testament, as commonly received among the Protestant Churches, do contain the revealed will of God, and that I do receive the same as the rule of my doctrine and practice.' Heavy penalties were imposed for lecturing after refusing to take this oath.[1]

III

Local societies for the discussion of technical and cultural problems took shape in Lincolnshire, a county whose capacities as a larder were being extended by scientific drainage. Following the establishment of a Gentleman's Society at Spalding in 1709 by Maurice Johnson, another took shape at Peterborough, in 1734, where William Elstob vigorously prosecuted mathematics and mapping,[2] and a third at Boston in 1750 where Nature was 'rack'd and improved ten thousand ways and made to submit to the powerful Laws of Mechanism'. Two members of these societies acquired a national reputation: William Stukeley, as a pioneer archaeologist[3] and Francis Peck, as an advocate of a special sustentation fund for science.[4]

Nonconformists and Anglicans alike joined such groups. Doddridge, for instance, played a leading role in one at Northampton in 1744 while the Rev. William Stukeley was active in that at Boston in 1750.

In London, such societies were often founded in coffee houses. At the 'Rainbow' a Botanical Society was formed in 1721 and a Society for the Encouragement of Learning in 1735. An Aurelian Society similarly took shape in the 'Swan' Tavern in the Cornhill in 1745 until a fire, three years later, destroyed it. In its resurrected form it used to meet at the York Coffee House in St James Street, and from this was formed, at the Marlborough Coffee House in 1788, the Linnaean Society.[5]

At the 'Bedford,' a coffee house even more directly concerned with science, James Stirling, F.R.S., and J. T. Desaguliers, F.R.S. lectured on experimental philosophy. Stirling was a friend of the Swiss mathematician Nicholas Bernouilli as well as of Isaac Newton, and later went on to become a mine manager in

Lanarkshire. Desaguliers also discoursed at large over the great piazza at Covent Garden to, amongst others, the Fieldings, Hogarth and Goldsmith, Woodward and Lloyd.

When John Houghton (d. 1705) remarked that the coffee houses had 'improved useful knowledge as much as the universities' he was prophesying shrewdly, for 30 years after he died Joshua Ward (caught by Hogarth in 'The Harlot's Progress'), made such good use of the scraps of gossip and information he picked up that in 1736 he was able to manufacture sulphuric acid at Twickenham by the bell process, greatly reducing its price. Ward was not the only chemist who professionally frequented coffee houses. Dr Morris had an 'elaboratory' at Roberts' Coffee House in the great piazza of Covent Garden where a number of crucibles were tested in 1757.[1] By 1782 a chemical society was meeting in the Chapter Coffee House in London.[2]

We know from Boswell that at the London Coffee House, in 1772, a club consisting of physicians, dissenting clergy and masters of academies used to meet to exchange ideas. There Boswell was to have met Benjamin Franklin on 26 March 1772, and did meet Joseph Priestley.[3]

At Jack's Coffee House in Dean Street and later at young Slaughter's Coffee House in St. Martin's Lane, a 'scientific club' existed in the 1780s under John Hunter, the surgeon. Amongst its members were Sir Joseph Banks and his protégés George Fordyce and D. C. Solander. Here Captain Cook and the great foreign naturalist J. C. Fabricius used to be seen on visits to London.[4]

Coffee houses also incubated local groups in the provinces. At Liverpool the Conversation Club used to meet in St George's Coffee House,[5] while the even more famous Manchester Literary and Philosophical Society met during its first year at the Assembly Coffee House (probably near the Exchange)[6] before getting premises of its own.

IV

Perhaps the best known of the coffee houses was Rawthmell's in Henrietta Street, Covent Garden. Haunted nightly by Martin Folkes (1690–1754), President of the Royal Society in 1741, it was a magnet for eavesdroppers. According to one Fellow, Folkes would choose the council and officers of the Royal Society from the 'junto of sychophants' that used to meet him there.

Here on 22 March 1754, a group of Fellows of the Royal Society at Rawthmell's listened to the proposal of William Shipley, a Northampton drawing master, to subsidise inventions by prizes, in much the same way as horse breeding was fostered by competition at the Northampton horse fair. Shipley was anxious to find substitutes for cobalt and madder, both dyes used in the cloth trade, both imported and both difficult to obtain. Meeting again at Rawthmell's on 29 March the group decided to make their meetings more formal and arranged to forgather regularly at a circulating library in Crane Court, Fleet Street. From this grew the Society for the Encouragement of Arts, Manufactures and Commerce, better known today as the Royal Society of Arts.[1] To diffuse a knowledge of new discoveries, the Royal Society of Arts issued a journal, organised competitions and encouraged effort by means of medals. But it chiefly worked through exhibitions, organising the first industrial exhibition in England in 1761. In this it was widely imitated in America and on the continent.

Anglicans like Stephen Hales and Nonconformists like Baker were leading spirits in its formation, whilst its frankly utilitarian, ameliorist programme attracted architects, botanists, but above all chemists of resource like Robert Dossie. Robert Dossie's *Elaboratory laid open* had so impressed Dr. Johnson (himself, for the briefest of periods, a schoolmaster) that he proposed him for membership. Dossie's frank admiration of French practice led him to envisage the Society of Arts becoming a centre of experimental research, as well as for the collection and dissemination of knowledge.[1] So it was fitting that the Royal Society of Arts should later help incubate the Chemical Society (in 1841) and the Institute of Chemistry (in 1877).

For chemistry was becoming fashionable and profitable. Private laboratories were growing. From about 1736 William Lewis sustained a teaching laboratory off Fetter Lane, and from 1747 at Kingston, where he planned to issue a periodical and proposed, by laboratory experiment, to find new materials and investigate uses for by-products with the help of Alexander Chisholm. His contributions, wrote Dr Gibbs, 'showed for the first time that great benefits could arise from the systematic application of scientific knowledge and method to industrial problems'. By differentiating between physics and chemistry Lewis showed how both were important to industrial development. The laboratory he described (and used) at Kingston has been also classed by Gibbs as 'unique in that it was the first designed specifically for research in applied chemistry and physics'.[2] Lewis also went on journeys to see ironworks in Rotherham, Staveley, Kitley and Coalbrookdale to investigate the use of coal and coke for the production of iron. So did Henry Cavendish, the wealthy private chemist.[3]

Dr. Johnson was described by Boswell, on 28 March 1772, as being 'very fond of talking of manufactures, or giving any instruction as to the matters of utility'.[4] Johnson possessed a refreshing belief in the educability of human beings, saying to Boswell: 'I do not deny, Sir, but there is some original difference in minds; but it is nothing in comparison of what is formed by education. We may instance the science of *numbers*, which all men are capable of attaining.'[5] Johnson was a great admirer of Thomas Braidwood, a teacher of mathematics, whose success in teaching deaf-mutes at Edinburgh to speak he described as a 'philosophical curiosity, a college of the deaf and dumb who are taught to speak, to read, to write and to practice arithmetic' by 'hearing with the eye'. Braidwood moved to London in 1783 where at Hackney he carried on his institution, with it is said, help from the King.

Whether influenced by the Society of Arts or not, large landowners and small farmers alike developed a desire to acquire new techniques, new machinery and new foodstuffs. Agricultural societies, like the Bath and West of England (1777), Odiham (1783) and Kent (1793), were formed, journals issued, lectures given and public demonstrations and exhibitions organised. These provincial agricultural societies were very concerned with education. The secretary of the Odiham society, James Huntingford, a friend of Robert Raikes, saw to the moral education of the members' employees and (with his society) provided much of the impetus which led to the foundation of the Royal Veterinary College in 1791.[1]

V

The increasing use of the steam engine to drain mines increased the clientele and repertoire of the travelling science lecturers.[2] One of them, James Ferguson, F.R.S., began to rhapsodise over the possibilities of mechanical energy slaves. His lectures on hydraulic engines (illustrated by plates of an engine at Blenheim), mechanical power, pile drivers, wheel carriages, air pumps and the like were given to select audiences of from 20 to 60 as widely dispersed as Bath, Norwich, Cambridge, Bristol, Liverpool, Scotland and Newcastle-on-Tyne. He was also intoxicated with the possibilities of electricity, and his *Introduction* to the subject reached a third edition by 1779. He looked on an electrical machine as a challenge to experiment. His Experiment XVI was a model of a triple pump mill (for raising the water by the force of wind), put into motion by electricity. Both Birkbeck and Brewster regarded him as the first 'popular' or 'elementary' writer, and in a preface to an edition of his lectures Brewster went further:

'to his labours,' he wrote, 'we must attribute that general diffusion of scientific knowledge among the practical mechanics of this country, which has in great measure banished those antiquated prejudices and erroneous means of construction that perpetually mislead the unlettered artist.'[1]

The centre traditionally first associated with the wholesale manufacture of the steam engine was Birmingham. Introduced by his American physician, Dr. Small, to James Watt, then working with John Roebuck on a steam engine, a local hardware manufacturer, Matthew Boulton, obtained the monopoly for manufacturing steam engines until 1800. Small, Boulton and Watt, together with other local industrial pioneers like Josiah Wedgwood, the potter-chemist and James Keir, the compiler of the first English chemical dictionary, formed a discussion group with local medical men like William Withering the discoverer of digitalis, and Erasmus Darwin the anticipator of the theory and ancestor of the proponent of evolution. This discussion, or dining, club was known after Small's death as the Lunar Society.[2] Reinforced by Joseph Priestley the Dissenter, Samuel Galton the gun manufacturer, ornithologist and grandfather of Francis Galton, Jonathan Stokes the physician and chemist, Thomas Day the author of *Sandford and Merton*, and Richard Lovell Edgworth, whom we shall meet in the next chapter, they enjoyed the stimulus of each other's minds and that of the foreign savants who used to visit Birmingham.

Similar groups formed in other industrial towns. At Manchester in 1781 Thomas Percival, M.D., a former student at Warrington, Edinburgh and Leyden, formed a Literary and Philosophical Society which incubated, two years later, a College of Science applied to the trades of the town.[3]

A third was founded in 1783 at Leeds, the original home of Joseph Priestley. A fourth took root at Newcastle under William Turner, a Unitarian minister. A fifth, formed at Derby in 1784, numbered amongst its members William Strutt, F.R.S., builder of the earliest iron-framed building in the world. A sixth, known as the Society for the Promotion of Useful Knowledge, was started at Sheffield in 1805 through Samuel Lucas, who had moved from Birmingham to Sheffield in 1787 to become a partner in a refining and smelting works. Lucas also corresponded with John Dalton, a member of the Manchester Literary and Philosophical Society.[1]

VI

With their salaries affected by the price rise, their monopoly evaporating with the lapse of episcopal licensing, and their only means of redress through slow and costly litigation in the courts (Shrewsbury was involved in a lawsuit which had lasted for 170 years by 1798), it is little wonder that masters either took private pupils as boarders, or held curacies and livings in plurality, or allowed their schools to disappear altogether.[2] Yet there were others who managed to utilise the rising price of land to enhance the value of their endowments, or took advantage of the improved communications to enlarge the area of recruitment of their schools and so escape becoming a mere local school for the 'petties'.

There was, however, no gainsaying the competition of private schools offering a curriculum more suited to commercial needs than that fixed for many grammar schools by their Tudor and Stuart founders. Such schools rose naturally, in the industrial towns. In Newcastle, the mathematician Charles Hutton established in 1760 a school of mathematics where 'persons may be fully and expeditiously qualified for business'. Others were opened at Salford in 1765, Bury and York in 1770, while another at Addiscombe became so famous that in 1809 the East India Company bought it for conversion into a college for engineers. In Manchester, Adam Walker established a school in 1762 'more adapted to a town of trade than the monkish system still continued in our Public Schools'. When he left Manchester for London (where he spent the winter lecturing and the summer constructing water-raising engines, wind and steam carriages, ploughs, house ventilators and rotating lights off the Scilly Isles), not only the Provost of Eton but the headmasters of Westminster and Winchester invited him to lecture at their schools: a role in which he was succeeded by his son Deane Franklin Walker.

The American War of Independence accelerated industrial growth, and also led to the relaxation of restrictions on Nonconformists. So after 1779, when the legal prohibition on their teaching in schools was lifted, many of them opened schools on lines which became so firmly incised that nearly a century later Matthew Arnold could poke fun at them through Archimedes Silverpump, Ph.D. in *Friendship's Garland*.

Since entry to the university was possible at the age of fourteen, 'preparatory' schools were founded to prepare boys for the university. The name 'preparatory' was given by John Trusler to a school at Marylebone which by the middle of the century was educating the sons, legitimate and illegitimate, of the nobility; recruited, rumour had it, by the midwife of the Princess of Wales. Perhaps the most famous preparatory school was that at Hackney where seven fellows of the Royal Society including Henry Cavendish, the famous chemist, were educated. Similar, if less notable academies were at Kensington, Bath and Ewell. Dr Hans has calculated that of the 200 or so private academies of this kind which existed, two-thirds were in London. Probably more than 1000 of these existed during the century, on an average of 200 at a time.

One preparatory school, which exists to this day under the name of its eighteenth-century location, Cheam, made a name for itself in the eighteenth century under William Gilpin, who became its headmaster in 1752. During the next 28 years, his enlightened and effective methods made quite an impression on educational thought, not least because Gilpin himself left us an account of them.

He banished the birch and appointed a jury of the boys to enforce school rules and fine those who broke them. The boys not only ran this jury but collected the fines through their secretary and librarian. The money raised was spent on buying cricket bats and balls, library books, seats in the playground, and fives courts. Gilpin also encouraged boys to play games, and cultivate gardens. Each boy owned his own plot, where he could cultivate what he wished. These plots were 'Projects' in a very real sense, for boys sold the produce to the school or to their neighbourhood. And when they left the school, they would either leave their plots to their brothers or friends, or sell them.

Gilpin held that it 'is of much more use to the boys to study their own language with accuracy than a dead one'. Yet such of his boys as did learn Latin and Greek at Cheam enjoyed it because they were encouraged to read as quickly as possible. Amongst his pupils were William Mitford the historian, his brother John, Lord Redesdale, the Addingtons, the son of the Earl of Dartmouth and Lord Kenyon. Gilpin himself was very probably portrayed in Smollett's *The Adventures of Peregrine Pickle* as Dr Jennings.[1]

VII

Since the universities used to accept boys at an early age (Jeremy Bentham came up to The Queen's College, Oxford, when he was twelve, and Edward Gibbon to Magdalen when he was fifteen), it is not surprising that later writers should accuse them of being 'moribund'.[2] Yet, though their youthful recruits later criticised them most severely, the universities were by no means insulated from the scientific or political interests and activities of the time, which were so evident at the University of Leyden, or those of Scotland, which all took a goodly number of English students.

Lectures on experimental philosophy at Oxford had, by 1729, become such 'a potential goldmine' that when the Savilian professor James Bradley decided to lecture in 1729, he bought the apparatus and goodwill from his predecessor. Up to 1760, the average attendance at his lectures was 57. One of his pupils was Gilbert White, author of the *Natural History of Selborne*.

Fresh endowments for science were also forthcoming. A chair of Botany was founded by William Sherard in 1728 and a Readership in Experimental Philosophy by Lord Crewe in 1749. Dr Radcliffe left his estate to build a 'physick library' (1737) and the Infirmary (1770). This latter led to Lord Lichfield's foundation of a chair of Clinical Medicine in 1772. In the latter years the

Radcliffe trustees also began to build the Observatory. Another Oxford medical practitioner endowed a Readership in Anatomy and a school built in 1767 outside the south of Tom Quad of Christ Church.

William Adams, the lifelong friend of Dr Johnson, attracted to Pembroke a number of chemists like James Smithson (who later founded the Smithsonian Institute in Washington), William Higgins (opposer of the phlogiston theory and enunciator of the law of multiple proportions) and Gilbert Davies (later a president of the Royal Society). Perhaps the most colourful lecturer in the subject was Thomas Beddoes, Reader in Chemistry from 1788 to 1793 who drew the largest number of auditors the subject ever had. Evicted from Oxford he opened the Pneumatic Institute at Clifton, near Bristol in 1798 to expose hypochondriacs, opium addicts, the scrofulous, asthmatics and the catarrhal to his 'factitious airs'. To manufacture these 'airs', Beddoes engaged, at the suggestion of George Watt, a young technician called Humphrey Davy. It was at this Pneumatic Institute that in 1799 Davy discovered the properties of nitrous oxide. Davy also got to know James Keir, F.R.S., who had originally wanted Beddoes to work with him.

Three further case-histories indicate an affiliation between Oxford and contemporary industrial developments. James Sadler, an assistant to Beddoes, by acquiring the art of filling balloons with hydrogen and having the intrepidity to fly them from the physic garden at Christ Church meadows became the first English astronaut. He later went on to serve as a technical adviser to the Admiralty, where his work on cannon and in small arms was invaluable in the wars with France that closed the century. Edmund Cartwright, elected a Fellow of Magdalen in 1764, invented amongst other devices the power loom in 1785, and the wool-combing engine in 1789: machines destined to transform the West Riding town of Bradford. Gowin Knight, also of Magdalen, made strong magnets by a secret process for the Admiralty, and his battery of 240 magnets was given to the Royal Society in 1776.[1]

But the Dissenters saw only the barriers erected against them.

As Priestley bitterly remarked in his *Letters to Pitt* (1787): 'thus while your Universities resemble pools of stagnant water, secured by dams and mounds and offensive to the neighbourhood, ours are like rivers, which taking their natural course fertilise a whole country.' Priestley was speaking with feeling, as some of his friends burnt their fingers badly at Cambridge. True, much went forward there, as at Oxford. Laboratories were established, Addenbrooke's Hospital was built, William Heberden tried to institute a rational system of *materia medica* and therapeutics, and important new chairs were founded. The examination of candidates became, during the century, increasingly sophisticated: by 1753 they were classified as wranglers or senior or junior optimes. The practice of examining all members of the same college together was discontinued by Dr Watson in 1763. Yet loop-holes for weaker candidates remained: they were allowed to 'huddle', i.e. go through mock exercises to get their degrees. Certainly the stiffening of the Cambridge curriculum led to a revival of mathematics in the schools with the result that by 1792 there was a complaint that several schools were studying mathematics 'to the neglect of the classics'. Dr Watson had other claims to fame. He was a keen chemist (being given £100 a year by the Crown to lecture on the subject and saving it £100,000 a year by a new process of making gunpowder), and he also supported the so called Feathers Tavern petition of 1771 for the abolition of subscription to the Articles and Liturgy of the Church of England.

The most energetic promoter of the Feathers Petition in Cambridge, John Jebb, eagerly campaigned for the establishment of an annual academic examination to be conducted by the university rather than the colleges; an attempt to universalise a practice earlier initiated at St John's College. This would, Jebb hoped, stimulate the study of mathematics, classics and natural philosophy. His scheme was defeated by a narrow majority in 1774 and soon after Jebb became a Unitarian and left the university for London where he took part in the formation of the London Society for Constitutional Information.[1]

By 1772 the Test Acts were discussed in the House of Commons, and the Solicitor-General hinted at Parliamentary action in case the universities did not do something about it themselves. Arguments for more efficient university examinations reverberated at Oxford too. By 1773 Napleton of Brasenose had suggested that degrees be divided into three classes on the results of more vigorous 'public exercises'. When John Eveleigh became provost of Oriel in 1781 the case for public examinations for the degrees found a champion, and nineteen years later a statute, largely of his drafting, instituted examinations for both the Bachelor's and Master's degrees.

VIII

The chief rewards available to the able and diligent university graduates lay in the church. Some pupils of the Nonconformist academies like Secker and Butler realised this and conformed, one becoming Archbishop of Canterbury, the other Bishop of Durham. Such diligence was best applied, not so much in theology as in the classics. Indeed after Bentley's death very few classical scholars exhibited any interest in doctrine. To a deistic age, the pagan theology of the classical authors was more diverting than strenuous wrestling with scientifically minded Dissenters.

For this was a deistic age. The classics not only eased the path to preferment in the church, but provided 'a most useful and necessary ornament' to gentlemen. 'Classical knowledge', Lord Chesterfield told his son, 'is absolutely necessary for everybody, because everybody has agreed to think and to call it so.'[1] Enthusiasts might claim that moral virtue, a love of liberty, patriotism and taste were nourished by study of the classics, but teachers believed that wit and accuracy were the real by-products. Thomas Gaisford (who went up to Christ Church in 1800), put the problem in its real perspective: 'The advantages of a classical education', he later remarked, 'are two-fold—it enables us to look down with contempt on those who have not shared its advantages, and also fits us for places of emolument, not only in this world, but in that which is to come.'[2]

Gaisford's remark explains why the better public and the grammar schools concentrated on providing a full classical education, and did it much better than the university. Such concentration did not inhibit imaginative teaching: Greek plays were produced in Parr's school at Stanmore in 1775. Intellectually, the age was much influenced by Greek poetry rather than philosophy, and it was a great age for Homer. Of the dozen or so translations of the *Iliad*, three were by eminent English men of letters: John Dryden (1700—Book 1), Alexander Pope (1715-20) and William Cowper (1791). Pope's was so profitable it enabled him to become a professional man of letters. Leigh Hunt had to learn great chunks of Homer by heart at Christ's Hospital at the end of the century.

Architecturally, even more than intellectually, Greek models left their mark on the schools and colleges that were to rise early in the following century. Downing College, Cambridge, the East India College at Haileybury and University College, London (designed by William Wilkins); the British Museum, the Royal College of Physicians and King's College, London (designed by Robert Smirke), the Taylor and Randolph Buildings at Oxford; and the old University Library at Cambridge (designed by S. C. Cockerell): all show how the buildings of classical Greece stamped themselves as models.

Yet all the time classical teachers were on the defensive. Joseph Cornish in *An attempt to Display the importance of Classical learning* (1783), argued that most technical terms used in physics, botany, chemistry, astronomy, architecture, mechanics, mathematics, rhetoric and grammar 'and almost every art and science are of a Greek original and numerous others of a Roman'. That he should be justifying Greek on these grounds is significant. For as Latin had ceased to be a living language, the practice of making boys speak it in school died out and with it dropped the composition of Latin letters. Though enthusiastic schoolmasters like John Clarke of Hull wished to preserve it by reading more literal translations and the work of the ancient historians,[1] in practice Latin became virtually a vestibule to Greek.

V

THE IMAGE OF THE FACTORY

1790-1826

I

To gain the goodwill of English Catholics in the American War of Independence the penal laws were moderated in 1778 and the threat of perpetual imprisonment was lifted from Catholic bishops, priests and schoolmasters. The onset of the second war against revolutionary France prompted further relaxations in 1791 whereby Catholics could publicly worship and become schoolmasters without fear of prosecution provided they took the oath of allegiance. Although they could still not hold office in an Oxford or Cambridge college, Trinity College, Dublin, relaxed its admission requirements in 1793 and allowed Catholics to enter, whilst in 1795 the Maynooth Act sanctioned the foundation of a college for them under Catholic auspices.

Ironically enough, though the Relief Acts now permitted English Catholics to send their children abroad for a Catholic education, the schools to which they might have been sent were 'coming home'. For the foundations which English Catholics had so laboriously encouraged for two centuries were now uprooted. St Omer (founded in 1593) was refounded at Stonyhurst in 1794; the English Benedictines, who had been at Dieulouard since the seventeenth century, founded Ampleforth in 1802, whilst those at Paris since 1605 founded Downside in 1815. The major clerical seminaries also returned: Oscott (1793), Old Hall at Ware (1794 which was the lineal descendant of Allen's English College at Douai founded in 1568), Ushaw near Durham (1808) and others.

Moreover, the Catholic 'poor schools' which had begun as early as 1763 as a triple charity movement for educating, clothing and apprenticing poor Catholic children in London and elsewhere could now show their faces. The Abbé Carron worked hard to build them up.[1] Of the Catholic victims of the French Revolution, many became tutors and teachers. The accretion of such a powerful conservative element in England—12,150 Catholic laymen and priests according to a government estimate of 1797—was by no means unwelcome at so dangerous a time, when not a few of the large towns were seething with 'Corresponding Societies' and 'Reform Clubs'. For the government had been indulging in a little conservative education on its own.

II

Encouraged by the fall of the Bastille, English Dissenters renewed their agitation for the repeal of the Test and Corporation Acts in 1789. Joseph Priestley openly attacked Edmund Burke and was followed by Tom Paine and William Roscoe of Liverpool. A responsive network of corresponding societies took shape to translate their principles into political action. To prevent this, 'Church and King' clubs were formed in opposition.

Naturally these two groups collided. In Birmingham on 14 July 1791 Priestley's house was looted and burned. In Manchester on 4 June 1792 the former headquarters of the Literary and Philosophical Society was similarly attacked. In Sheffield in 1794 the editor of the local paper narrowly escaped being arrested for treason. The climax came with the trial of all three London leaders of the movement.

In 1796 the great blow fell: the magnificent Nonconformist academy at Hackney was closed because of the sympathy of some of the staff and students with the French Revolution. Only ten years old, Hackney College had been launched with a large capital fund and a long list of supporters, in Homerton Hall, with accommodation for 70 students. Intended for 'youth in general, whether they are intended for civil or commercial life, or for any one of the learned professions' it numbered a Roman Catholic and several members of the Established Church amongst its students. After the French Revolution broke out, Edmund Burke described it as 'the new arsenal in which subversive doctrines and arguments are forged'. The subversive arguments were those of one of its tutors, Richard Price, whose warm approval of the French Revolution evoked his own *Reflections on the French Revolution.* If Price annoyed Burke, another tutor, Thomas Belsham annoyed the Dissenters themselves, for he was both an Arian and a suspected republican. A republican supper at the College with Tom Paine as the guest of honour led to the arrest of an ex-student for treason, and the imprisonment of one of the governing body for attempted rebellion. This was too much for the trustees, so in Midsummer 1796 the college was dissolved, its buildings sold and the students dispersed.[1] The intellectual impetus of the dissenting academies, however, continued in the persons of old students like William Godwin, William Hazlitt and William Johnson Fox[2] and because its institutional embodiment was confined to sectarian theological colleges restricting admission to students who intended to become dissenting ministers, the more forward looking of them were by 1809 to discuss the possibility of a university.[3]

Sympathy with the French revolutionaries was the kiss of death for even a reputable school. Thus Vicesimus Knox the second, headmaster of Tonbridge, found that the pamphlets he wrote in favour of events in France lowered his numbers from 85 to 28 (in 1793) and when he retired in 1812 they were only 41.

III

One of those who had 'conceived an utter aversion to liberty according to the present idea of it in France'[4] was Hannah More. She had experienced the hard lot of a well-meaning pioneer. When she had deserted the life of a literary lioness to open schools for children and adults in the Mendip industrial towns of Shipham, Nailsea and Drayinst, she found that adults were bribed with gin not to attend her classes, that farmers wanted (as one said) 'workmen, not saints', that clergymen suspected her of being 'methodistical,' and that the Methodists themselves suspected her of encroaching on their territory. Indeed she was herself accused of 'entertaining French principles'. She was guilty of that cardinal eighteenth-century vice, enthusiasm, as she doggedly made her way around the bowels of the Mendips seeking to establish other skeletal institutions for the welfare of their occupants, like friendly societies for women. Through the dissolution and reformation of her schools she stoically went her way, beginning afresh as the French threat evaporated. She told her great friend Wilberforce that his sister would have been shocked to see 'the petty tyrants whose insolence I stroked and tamed, the ugly children I fondled, the pointers and spaniels I trained and caressed, the cider I consumed, the wine I swallowed'.

As the campaign against 'French principles' intensified, Hannah More, helped by the Clapham Sect, began to issue sedative ballads and tracts, like Paine's in format, but the very reverse in content. Selling at a halfpenny (over 50 of them came from Hannah's pen alone), their enormous circulation between March 1795 and September 1798 led Professor R. D. Altick to observe that through their publication 'middle-class Englishmen got their first experience in the mass production and distribution of reading matter'.[1]

Such distribution was the express concern of the Religious Tract Society, founded in 1799 with inter-denominational support. An early secretary, the Rev. Legh Richmond, set the standard with his *Dairyman's Daughter* (1809). Five years later in 1804 a second interdenominational body, the British and Foreign Bible Society began to distribute the scriptures on a massive scale. A moving spirit in these, as in the London Missionary Society, was David Bogue, who hoped for a university in London.

On this tide Mrs Sherwood launched her work. Wife of a paymaster of the 53rd regiment in India she sent home a story called *Little Henry and his Bearer*. Sold to a Shropshire publisher for £5, it inaugurated Mrs Sherwood's literary career just as that of her old schoolfellow, Jane Austen, was closing. What Jane Austen became for Victorian adults, Mrs Sherwood became for their children. *Little Henry* marked the first impact of her work on a society where the nursery and the governess were soon to flourish. Like Jane, Martha Mary created a literary genre of her own. Taking the Gothic horrors of Mrs Annie Radcliffe (whose *Mysteries of Udolpho* first whetted her literary appetite), she wove them into the simple pattern of the cautionary tale.

As a girl, she had once been introduced to the uxorious and inventive Richard Lovell Edgeworth, who had taken one look at the little giantess and tapped his head sadly, remarking 'She wants it here, she wants it here'. Edgeworth's usual perspicuity must have deserted him, for Martha Mary grew to rival his daughter Maria as required reading for future Victorians.[1] Indeed, none of Mrs Sherwood's contemporaries could rival her in classic evocation of childhood sins. Perhaps her masterpiece was the *Fairchild Family*, published in 1818 when she was 43. These sins fill over 300,000 words of print. What can we make of Lucy Fairchild (aged nine), who gets tipsy on cider with her sister (aged eight), who kept a journal of truly Buchmanite intensity and feeling, and who could supplement this by asking 'Papa! May we say some verses about children having bad hearts?'?

Indeed, Lucy could voice Mrs Sherwood's innermost convictions, especially when she prayed 'My heart is so vile, so full of sin, that even when I appear to be good, even then I am sinning. When I am praying or reading the Bible, even then I am sinning. When I speak, I sin, and when I am silent, I sin.' Such a preoccupation with the innate depravity of the child mind moulded the form of over 300 tracts which the industrious Mrs Sherwood wrote for the remaining 35 years of her life. For instance, the Sherwood version of the *Pilgrim's Progress* begins with three children left alone in the City of Destruction: Humble Mind, Playful and Peace. Unasked, a fourth comes to dance with them and cause the difficulties which form the core of the book. Its name—Inbred Sin.

It is easy to smile at the hard outlines of such a theology, but it is a historic fact that her books were the staple reading of children until the more frolicsome *Alice in Wonderland* was published in 1865. For, clouded as her stories were with minatory exegesis, the radiant prose of her description of childish pleasures (especially that of eating), ensured her a steady public in the days when governesses and parents had the time to read aloud to children. Each chapter of *The Fairchild Family* is a self-contained bedtime story, with sufficient continuity to last for months.

Nor should the missionary zeal of this remarkably industrious woman be despised. For she was a born teacher. Before her marriage she ran a Sunday school at Bridgnorth (in the days when such schools were novel), so well 'that the parents brought the children in crowds'. As she wrote in her diary, 'we made bonnets and tippets for our girls; we walked with them to church; we looked them up in the week-days.' After her marriage she taught on the troop-ship going out to India, although her own quarters were intensely uncomfortable: 'the cabin just the width of one gun, with a little space beside for a small table and a single chair. Our cot was slung sideways over the gun.' The pioneer work in army education that began in this canvas partition (for it was nothing more), continued when they got to Dinajpore, where her house became the regimental school. With the help of Sergeant Clarke she ran this school for 50 children, and later at Berhampore organised another for coloured children. At Cawnpore her school had four classes. Over and above this steady ameliorative routine she wrote extensively for evangelical circles, among whom moved her great friend the missionary Henry Martyn. These works, like *The Indian Pilgrim* and the *Ayah and the Lady*, were translated into Hindustani. Undoubtedly, the circumstances attending their composition, as well as her friendship with Henry Martyn, intensified the rigidity of her theology.

That the author of *Erewhon*, like many another late Victorian rationalist, should have been brought up on the *Fairchild Family* is illuminating. Samuel Butler, both in his life and writing, avenged himself on his boyhood mentors.

IV

The Sunday schools of Mrs Sherwood's young womanhood (and of that of Hannah Ball at High Wycombe), were growing rapidly. Priestley's radical friend Theophilus Lindsey had run one at Catterick in 1763. As local experiments they acquired, through the publicising flair of the editor of the *Gloucester Journal*, a national significance, when on 3 January 1783 he wrote: 'the misuse of Sunday appears, by the declaration of every criminal to be their first step in the course of wickedness'. This editor was Robert Raikes. One of his brothers was a director of the Bank of England; another was a curate who used to roam the streets with a lantern looking for fallen women who needed reclaiming. Raikes launched his ameliorative campaign by establishing the Sunday School Society in 1785 which enlisted the support of Anglicans like William Cowper and of John Wesley himself. By 1795 there were three-quarters of a million children in Sunday schools, representing, as one distinguished modern editor has said 'one of the first unconscious triumphs of the press'.[1]

Raikes paid his teachers a shilling for a twelve-hour day (including church services), and like Hannah More, encouraged parents with clothing clubs, meals and combs. Also like Hannah More, he encountered opposition. From 1797 on the *Gentleman's Magazine* attacked them as raising discontent and fomenting rebellion. Jonas Hanway, himself a philanthropist, thought they would teach children to despise manual labour, and encourage them either to refuse to work or to take employment from middle-class children. To do Hanway justice he subsequently revised his opinion in favour of teaching the young to read the Bible, for as he put it, 'religion is the prop of government'.

An institution was formed in Birmingham in 1789 to further the education of youths who had finished the normal Sunday school. It developed by 1796 into a Brotherly Society. Ostensibly, it was to train Sunday school teachers, but it was much concerned with furthering scientific knowledge amongst the mechanics. For this members were known as 'the Cast Iron Philosophers'. They established a popular library for themselves and another for artisans.

The interdenominational idyll of co-operative effort did not last. By 1800 Samuel Horsley, Bishop of Rochester, warned the House of Lords that 'schools of jacobinical politics abound in this country. In these the minds of many of the lowest orders are taught to despise religion and the laws of subordination.' He proposed that the clergy should take control of them.

Such admonitions were also directed against imaginative literature when it did not buttress Christian faith and character. To the republican Baptist minister, John Foster, and even more to Southey's friend Henry Kirke White (who died from overwork in 1806), 'literature has, of late years, been prostituted to all the purposes of the bagnio'. Shakespeare himself was trimmed down to the needs of evangelical propaganda by the egregious Dr Bowdler, whose brother John was one of the founders of the Church Building Society.

The Napoleonic war facilitated the entry of the newspaper into the lives of the working classes, who, hungry for news and avid for sensation, would even buy them when a day or two old, often by clubbing together. Their appetite was whetted by William Cobbett's *Political Register*, started in 1802. This became in spite of its price (1/0½) so appreciated that from 2 November 1816 he issued a second version to be read at home. Boosted by an efficient distribution, more than 70,000 copies of his new *Political Register* circulated. When threatened with arrest he had to decamp to America, leaving the field open. Similar fare, salted by even more radical comment, was served up to working-class readers by T. J. Wooler, whose *The Reasoner* began publication in 1808, and who succeeded Cobbett as editor of *The Statesman*. Wooler was the precursor of many others, notably William Ellis, who after being acquitted on a charge of publishing seditious libels in 1817 was helped by public subscription to set up a bookshop on Ludgate Hill where he enjoyed the services of

Cruikshank the famous cartoonist. To prune and control so many radical papers the government passed an Act in 1819 which imposed a tax on all cheap papers except those which contained 'matters of devotion, piety or charity'. This 'tax on knowledge' was to rankle.[1]

V

Sunday schools, by definition, only attacked the problem of children when they were not employed. By holding them on Sunday their promoters showed that they could or would not interfere with employment of children. Yet it was this very employment which troubled the consciences of evangelicals.

'I cannot think,' wrote Mrs Trimmer, the wife of a brickfields owner, 'of little children who work in the manufactories, without the utmost commiseration.' The physical and moral condition of children excited this mother of ten to start secondary schools at Brentford to civilise the street arabs. Having a quick pen and a lively imagination, she publicised the work in her *Oeconomy of charity* (1787). The gift of a spinning wheel for the Sunday school led her to form a spinning school for week-days. This, as one of her correspondents wrote, would 'inure them early in life to industry'.

Other schools followed, one for knitting, one for winding cotton, and one for boys. Mrs Trimmer wanted rate aid for each parish school of industry. This concept of the parish as the responsible unit for undertaking such work was to haunt politicians for a generation or more.

Those who wished to cope on a national scale with the problem could see no further than the parish pump. Even Pitt, Prime Minister in 1796, envisaged every parish sustaining a school of industry. So did Samuel Whitbread, who in 1797 introduced a Bill whereby they could be established on a parish rate. So did Brougham, who in 1820 introduced another Bill which was equally unsuccessful. Such progress as was made in parishes came from individual endeavours rather than by state stimulation. The

Reverend William Gilpin's schools at Boldre in Hampshire found many imitators in his own native county of Cumberland as well as in Westmorland, Lancashire and North Yorkshire.

Meanwhile, other more successful attacks on the evils consequent upon the exploitation of the agile bodies and nimble fingers of children had been made. The employment of 'climbing boys' to scale the flues of great houses was a public scandal. For, from the age of 5, these little human brushes acquired the skills which made them such objects of compassion to Jonas Hanway that in a *Sentimental History of Chimney Sweepers* (1785) he argued that they should not be employed until they reached the age of 8 and then only under better conditions. Though an Act of Parliament was passed to this effect in 1788 it was so ineffective that in 1803 a Society for Superseding the Necessity of Climbing Boys was formed, which tried to persuade chimney sweeps to use a machine.[1]

No machines, however, could be used in place of the nimble fingers of children in the cotton factories of South Lancashire. Housed in gaunt and comfortless 'prentice houses' to which most of them had been sent by the overseers of the poor as paupers, their welfare depended entirely on their employers. Some of these employers, like Arkwright, Oldknow or Greg, treated them as human beings, but they were exceptions. For the early cotton factories, being driven by water power, were sited in lonely places where water was plentiful and labour was scarce. Lack of oversight bred promiscuity and degradation amongst the children. When taxed with this, cotton manufacturers often pleaded that they were too busy to appreciate how bad things had become. Thus, Robert Peel confessed that he rarely found time to visit his factories, but when he did, he was 'struck with the uniform appearance of bad health, and, in many cases, stunted growth of the children'.

Public attention was drawn to the exploitation of children by Dr Percival, a former pupil of the Dissenting Academy at Warrington, who, with his fellow doctors, formed the Manchester Board of Health in 1795.

VI

War-time demands exacerbated the labour problem in the large cotton factories established near and round the towns, where in Dr Percival's opinion, conditions tended 'to diminish future expectations as to the general sum of life and industry, by impairing the strength and destroying the vital stamina of the rising generation' and by giving 'encouragement to idleness, extravagance and profligacy in the parents, who, contrary to the order of nature, subsist by the oppression of their offspring'.

Armed, and perhaps alarmed, by these findings, Sir Robert Peel who, in the year he was made a baronet (1800), was employing more than 1,500 hands, introduced an Act of Parliament on 6 April 1802, to remedy this state of affairs. His Bill took its title from its intention: 'The Health and Morals of Apprentices Act.' Neither *Hansard* nor the *Annual Register* deigned to mention its provisions. These were intended to shorten hours of work, to discontinue night work, to ensure separate sleeping apartments for males and females, and certain minimum hygienic standards (like the whitewashing of walls) for all. For the first four years apprentices were to be instructed 'by a discreet and proper person' in the three Rs. A J.P. and a clergyman, appointed at midsummer sessions, were to see that the Act was observed and were to report to the quarter sessions. The respect these worthy 'inspectors' might command did not dissipate the very real fears of the manufacturers that manufacturing secrets would be revealed, cheap labour would be lost and their business destroyed by busybodies.[1]

As with the climbing boys, mitigation of the lot of the cotton factory children began when the steam engine brought factories back into the towns, where child employees could live at home. But steam-powered factories created a fresh problem, because of the system of paying overseers according to the amount of work done. Grasping employers could plead that they were helping the war effort by working employees as hard as they could go.

When the war ended in 1815, matters came to a head. Another factory owner, who had tried the system of shortening working hours and withdrawing all children under twelve from the works, contacted Sir Robert Peel. This experimenter, himself nurtured in the Manchester atmosphere, was Robert Owen. With the help of the same Quakers who supported Joseph Lancaster (*infra* § XI), he had bought his father-in-law's mills at New Lanark where he opened an Institution for the Formation of Character on New Year's Day 1816, with an infant school, a day school for children and evening schools for adults. In these, teaching was on activity methods on Pestalozzian lines.

Owen drafted a Bill with legal sanctions and Sir Robert Peel, in printing and circulating it in 1815, confessed that it was experimental. He spoke truer than he knew at the time. After four years of opposition, during which time both the Houses of Parliament set up committees to hear evidence for and against legislation, a second Factory Act found its tortuous way to the Statute Book. In this Act in 1819, the teeth of the Bill drafted four years before were carefully drawn. It did *not* apply to all factories, as intended, only to cotton mills. It did not raise above 9 the minimum age at which labour could begin. It did not allow any provision for education, where the draft had made special provision for those children between 10 and 14 to spend half an hour a day in being instructed. Worst of all, the provision on which both Peel and Owen had depended to work their Bill was dropped: that of paid inspectors. For in 1815 Peel had lamented that the voluntary inspectors 'had been very remiss in the performance of their duty' and suggested that they should be paid. Such inspectors were not set up until 1833, three years after Peel's death. But the principle had been established 28 years before. His two Factory Acts provided the foundations for the legislative superstructure which was to be raised over the century to shelter children.

VII

The manufacturers and inventors were, in this twenty-year-war boom, conjuring up marvels that outstripped the *Arabian Nights*. To Robert Lovell Edgeworth's daughter Maria, they were heroes, and she wrote stories like *Rosanna and the Manufacturer* in which they played the part of Prince Charming. Small wonder Lord Byron groaned 'Miss Edgeworth's Cupid must be a Presbyterian'. Only Cupid was a stranger to Miss Edgeworth. She never married, for she shunned matrimony to devote herself to the teaching of her father's 22 children. Her father, rewarded by the Society of Arts and elected to Fellowship of the Royal Society, gave great attention to innovations like telegraphy, caterpillar traction and shorthand. She, denied these masculine fields of enterprise, confined her considerable gifts to helping her many half-brothers and half-sisters to take the same interest in the structure of things as he did.

For matters educational, father and daughter had complementary experience. Maria was still teaching her half-brothers when she was 50. Her father, on the other hand, had six years' experience as a Royal Commissioner on Irish education, and in 1800 had suggested the formation of an association which should establish 'secondary' schools throughout the country—a use of the word which the late Sir Michael Sadler rightly pointed out as surprisingly modern.

Their joint testament was *Practical Education*, published in 1798, a year before the birth of the seventeenth Edgeworth child. It was based on an actual record initiated by the second Mrs Edgeworth 22 years before. This register was indeed pioneer work in child study. But *Practical Education* is more than a chronicle of these long-term experiments; it caught up and made current other contemporary ideas. Rousseau was suitably modified in view of the failure of his theories as applied to the education of the eldest Edgeworth child (born three years before Maria).

The opening chapter—on 'Toys'—set the tone of the book. Written, like sixteen of the other chapters, by Maria herself, it applauds the initiative which prompts a child to dissect a speaking doll.

Learning, in Edgeworth eyes, was a very active process, and if the spontaneity of the play impulse was checked, mischief of a more serious kind would invariably follow. It remained for Froebel to restate this with such effectiveness that it is now a commonplace. To Maria's sixteen chapters (mainly philosophical), her father added six of his own composition (mainly practical), while her half-brother Lovell (sixth in the family) contributed one on the teaching of chemistry. Only one chapter was written by both father and daughter—that on 'Tasks'. The question of religion was ignored: indeed their silence on the question provoked the reproaches of their French translator Pictet, some three years later. Nor did fairy tales fit into the Edgeworth scheme of things. 'Why should the mind be filled with fantastic visions instead of useful knowledge?' asked Maria.[1]

From small beginnings (a slate in the drawing room at Edgeworthstown), these stories grew in number till they filled the six volumes of the *Parent's Assistant* (a title which Maria herself 'disliked particularly'). *Moral Tales*, another collection, with its insistence on tact, its theme that boys and girls should mistrust appearance and despise self-indulgence and uncontrolled emotion, has a contemporary pertinency of its own. In spite of Byron, her stories had a wide and effective circulation. Thomas Moore used to read them to his pretty actress wife at Mayfield, while Walter Scott confessed to a friend that after reading *Simple Susan* 'there is nothing for it but to put down the book and cry'. Her writings prompted Thomas Arnold to complain 'it does seem to me as forced and unnatural in us now to dismiss the principles of the Gospel and its great motives from our consideration—as is done habitually in Miss Edgeworth's books—as it is to fill our pages with Hebraisms, and to write and speak in the words and style of the Bible'.[2]

VIII

Maria mirrored a mood that found expression in the towns where factories were booming.

A strong desire to introduce utilitarian subjects like algebra, mathematics, French and German into the curriculum of Leeds Grammar School against the wishes of the master led the Governors to take the case to the Court of Chancery in 1795. After some ten years a circumspect and oracular judgement was finally given in 1805 by the Lord Chancellor (Lord Eldon), to the effect that the 'new subjects' would be taught only as 'ancillary' to the 'fundamentals' of the classical languages. The length, expense and unprofitable results of the Leeds suit did perhaps as much as Lord Eldon's judgement itself to deter other schools from seeking a change. Other foundations, however, like that of King Edward VI at Birmingham were enriched by industrial growth. Here an elementary school (in 1775), an evening school (in 1790) and exhibitions to the universities were established as well as teachers' salaries raised. Its secretary was held to be 'largely responsible' for the antipathy to the Dissenters that led to the burning of Priestley's house in June 1791.[1]

Eleven years later, one of Priestley's friends (who had tried to save his house from the mob) bought a school at Hill Top, Birmingham. His eldest son, Matthew Davenport, was 10 years old; his second, Edwin, was 9; his third, Rowland, was 7 and his daughter, Caroline, was but a baby. Other children were to follow: Frederic (born that very year), William Howard (born two years later) and Sarah (born in 1807). But to Hill, the boundary line between his family and his school was but thinly drawn, if at all. For him as for other great educational reformers, his school was the community which embraced all loyalties, and his children began to assist him when they had barely reached their teens. Matthew would attend him as he taught the natural sciences to boys of the local grammar school. Rowland's first purchase—at the age of 9—was Maria Edgeworth's *Parent's Assistant*, and within two years he too was teaching—out of Mrs Barbauld. The Hill boys all learnt by teaching, and all became distinguished men. Matthew became the first recorder of Birmingham, Edwin invented a machine for folding envelopes which was exhibited at the Crystal Palace in 1851, Rowland invented a rotary printing press and secured the national adoption of penny postage, whilst Frederic carried out educational investigations for the Manchester Statistical Society and became one of the first inspectors of prisons. Not only Hill's sons, but his pupils did him credit. Samuel Beale became M.P. for Derby and chairman of the Midland Railway, and A. F. Osler, F.R.S., invented the anemometer, and made a name as a glass manufacturer. Hill Top developed into a virtual republic, administered, judged and operated by the boys—an educational refraction of Priestley's ideas.[1] Lubricating the machinery was a school currency, in which industry was rewarded and slackness penalised. This cash nexus had no value in the community outside, though it reflected the utilitarian mentality of the boys' parents who were turning the city into one of the workshops of the world. But it was not so much the currency which steadied the schoolboy community as the responsibility it entailed. For the fines and rewards were distributed by a schoolboy court, and their scale determined by a popular code. Payment by results on these lines held no injustices for teacher or taught since all had a voice in determining what those results should be. The test of language was speech, whether in the vernacular or not; while for those to whom the ample scientific and mathematical course proved difficult, rewards in the school currency could be earned by voluntary work on models, etching, versifying or reading. Though the masters ruled in the classroom (itself a novelty in the days when large halls were still the vogue), the boys ruled elsewhere. Corporal punishment was unknown.

Rowland, the third son, became the moving spirit after the departure of Matthew for the bar. In the decade following Waterloo he even supplanted his father. Speech Day was superseded by an exhibition. A trigonometrical survey of Birmingham was undertaken. Visits to coal mines and canals were organised. A weekly staff meeting was instituted to discuss 'improvements to be introduced'. Of this Rowland wrote, 'I find the conference a most powerful engine'. The youngest children learned the school code with the alphabet so that 'school morality' could be 'imbibed with the pupils' earliest letters'. It was Rowland, too, who designed the new buildings at Hazelwood, into which the school moved in 1819. By then he could write, 'a few days ago, without any solicitation, or even hint on my part, my father took me into partnership: that is to say, all our business since has been carried on under the firm of Thomas Wright Hill and Son.'

Rowland caught the public eye, and in 1821, took his brother Arthur to Edgeworthstown to see Maria, who advised them to tone down the 'republicanism' of Hazelwood school. The publication of *Plans for the Government and Liberal Instruction of Boys in Large Numbers, drawn from Experience* (1822) attracted Jeremy Bentham, who induced the Hills to move the school to Bruce Castle, Tottenham. By now Edwin and Frederic were teaching in the school, together with F. C. Ruinet, a French language teacher, and E. W. Brayley, who specialised in the physical sciences. Brayley was an interesting product of the Royal Institution, and in 1831 published *The utility of the knowledge of nature considered with reference to the general education of youth*: a powerful anticipation of Huxley's memorable address a generation later. Bruce Castle became a mecca for the educationalists of the day. Wilberforce, Grote, Count Frölich of Sweden, Professor Save of Uppsala, Dr Maltby, Joseph Hume, Nassau Senior, W. J. Fox, Basil Hall, Babbage and Lardner were some of the many who approved. Articles in the *Edinburgh Review* (1825) and the *London Magazine* (1826) helped to spread the knowledge of the school's educational expertise. Thomas Jefferson made enquiries, and the President of Haiti showed great interest. But perhaps the strongest tribute of all came from Robert Owen, who urged Rowland to undertake the management of one of his communities. Rowland refused, preferring to employ his energies in establishing a remarkable anticipation of the Peckham experiment. But on this Thomas Wright Hill did not look with a very enthusiastic eye. 'My dear Rowland,' he told his son, 'you and your brothers are the last men to make monks of.'

So through the top-soil of custom and tradition, new ideas sent down roots, even in established schools. Oundle, for instance, which was revived in 1796, offered boys 'a competent idea of the several manufactures and the metals from the rude material and the mines to their last improvement'. At Sherborne, Manchester Grammar School and other schools, similar pressures registered.

IX

'All this avails but little,' complained Vicesimus Knox, speaking of the 'fashion' for science, 'if there is no foundation, or a very slight one, of grammatical or classical literature.' Like many of his contemporaries Knox held that 'the very terms of the sciences, as well as of the arts, are almost entirely Latin and Greek, with slight variations' and argued, 'to initiate boys in the exact sciences without giving them a knowledge or taste for philology' was 'to disgust them with difficulty and to prevent them from ever making their science acceptable to others, by the elegance of the vehicle'.[1]

Classical teaching was reanimated during the French wars by Samuel Butler, who became headmaster of Shrewsbury in 1798. Through regular written examinations to test and grade the boys they came to feel 'that Latin and Greek were the one thing worth living for'. They won for themselves a stream of scholarships to the universities and for Butler a bishopric. The headmaster of Harrow, C. T. Longley, came in the first flush of his appointment to see how Butler's system worked, whilst H. J. T. Drury, also of Harrow, told Butler that 'the advance of learning amongst the young has decidedly, at all English schools of any note, generally taken its impulse from you'.[2]

The diminutive but no less powerful Keate (who had unsuccessfully competed with Samuel Butler for the Craven Scholarship in 1793) assisted by only nine masters coped manfully with 500 boys at Eton, where he was headmaster from 1809 to 1834, by encouraging debating societies. When boys got out of hand he flogged them. Flogging was indeed no indication of a lack of liberal ideas, for Richard Valpy flogged too: yet he encouraged school drama at Reading (where he was headmaster from 1781 to 1830) and adapted plays from English, Latin and Greek for them to act for the benefit of local charities. By the time Nicholas Carlisle came to publish his *Concise Description of the Endowed Grammar Schools in England and Wales* (1818) many smaller grammar schools were not teaching classics at all. He lamented: 'In an age, when so many Theories are entertained with respect to the *universal Necessity*, or the *expeditious Acquirement*, of Learning, when ... even WESTMINSTER has been strangely classed in the Report on the Education of " *The Lower Orders* in the Metropolis," it may well become some able and scientific pen to protect and exemplify the rights and importance of our PUBLIC GRAMMAR SCHOOLS; and put a bold stop to the havoc of ignorant or fanatic Trustees, before they impair those Venerable Institutions, where the true sense of the Learned Languages may in youth be obtained'.

x

Vicesimus Knox pointed out that the war with France had stimulated the study of science.

It appears that, in imitation of the French, especially since the Revolution, the sciences which Bonaparte encouraged (chiefly for the sake of raising engineers, gunners, surgeons and all other description of people who assist in sieges and the works of slaughter), are becoming in England the fashionable study to the exclusion or at least the comparative neglect of, polite literature.

From its outbreak to long after Waterloo, French ideas and practice found imitators. John Anderson, Professor of Natural

Philosophy at Glasgow university, sent the French revolutionary government a new type of gun, together with suggestions for using paper balloons to disseminate their ideas in Germany. And just as the French set about establishing institutions for the training of scientists (ultimately to culminate in the École Polytechnique in 1794), so did he. His scientific apparatus (which was considerable), and his fortune (which was very small), he bequeathed as the nucleus of a university which was to bear his name. Anderson's university duly took shape in 1796 with the appointment of Thomas Garnett, M.D. to deliver three lectures on popular science and its applications. One course attracted 500 students.[1]

Garnett left for London to teach in a similar institution, founded in Albemarle Street, London, in 1799 by an American expatriate, Benjamin Thompson, Count Rumford, and known as the Royal Institution. Rumford, hoping to marry the skills of scientists with those of artisans, built a separate staircase to, and a special gallery in, his lecture theatre so that though commonly engaged they need not have to sit together. But even this ingenious concession to class prejudice did not placate the hostility of certain influential patrons of the Royal Institution who let it be known that the mixing of masters and men had to be dropped 'as quietly as possible', as it was 'thought to have a dangerous political tendency.' Dropped it was.[2]

That the Royal Institution was a success was due to the subsequent appointment of Humphrey Davy, formerly assistant to Thomas Beddoes (the son-in-law of Richard Lovell Edgeworth) as professor of chemistry. Using the great voltaic pile built up by the first secretary of the Institution, Davy decomposed potash to obtain potassium and subsequently obtained sodium, calcium, barium, strontium and magnesium by similar means. One of his assistants, Frederich Accum, published in 1803 the first English chemical text book to be based on Lavoisier's principles. His subsequent work at popularising science at the Surrey Institution attracted the attention of Rowlandson the cartoonist, and distinguished Americans like Benjamin Silliman.[3] Another of Davy's assistants, Michael Faraday was to improve on Davy's work in electricity by discovering in 1831 the principles of the dynamo and the electric motor.

Emulation of French technological discoveries, like Leblanc's soda process or Appert's food canning led to further English experiments in technical training. The introducer of the Leblanc process into England, James Muspratt, also founded a chemical college at Liverpool, while the introducer of food canning into England was a strong supporter of the Royal Institution.[1] Perhaps more directly germane to our story, however, was the introduction, by its French inventor N. L. Robert, of the mechanical manufacture of paper into England where it was vigorously exploited by the brothers Henry and Sealy Fourdrinier from 1803 onwards at Frogmore and by John Gamble at St Neots. It increased output tenfold and reduced the price by a third. With stereotyping (invented by Earl Stanhope in 1805), and with the introduction of the mechanical press and steam printing, the production of cheap books now became possible.[2]

In the universities too, such ideas spread. When William Farish was elected to the chair of chemistry at Cambridge in 1794 he decided to lecture upon the application of chemistry to the arts and manufactures of Great Britain. He too drew crowded audiences.[3]

In more official circles French practice found sedulous imitators. Officers for the army fighting against France were provided by new military schools at High Wycombe (1799) and at Great Marlow (1802);[4] those for the navy by a college at Portsmouth (1809), while the extensive losses in horses sustained by the army led the government to award the veterinary college established in 1792 an annual grant of £1,500, to train veterinary surgeons for each regiment of cavalry. Paid from 1795 to 1813, this grant was an early example of public funds being used for scientific training.[5]

The East India Company, then the largest joint-stock enterprise in the world, opened a private engineering college at Addiscombe, near Croydon, in 1809 to supply, on the lines of the French École des Ponts et Chaussées, skilled men to cope with the needs of the sub-continent then under its jurisdiction. Addiscombe produced the engineers like A. T. Cotton, and J. V. Bateman-Champaign, who harnessed India's rivers and built its roads. One of its pupils whom we shall meet later in these pages was J. F. D. Donnelly. William Sturgeon, discoverer of the soft iron electromagnet, taught at Addiscombe. He subsequently founded the *Annals of Electricity* (the first electrical journal in England) and went on to teach the subject in London and Manchester.

The first realistic attempts made to teach the blind by using letters printed in relief by Valentin Haüy were translated into English, but not published, by the poet Blacklock, himself blinded by smallpox in 1786. Six years later in 1791, Edward Rushton, blinded by malignant ophthalmia contracted on a slave ship, started the first English school for the blind at Liverpool. Two other schools were founded in Edinburgh and Bristol in 1793 and a third in London in 1799. Other provincial towns like Norwich, Glasgow, Aberdeen and Birmingham, followed suit.

But these institutions were retreats or asylums rather than schools for training the blind. The necessary metamorphosis was made possibly by a French artillery officer, Charles Barbier, who, to enable soldiers to transmit messages in the dark, developed a phonetic speech-sound method of expression whereby embossed dots could be used for letters.[1] On a visit to Haüy's school Barbier met young Louis Braille, who cut down his twelve dot system to six, varied in 63 different combinations. Braille liberated the fleeting fingertips of the blind in 1829, when he published the system that from then on was known by his name. The propagation of Braille in England was largely due to Dr T. R. Armitage, who founded in 1868 The British and Foreign Blind Association (now the National Institute for the Blind).

XI

Exhilarated by factory techniques, some tried to apply them to schools. The monitorial system was, to Sir Thomas Bernard (one of the founders of the Society for Bettering the Condition of the

Poor in 1796) 'the division of labour applied to intellectual purposes'. 'The principle in schools and manufactories,' he wrote, 'is the same.' To Samuel Taylor Coleridge, perhaps the least mechanistically minded thinker of his age, the monitorial system was an 'incomparable machine', a 'vast moral steam engine'.

In essence monitors began as an expedient for coping with large numbers of children; only later did they become a 'system'.[1] An Anglican chaplain to the Indian Army, Dr Andrew Bell, trying to cope with his many duties as superintendent of the orphan asylum at the Egmore Redoubt at Madras and chaplain to five regiments, employed an intelligent pupil, Johnnie Frisker, to teach his fellows to write and draw in sand. The boy lived up to his name and proved as capable a teacher as he had been a pupil. This 'discovery' Bell publicised in *An Experiment in Education* (1797).[2] But the system made little headway until Joseph Lancaster, son of a private in the American War of Independence, began in 1801 to utilise it in a one-room school at Borough Road, where he taught as to a thousand children through a system of 'drafts not classes' and published his results in *Improvements in Education* (1803).

As a system of mass instruction, it enabled the vast increase of the child population to be coped with.[3] When Lancaster asked in 1805 that the national education should be based on the 'grand basis of Christianity', and that a new voluntary society should be formed to encourage existing schools and create new ones, he outraged the formidable Mrs Trimmer. She promptly drummed up Dr Bell out of his comfortable living at Swanage to oppose Lancaster and a caustic exchange of epithets ensued. Poor Lancaster, a weak vain creature at the best of times, ineptly castigated by Mrs Trimmer, a charitably disposed lady of Brentford, as 'the Goliath of Schismatics', fell into debt in a mood of euphoria following an audience with George III (who had promised him support).[4] He had to be rescued by two Quakers, Joseph Fox and William Allen, who in 1808 took over his school and formed the Institution for Promoting the British System for the Education of the Labouring and Manufacturing Classes of Society of Every

Religious Persuasion. In 1814 this formidable name was shortened to the British and Foreign Schools Society.

This pamphlet warfare and the increasing need of educating the children in the mushrooming industrial towns affected the S.P.C.K., which reported in 1810 that two-thirds of the children of the poor had no schooling at all. At his anniversary sermon the following year the Lady Margaret Professor of Divinity at Cambridge urged the laity and clergy to combine and remedy this state of affairs. The instrument to their hands he pointed out, had been provided by Dr Bell. So members of the S.P.C.K. met on 16 October 1811 and decided to form The National Society for the Education of the Poor in the Principles of the Established Church throughout England and Wales. Unlike its parent, the S.P.C.K., the National Society was more than a merely advisory body, for after incorporation in 1817 it moved with force and vigour. Taking over the charity schools, it also began to issue its own books and school material (after 1845). Its aim was heroic; nothing less than shouldering the whole burden of the national education at a time when that burden was increasing very rapidly.

These two, the British and Foreign Schools Society and the National Society, paced each other in the establishment of schools for the children in the manufacturing towns. In this race the National Society had the very considerable advantages of a diocesan and parish organisation already set up by the S.P.C.K., a formidable number of charity schools to start with and the patronage of the Archbishop of Canterbury. By 1814 it had 230 schools and 40,484 pupils. These advantages were to be resented by the Nonconformists in subsequent decades.

The monitorial system itself spread to grammar and public schools.[1] At Charterhouse John Russell, headmaster from 1811 to 1832 took the top 120 boys before allowing them to go to work on their juniors, which they did to the great dudgeon of young Thackeray and Martin Tupper, their pupils at the time. It also spread to the United States. It is not unlikely that it subconsciously influenced Thomas Arnold (a great admirer of Coleridge).

Machine-like though the monitorial system might be, as a

system it had to be acquired, and so the teaching of monitors became important. Lancaster began in 1805 to board a selected number of monitors as 'apprentices'; by 1808 he had 24 and by 1811 he had 50. In the following year this led to a quarrel between himself and his sponsors, so he migrated with most of the trainees to a private school in Tooting, leaving his sponsors to manage the training at Borough Road. Meanwhile the National Society, on its formation in 1811, developed a multi-purpose school at Baldwin's Gardens under the Rev. W. Johnson, from Bell's own very modest beginnings at Gower's Walk. Baldwin's Gardens served as a centre of the movement, training both organisers and monitors. The efforts of the National Society were supplemented by the establishment, by the Bishop of Durham in 1810, of a similar dual-purpose 'training school' at Bishop Auckland, admitting trainees at 14. This, known as the Barrington school, was opened by Dr Bell and descanted upon by Sir Thomas Bernard.

So the two societies also launched a programme of teacher-training in England.[1] That of the National Society quickly spread to various diocesan 'central' schools, embryos of the training colleges of two decades later. That of the British and Foreign Schools Society affected, of all places, Ireland, where a Lancastrian trainee, John Veevers, took part in the establishment of a training centre in 1814 which five years later joined the model school in Kildare Place to train Roman Catholic and Protestant teachers.

XII

The precepts of Priestley and the practice of Bell and Lancaster stimulated Jeremy Bentham to devise a plan for an institution based upon his own unique utilitarian calculus of pleasure and pain. Called *Chrestomathia* it offered an architectural, administrative and pedagogic blue-print for a new type of 'day school' for the use of the 'middling and higher ranks of life' based on vocational training through science and culminating in 'a school of technology'. Since to Bentham all knowledge had a social purpose (the Classics being suitable only for the learned professions), science was to be diffused in it by exhibitions, experiments and working models. The progress of this diffusion he plotted in an encyclopaedic table.

Embedded in this remarkable book are many principles that were subsequently to engage teachers: the 'place-capturing principle', charts and wall diagrams, minimal rewards and no corporal punishment. Self-government on the part of the children was advocated to prevent conspiracy against their teachers.[1]

Bentham's ideas were applied by his disciples, James Mill especially, who wrote a pamphlet entitled *Schools for All* in 1812, amplified it in an article for the *Edinburgh Review* in 1813, and then, in the *Encyclopaedia Britannica* of 1818, gave it philosophic form. The *Edinburgh Review*, to which Mill began to contribute in 1808, had been established by Henry Brougham, Francis Jeffrey and Sydney Smith, nuclear members of a student 'Academy of Physics' in Edinburgh at the close of the preceding century.[2] Mill found that Brougham was, if not a cold-blooded utilitarian, at least a warm ally.

Brougham tried to make the Lancastrian movement a public one as early as 1810. Failing in this, he secured the appointment of a select committee to investigate the education of the lower orders in London in 1816. The money spent on it was the first governmental expenditure on education since the days of the Commonwealth. He extended it to survey the schools of the country. He sent questionnaires to 11,400, and all but 200 were completed and returned. From these he found that 3,500 parishes had no school at all. So he suggested that schools should be provided from State funds with masters appointed and paid by the parish. But both Dissenters and Catholics argued that this would merely strengthen the Anglican church and his Bill was withdrawn. Meanwhile in 1819 he secured the appointment of a Royal Commission to survey all educational charities. As it began to gather its information (a task which was to take 24 years to complete) trustees began to stir. As the *Edinburgh Review* gloated, 'the culpable are reforming from fear of exposure and punishment; the indolent and inattentive from shame'.

Brougham and Mill also in 1818 established the first infant school in London (and England), modelled on that established by Robert Owen at his factory in New Lanark. For Brougham, like a true man of action, caught up the best from all reformers with whom he was brought into contact.[1]

XIII

If Bentham was primarily interested in the truth which broke with the past, Coleridge was interested in finding the truth underneath the past.[2] By the vulgar, Bentham was often regarded as an innovator, and Coleridge a conservative. The polarity between their followers persisted down to our own times. Coleridge's 'conservatism' was essentially English: history to him presented no contradiction between old and new. He had an acute appreciation of the two-handed impact of technology on human life. Visiting the dockyards at Portsmouth he noticed the 'pitiable slaves' who became 'old men in the prime of manhood'.

A pin machine has been lately introduced, after a rebellion among the men, & but for the same Deplorable delusion, 2 thirds of that Labor might be done by machines, which now eats up the Rope-men like a Giant in a fairy-tale.[3]

Coleridge also passionately admired Davy. He wrote:

O how gladly I would resign my life to procure for mankind such health and longevity to H. Davy as should enable him to discover the Element of metals, of Sulphur and of Carbon. O! he will do it! Yea and may perhaps reveal the synthetic idea of the Antithets, Attraction and Repulsion.[4]

He attended and took notes at Davy's lectures at the Royal Institution in 1801–2 and helped him to read new German scientific works.[5] He argued that chemistry 'united the opposite advantages of immaterialising mind without destroying the definiteness of Ideas

—nay even while it gives clearness to them'. He even proposed to set up a chemist's laboratory himself with William Calvert. But he found chemistry could 'never possess the same kind of certainty with mathematics',[1] and though he obtained, by his own confession, images for poetry 'from his chemistry', he warned his two sons Hartley and Derwent to profit from his experience and study mathematics.

O! With what bitter regret, and in the conscience of such glorious opportunities, both at school under the Janus Mathematician, Wales, the companion of Cook in his circumnavigation, and at Jesus College, Cambridge, under an excellent mathematical Tutor, Newton, all *neglected* with still greater *remorse*!

Lamenting that there was abundant reason for 'excluding from all philosophy and theology not merely practical those who were ignorant of Mathematics', he groaned, 'O! with what toil must the essential knowledge be *anguished-out* without the assistance of the technical!'[2]

Coleridge's whole life was spent in 'anguishing-out' essential knowledge, and the process is still being charted.[3] His idea of 'essential knowledge' first appears in a plan to form a private class in 1796. He took the theme up again 26 years later with members of a philosophical class to educate them for 'any of those walks in life in which the possession and display of intellect are of special importance'.[4]

Coleridge scorned the 'contemptible arrogance' of the 'boy-graduates in all the technicals, and in all the dirty passions and impudence of anonymous criticism', and developed the exciting concept of a lay clerisy: a body of men and women who conserve and carry forward the spiritual traditions of the country. This concept was to excite and animate such followers as Dr Arnold.[5]

His passionate concern with the 'human condition' led him to work feverishly for the Factory Bill of Robert Peel, which he thought had been brought forward 'injudiciously . . . without due proper action of the public mind—and without due parliamentary arrangements'.

'God forbid,' he told a friend on 21 February 1818, 'that I should even suspect the possibility of his not being in earnest; but really I cannot with my experience of the world wonder that others suggest the probability.'[1]

In his rich, tumultuous and often tortured prose, he wrestled with the problems posed by technological change: a militant utilitarian philosophy, the 'plebification' of knowledge, the cult of the trivial and the passion for entertainment and instruction at small cost. These things depressed him as they were to depress his disciples down the *via dolorosa* of Victorian England. For though he condemned 'the disposition to think that the peace of nations . . . may be re-established by excluding the people from all knowledge and prospect of amelioration', he also condemned the 'spinning jennies for the cheap and speedy manufacture of reading and writing'. To him, the real answer lay in true religion which 'through her sacred oracles answers for all that effective faith pre-supposes, knowledge and individual conviction'.[2]

Coleridge's friend Wordsworth also condemned exclusive dependence upon the intellect and upheld the higher claims of imagination and intuition. For Wordsworth also believed that childhood held the key to later life, and that the State should recognise this and promote the education of children. 'I wish to be considered as a teacher or nothing,' he wrote. It ruined his poetry, but it made him more effective.[3]

Coleridge's 'disciples' humanised what the Benthamites made efficient. Dr Arnold of Rugby, Arnold's pupil and biographer A. P. Stanley, Arnold's successor Frederick Temple, Thomas Carlyle and F. D. Maurice were all Coleridgeans. And though his philosophy was dismissed by Victorian evangelicals as 'semi-pagan' and 'mystical' 'baptised with a christian and biblical nomenclature,'[4] it enabled the Church to change and accommodate itself to the needs of the nineteenth century.

VI

MALTHUSIANISM AND THE MECHANICS
1826–1851

I

A cold douche to the perfectibilist optimism of the 'educationists' was administered by the Reverend T. R. Malthus, who pointed out that the population was increasing faster than it could be sustained. Amongst the positive insurances against such a 'flood of life' Malthus included 'all unwholesome occupations, severe labour and exposure to the seasons, extreme poverty, bad nursing of all kinds, the whole train of common diseases and epidemics, wars, plague and famine.'[1]

Malthus was challenged by (amongst others) Thomas Hodgskin, who argued that the increase was reciprocal with the progress of man in knowledge and happiness. To provide working men with 'Accounts of all new Discoveries, Inventions and Improvements,' together with 'Plans and suggestions for the Abridgement of Labour,' Hodgskin established *The Mechanics' Magazine*, a weekly in which he suggested on 11 October 1823 that a Mechanics' Institute should be established in London, modelled on one established earlier that year in Glasgow.[2]

Malthus was also challenged, in deed if not in word, by those who both analysed and endeavoured to cope with the problems posed by hasty urban development. As a result of an Act of 1815 (55 Geo. III. c. 194) a corps of qualified general medical practitioners appeared: all from that year examined and licensed by the Society of Apothecaries. Teachers in the various private venture schools in London and the provinces which arose to prepare students for this examination also played a leading role in the assault on Malthusianism, notably Dr George Birkbeck of the Aldersgate School of Medicine, C. T. Thackrah of the

Leeds School of Surgery and Dr James Kay of the Ardwick and Ancoats Dispensary.[1]

Engineers were supplying an even more positive answer to the gloomy forebodings of Malthus. Their canals, dams, engines and various devices for bending the forces of nature to the service of man demanded professional skills, as the civil engineers said when they formed their professional association in 1818. Some of them, like Bryan Donkin, inventor of devices for the canning of food, joined Dr George Birkbeck and Thomas Hodgskin in their schemes for the education of mechanics. That is why the London Mechanics' Institute opened its doors in 1824 in a disused chapel in Monkwell Street. Within a year it had 1,887 students.

II

Like so much else in England, mechanics' institutes embodied the results of Scottish experience, tempered by French practice.[2] The 'mechanics' class' at Anderson's Institution had leased a disused chapel in Shuttle Street, Glasgow, in 1823 for an independent Mechanics' Institution and chose Dr Birkbeck, a former lecturer at Anderson's, as their president. The Glasgow institute was, however, not the first, for others had been founded at Chester in 1810 and Perth in 1814, and one had been proposed in London by Timothy Claxton in 1817. At Edinburgh, thanks to Leonard Horner's adoption of suggestions by Thomas Dick in the *Monthly Magazine* in 1814 and Dugald Bonnatyne (director of the Glasgow Gas Company), in the *Encyclopaedia Britannica* in 1818, a school of arts took shape in 1821. 'Arts' in Horner's mind included instruction in practical science for mechanics by mechanics. Yet another pioneer venture had been established at Haddington four years earlier, where Samuel Brown, a public-spirited merchant, had utilised some balances of militia insurances for which no claimants had been found to start a travelling library in East Lothian, around which developed a strong school of arts in 1823.

The Glaswegian spore spread. Liverpool, Sheffield and Kilmarnock and Greenock had institutions of a similar kind growing before the end of the year 1823. By 1826 over 104 other mechanics' institutes were in existence, yet by 1831 there were only 101. Of the many individual causes of this—shortage of money and of lecturers, mechanics' suspicions of the sedative techniques of their employers and their employers' contempt for the subversiveness of 'bookish learning'—one stood out: the impossibility of teaching untutored (and in some cases uninterested) audiences who clearly preferred political to physical science.

Institutes grew rapidly in the industrial areas of the West Riding and Lancashire where 27% of all the British institutes were formed. The emergence of American type Lyceums (with their regional organisation and provision for women members), and provincial Athenaeums (for middle-class merchants and clerks), led mechanics' institutes to form unions. The West Riding, later known as the Yorkshire Union (1837), led, followed by the Manchester, later the Lancashire and Cheshire, Union (1847), Kent (1847), Midlands (1847), the Northern (1848), Devon and Cornwall (1850) and Leicestershire (1853) Unions.

By 1852 a National Union was established by the Royal Society of Arts with a central clearing house. Through this the Royal Society of Arts inaugurated in 1856 a system of examinations. These examinations were adopted by regional unions. Not only do the examinations of the Union of the Lancashire and Cheshire Institute survive, but the Union itself is still a consultative and examining body for the Local Education Authorities.

The institutional progeny of the mechanics' institutes illustrates how widely they ranged in their heyday. The London Mechanics' Institution became Birkbeck College, that at Manchester became the College of Advanced Technology, that at Leeds became the College of Technology, those at Bolton, Crewe, Huddersfield, Keighley and Preston became technical colleges, and that at Liverpool became a college of art. Itinerant libraries circulated in Lancashire, Cheshire, Yorkshire and the North entirely through

99

mechanics' institutes, and their unions provided what was virtually the same service as is now discharged by the county library. And when the lethargy of local authorities was over-come (only 80 of them had taken advantage of the Act of 1850 which enabled public provision to be made for libraries by 1877), it was from the mechanics' institutes that many public libraries began to operate. Blyth, Gateshead, Newcastle, South Shields and Tynemouth in the north, Newport (Mon.), in the west, Basing-stoke in the south and Beccles in the east were some of the many local libraries that began in this way.

Least known, but none the less important, were the day schools started, sustained and ultimately handed over to the local authorities, by certain mechanics' institutes. The Liverpool In-stitute High School for Boys (and its counterpart for girls), the Leeds Modern School for Boys (and its counterpart for girls), and the Keighley Grammar School for Boys were perhaps the best examples.

Some of the suggestions made for the improvement of the institutes were later taken up on a national scale. The Northern Union, for instance, planned a system of examinations (which never materialised), before the Society of Arts took up the idea. Moreover, the chief organiser of the East Lancashire Union actually suggested a system of payment by results.[1]

III

In the institutes educability was eagerly canvassed. The tireless labours of the brothers Combe spread the belief that there was a relationship between the human faculties and the shape of the brain and skull. George Combe had founded the Phrenological Society in 1820 and a *Phrenological Journal* in 1823, supported by his younger brother Andrew, a physician to Queen Victoria. The belief, like many other quasi-scientific ideas of that time, was brought back from France by George Combe in 1817, and in the subsequent eruption of radical ideas the possibility of selecting man for particular kinds of training or of enabling them to assess their own talents vastly increased the sale of plaster casts of heads and cheap 'self-instructors'. Mechanics' institutes responded so readily to lectures that by the 1840's phrenologists were sure of bumper audiences. Even the novelist George Eliot had her head shaved so that her bumps could be read.[1]

There was another belief abroad which, though it did not elicit such popular interest, was even more fundamental to the work of the mechanics' institutes and their successors. James Mill wanted to 'make the human mind as plain as the road from Charing Cross to St Paul's'. 'Till recently', he wrote in the *Encyclopaedia Britannica*, 1818, 'it was denied that intelligence was a desirable quality in the great body of the people, and as intelligence is power, such is an unavoidable opinion in the breasts of those who think that the human race ought to consist of two classes, one that of the oppressors, another that of the oppressed. As we strive for an equal degree of justice, an equal degree of veracity, in the poor as in the rich, so ought we to strive for an equal degree of intelligence.' The corollary to this belief was democratic government based on universal education, and a belief that 'intelligence could be affected by education.'

IV

An early by-product of the mechanics' institutes was the Society for the Diffusion of Useful Knowledge. Formed in 1826 with Brougham as a prime mover, it preached salvation, but salvation through science, and it worked in the same way as the S.P.C.K. by issuing tracts and a 'penny encyclopaedia'. Indeed, James Mill was said to have suggested that the Church of England should be turned into a mechanics' institute.

Motivated by a mixture of benevolence and self-interest, many manufacturers followed the example of Robert Owen and established minuscule welfare communities around their factories. Near Manchester, the Ashworths (of Turton), the Ashtons (of

Hyde), the Gregs (of Bollington), and the Whiteheads (of Rossendale) established day schools, evening classes, libraries and even baths. Bankers too, like Benjamin Heywood, regarded 'the improvement of the working classes' as 'an object of paramount importance'. He told the Manchester Mechanics' Institute 'as it is the duty of every man to mark out for himself some sphere of active usefulness to his fellow-men I would select the furtherance of this object for mine'.[1]

A taste for political rather than natural science was sedulously cultivated by the Universal Society of Rational Religionists, a body formed by the disciples of Robert Owen. This divided the country into secular dioceses under 'missioners', each centred on a Hall of Science. From places like Salford (1836), Manchester (1839), Huddersfield (1839), Sheffield (1839), Stockport (1841), Halifax (1841), Birmingham (1841), Bristol (1841) and Lambeth (1842), these 'missioners' organised public meetings, wrote books and conducted day schools, raising funds for an Owenite community at Queenwood in Hampshire. This was built later and sustained by the contributions of the faithful. When abandoned by the Owenites, it became a boarding school, for boarding schools were, in principle, favoured by Owenites because they 'removed the rising generation from the vicious and degrading circumstances, by which they were everywhere surrounded'.[2]

Further reaction, partly against the utility of the mechanics' institutes but chiefly against the secularity of the halls of science led Anglican clergy to establish rival institutes for their own members. The Coventry Religious and Useful Knowledge Society was one of the first of such foundations. Seven years later in 1842, a Congregationalist minister founded a People's College in Sheffield. This was in turn imitated at Nottingham and Leicester. It caught the imagination of F. D. Maurice and the Christian Socialists in London, who founded the Working Men's College in 1854.[3]

Such reaction and abreaction amongst these adult educational groups mirrored the great debate going on in society at large, and much field work in the local history of each town is needed before the pattern can be filled in.

V

A second institutional expression of the same secular enthusiasm was the formation of a University of London in 1826. Here too, it was not so much a new idea (for there had been a number of proposals before Thomas Campbell's letter in *The Times* of 9 February 1825), as the same old driving forces: Brougham and Birkbeck, helped by Francis Place the radical tailor of Charing Cross, and Isaac Goldsmid, the financier and philanthropist. A disused rubbish dump in Gower Street was selected for the building which was, at first, little more than a joint-stock medical school, for by 1834, 347 of its 469 students were medicals. Attempts to enlist further professional groups failed: chairs of mineralogy, engineering, design and education, though canvassed, were not created.

But in another respect London initiated a revolution, for it was the first university institution in England to admit students without a religious 'test'. The challenge of its 'Godless' curriculum provoked the rector of Lambeth to enlist the support of the Duke of Wellington, the two archbishops, some city financiers and surgeons to found King's College in the Strand. This, though specifically Anglican, offering 'religious and moral instruction', yet made similar concessions to preparation for the professions and, as in Gower Street, medical students in 1834 comprised 241 of the 446 students.[1]

Three of the first five professors appointed were, like Brougham, graduates of the University of Edinburgh: Anthony Panizzi, an Italian political refugee who later built up the great reading room of the British Museum, Leonard Horner, founder of the Edinburgh School of Arts, who became Warden, and J. R. McCulloch, expositor of the 'Wages Fund' theory. At King's College J. F. Daniel, inventor of the hygrometer, took the Chair of Chemistry in 1831 and Charles Wheatstone, the pioneer of spectrum analysis and submarine telegraphy, took the Chair of Physics in 1834.

With so much in common (except religious convictions), it was natural that the two colleges should draw together. Their juncture was sealed by charter in 1836, when the institution in Gower Street relinquished the title of London University for that of 'University College'. By 1851 the new University of London gathered under its academic umbrella 29 general and nearly 60 medical colleges all over England.

To anticipate the radicals, the chapter of Durham Cathedral enfranchised their property in South Shields (now developing rapidly as an industrial centre), to finance a college in Durham Castle, for which the bishop obtained a charter in 1837.[1] At Durham, too, science was well to the fore; agricultural chemistry was founded there by J. F. W. Johnston.[2] Externally, a minuscule copy of Oxford and Cambridge,[3] with colleges like Hatfield Hall (from 1846), and Cosin's Hall (from 1851), Durham University responded to the needs of its region.

Regional needs in Manchester led to the formation in 1833 of a statistical society, the first of its kind in the country. One of its four founders, William Langton, helped establish four years later the Manchester Society for National Education, and in 1846 was secretary of a committee which aimed at founding a university. A legacy of £100,000 from John Owens, a Manchester merchant, who died in the latter year was promptly used to found a college which opened its doors in Richard Cobden's old house in Manchester in 1851. One of Langton's daughters married its first principal.[4]

VI

The 'joint-stock' University College of London was followed by joint-stock middle-class schools, and University College School took shape in 1828,[5] followed by King's College School in 1829.

Other middle-class schools appeared in the industrial areas. In Birmingham, as a result of an Act of Parliament in 1831, a new school on the grammar school foundation was built to teach science and modern languages. In Sheffield the churches supplied the schools: Anglicans, the gothic Collegiate School (1836) and Wesleyans, the palladian Proprietary Grammar School (1837).[1] At Leicester, a similar palladian Nonconformist proprietary school (1837) was followed by the gothic Anglican Collegiate School (1838). At Hull a proprietary school (1837) was modelled on University College School, London.

Fostered and promoted by parents and townsmen who, as proprietors, were able to control the curriculum more effectively than they could in either the grammar or private schools,[2] these proprietary schools, and others like them at Blackheath (1830), the West Riding (1834) and, later, the City of London School (1837) flourished. So well, in fact, that Samuel Butler, who had given his life to building up Shrewsbury, lamented that 'the traffic in joint-stock company schools, is ruining, and will ultimately ruin, the old foundations'.[3] Butler's successor, B. H. Kennedy also attributed the fall in the number of boys at Shrewsbury to the competition of 'the new proprietary colleges' like Cheltenham (1841) and Marlborough (1843). By Kennedy's time proprietary colleges tended to become boarding schools, a new mutant: Cheltenham taking as day boys the sons of local people, and boarding boys from elsewhere. The growing desire for 'boarding facilities' led a group of merchants in Bristol to found Clifton College in 1862, because the Bristol Grammar School (revived in 1845) would not take boarders.

The churches were active in promoting both day proprietary schools and proprietary boarding schools. Roman Catholics founded Mount St. Mary's (1842), Ratcliffe College (1847), The Oratory School (1859) and Beaumont (1861). Nonconformists founded Queen's College, Taunton (1843), Taunton School (1847), Bishop's Stortford College (1868), The Leys (1875), Ashville College (1877), Truro School (1879) and Kent College (1885). The Quakers founded one at Ackworth in 1842. Anglicans were also active with Brighton College (1845), Radley College (1847), Bradfield College (1850), St John's School Leatherhead (1851) and Trent College (1866).

Anglican influence was strongest in several of the 'corporations' set up to provide schools for the middle classes.[1] A Middle Schools Corporation was founded by the Rev. William Rogers which founded the Central School at Finsbury among others. An even more ambitious corporation, that of SS Mary and Nicholas, was founded by the Rev. Nathaniel Woodard, a curate, who founded Shoreham Grammar School in 1847. Ten years later it was rechristened St Nicholas's, Lancing. In *A Plea for the Middle Classes* (1848), he forecast:

By neglecting the employer you are, in the present pressure of civilisation, hastening on a very general state of barbarism.

By devious means like luncheons and public meetings, where the socially aspiring could rub shoulders with the aristocracy,[2] he raised money to found another school for 'the lower middle class' in 1850 (which became St. John's Hurstpierpoint in 1853), and a school for the 'poorest members of the middle class' (which became St Saviours, Ardingly in 1870). To unite the three a great chapel was begun at Lancing in 1868.[3] The Woodard pattern was extended from Sussex to the North until by the beginning of the first world war it was the largest governing body for secondary schools in the empire. Though he aroused strong criticism, he was fortunate in his patrons, and his schools, with two exceptions, exist today.[4]

Even the National Society, engrossed as it was in the heavy task of expanding its elementary school network, was brought into the 'middle school' movement. Egged on by the 30-year-old H. E. Manning, then an Anglican clergyman, and his friends, it undertook in 1838 to establish 'middle' or 'commercial schools' for those pupils from their own schools who 'from their ableness to learn and to teach might be considered as proper persons to be admitted to its higher advantages'.[5] These new schools were to be added to existing national or grammar schools. But the idea did not survive in face of the other heavy demands (notably the need for training colleges), and not until 1866 did the Society sponsor a fund to found them.

VII

A potent advocate and exponent of middle-class boarding schools was Thomas Arnold, headmaster of Rugby from 1828 to 1842. He won the mercantile and middle class by his broad theology, advocating a union between the Anglicans and the Nonconformists in a true Establishment which would cope with the social and educational problems of the towns. Even the Unitarians (for whom Arnold had little sympathy) said that his proposals, had they been carried out in 1688, would have healed the breach between the two parties.[1] 'When we consider,' Arnold wrote, 'the inadequacy of the Establishment, as it now stands, to meet the wants of the great manufacturing towns and districts, it may be said that in those portions of the kingdom our business is not so much to reform the Church as to create one.'[2] He wanted lay clerical ministers in each town and in each town a bishop.[3]

Arnold was apprehensive of what he called 'the Movement' —Jacobinism and utilitarianism. While he was a curate at Laleham, he had 'indulged in various dreams of attaching himself' to the University of London and 'trying as far as possible to influence it'. He also wanted to give the *Penny Magazine*, the publication of the 'Useful Knowledge people' (as he called them), a 'decidedly Christian character', for then, he wrote, 'I think it would suit my notions better than any other'. 'The slightest touches of Christian principle and Christian hope in the Society's biographical and historical articles,' he argued, 'would be a sort of living salt to the whole.'[4] By founding his own short-lived weekly paper *The Englishman's Register* in 1831, in contributing to others like the *Sheffield Courant* and the *Hertford Reformer* and in his writings he tried to 'pull the bell, as it were, and try to give the alarm as to the magnitude of the danger'.

He even tried to form a society of his own to collect information 'on the condition of the poor throughout the kingdom, and to call public attention to it by every possible means, whether by the press or by yearly or quarterly meetings'.

He looked to education to hold back Catholicism, Jacobinism and utilitarianism, all of which he detested. But the education had to be provided by a National Church and a strong central government. 'I hope,' he wrote in 1826, 'to be allowed before I die, to accomplish something on Education, and also with regard to the Church, the last indeed, even more than the other, were not the task, humanely speaking, so hopeless.'[1] And again, 'The *Idea* of my life, to which I think every thought of my mind more or less tends, is the perfecting of the idea of the Edward the Sixth Reformers—the constructing of a truly national and Christian system of education'.[2] For the working classes were, in his opinion, liable to 'alienation' and 'active hostility . . . in a moment'. Their language bore, in his opinion, 'the certain marks of slaves . . . all but insanity'. His life was a kind of one-man sortie in a mood of spiritual hopelessness. 'When I think of the Church,' he wrote in 1839, 'I could sit down and pine and die.'

As headmaster of Rugby he inspired a body of disciples who carried his ideas into the forward areas of public life in England and the Empire.[3] Like all disciples, they made the Arnold myth even more powerful than the man had been. The myth spread, especially in the public schools, as Moberly, headmaster at Winchester from 1835–66, told A. P. Stanley (Arnold's pupil and first biographer):

I am sure that to Dr Arnold's personal earnest simplicity of purpose, strength of character, power of influence, and piety, which none who ever came near him could mistake or question, the carrying of this improvement into our schools is mainly attributable. He was the first.[4]

The 'improvement' to which Moberly referred was not only effected by Arnold's writing, preaching or teaching, vivid, regular and dramatic though they were, but by his fanatical cult of physical fitness. At Rugby Arnold imported a 'gallows' on which he used to swing. Cricket was his 'great refreshment', the

ground a hallowed place 'where no profane person may approach.'
In 1840 the Rugby School Cricket XI played at Lord's for the
first time, captained by Thomas Hughes, later to immortalise
Arnold in *Tom Brown's Schooldays* (1857): the first of the schoolboy novels. Arnold would also bathe, garden and visit the sick,
constantly reiterating that daily exercise was essential. 'I must
have my hour or two of thorough relaxation if I am to do my
work,' he wrote. That was why he purchased Fox How near
Ambleside in 1832 and there he would spend his vacations on
long mountain walks varied by writing.[1] He endowed the
profession with the prestige of his name because he saw clearly
that the professional status of schoolmasters was not secure. 'It
has not yet obtained that respect in England', he wrote, 'as to
be able to stand by itself in public opinion as a liberal profession;
it owes the rank which it holds to its connection with the profession of a clergyman, for that is acknowledged universally in
England to be the profession of a gentleman.'[2] He feared the
example of America.[3] His pupils made teaching and public
service their vocation too.

In the universities (John Conington, H. H. Vaughan and
Bonamy Price), the colonies (C. H. Pearson, J. P. Gell and
Arnold's younger son, William Delafield Arnold), the army
(Hodson of Hodson's Horse), the Church (A. P. Stanley, W. C.
Lake and Septimus Hansard), the co-operative movement
(Thomas Hughes) and, of course, the public schools (Prince Lee
of King Edward's Birmingham, G. E. L. Cotton at Marlborough,
Herbert Hill at Warwick and Charles Vaughan at Harrow),[4] old
pupils carried forward his ideas. Even Arnold's descendants
seemed to have had a dynastic interest in preserving the tradition,
for his sons Matthew and Thomas Arnold, his son-in-law W. E.
Forster, his daughter Mrs Humphrey Ward, his grandson H. O.
Arnold-Forster and great-grandsons Aldous and Julian Huxley
all exhibited his pedagogic flair. That three times as many public
schools were founded in the 30 years after his death as in the
whole century before was an indication of how the new industrial
middle class looked to Arnold's ideas.

VIII

In company with many others Arnold condemned the condition of the manufacturing towns[1] where the Factory Act of 1819 was a dead letter. Only two convictions under it had been secured, and attempts to tighten up its administration in 1825 and 1831 had both failed. In a letter to the *Sheffield Courant* in 1831 Arnold described them as

... places where men have assembled together, not for the purposes of social life, but to make calicoes or hardware or broadcloth. A man sets up a factory and wants hands: I beseech you, Sir, to observe the very expressions that are used, for they are all significant. What he wants of his fellow creatures is the loan of their hands: of their heads and hearts he thinks nothing.

Another argument for improving conditions in them was advanced by Michael T. Sadler, M.P. for Leeds, who in *The Law of Population* (1830) showed that a growth in security and comfort, by actuating prudence, lowers the birth rate. For this reason he accepted the invitation of the ten-hour committees and introduced a Bill on their behalf in 1831. When he lost both his Bill and his seat in the ensuing general election, an even more influential champion was forthcoming in Lord Ashley.

When Ashley introduced his Bill in 1833, the manufacturers secured the appointment of a Royal Commission to clear themselves of charges of exploitation. To this commission Dr Southwood Smith and Edwin Chadwick were appointed; one a doctor who had worked in Whitechapel, the other the literary secretary of Jeremy Bentham. Both were responsible for the revolutionary educational clauses of the subsequent Factory Act of 1833 whereby children could no longer be employed in two different factories on the same day and, moreover, were to be equipped to adapt themselves to other employments should 'the vicissitudes of trade or other causes' make it necessary. To ensure that no children under 9 were employed, four alert and enthusiastic inspectors were appointed with the considerable emolument of £1,000 a year. But just as important, they had to ensure that those between 9 and 13 attended school for two hours daily, six days a week. Of these four Leonard Horner, formerly Warden of the University of London was outstanding. From 1833 onwards he and his colleagues ensured that each child presented a voucher every Monday certifying that he had been to school in the previous week.[1] These vouchers were a source of further trouble, for, despite penalties, there were many forgeries. Employers objected to financing a factory school where no other was provided; parents resented the curtailment of their children's earnings, while the children did not find schools at all congenial. There was, until 1837, when registration of births was made compulsory, no means of trapping those who broke the age-restriction clauses. So the inspectors sponsored the relay system of half-time education.

After 1839, when the government increased their grant to the two voluntary societies to £30,000, more schools could be built; for under section XXII of the 1833 Act, inspectors had the power to establish such schools. But the type of school elicited bitter comment from Leonard Horner, who reported:

I have to reject the school voucher of the fireman, the children having been schooled in the coal hole (in one case I actually found them there), and having been made to say a lesson from books nearly as black as the fuel, at intervals between his feeding and stirring the fire of the engine boiler. . . . It occurred where a large capital must be embarked.

Yet another, Robert Saunders, commented on the utter indifference of parents to the training of their children, remarking that 'the worship of Mahomet or the worship of blocks and stones' could be inculcated without their concerning themselves in the matter.[2] Both of them persuaded the National Society to build and provide maintenance grants for some seventeen schools in their areas, a scheme that was so successful that it was written into a Factory Act that Sir James Graham hoped to pass in 1843. But Nonconformists objected so violently that the scheme was dropped.

After considerable legislative wrangling the inspectors obtained, in 1844, the power to annul the certificates of unsatisfactory schoolmasters. By the same Act children were henceforth to work for half a day (or 'an average of six hours of labour in each day'). As a result, not only attendance rose, but the character of the education improved. The numbers of children attending schools run by the voluntary societies also rose.[1]

IX

Of the four inspectors, Horner was the most far-sighted. He sharply criticised the monitorial system, and urged that English education should be brought abreast of practice in Holland, Germany, France and the U.S.A. by the establishment of a central board of commissioners with power to establish normal schools and recruit teachers. This more than anything would, he foresaw, foster minimal standards of health and well-being.

Horner's idea of a central board was taken up in the House of Commons by Sir Thomas Wyse, himself a promoter of inter-denominational education in Ireland, whereby poor Protestant and Catholic children were educated in common or 'mixed' schools.[2] Wyse's project, after endorsement by a select committee of the House of Commons in 1829, had been inaugurated in 1831. As part of an even grander design involving the establishment of middle schools and university colleges, under a grant-giving administrative national board of Catholic and Protestant clergy and laity, it engrossed Wyse's life.

These Irish interdenominational schools were so successful that the Corporation of Liverpool adopted a similar scheme for two schools of their own.[3] When Wyse lost his seat in the Commons, his scheme for a state board in England, indeed a Ministry of Education, was taken up by J. A. Roebuck who wrung an annual grant of £20,000 from the government for the two voluntary societies in 1833.

Returning to Parliament in 1835[4] Wyse was harnessed by

pressure groups in England, like The Central Society of Education (founded in 1836) which he served as chairman and author of their three most important papers. He was in great demand at mechanics' institute meetings all over the country. Because of such work he was jocularly known as the 'member for Education'[1] just as his great opponent in the house Sir Robert Inglis, the M.P. for Oxford, was known, in view of his frequent references to, and apparently intimate knowledge of, the Almighty's intentions, as 'the member for Heaven'.

Embroidering arguments made in the Commons by J. A. Roebuck six years before, Wyse spoke powerfully for an English National Board on 14 June 1838, when his statistical exposure of the educational lag between England and the other countries, especially America, so impressed the House of Commons that his proposition for an address to the Queen asking for the appointment of such a board, and for teacher training colleges, was lost by only four votes.

Meanwhile the 'Irish system' was working so well in Liverpool that Lord John Russell paid a visit to one of the schools on 3 October 1838 and even attended a period of religious instruction there. If the lesson he learned there was lost on him, the paper *Morning Advertiser* rubbed it in on 11 January 1839 by publishing a report of the Liverpool 'mixed' schools, and James Simpson reinforced it in *The Courier* a fortnight later.[2]

On 12 February 1839, Lord John Russell announced the government's decision to set up a committee of the Privy Council to distribute the grants for education and suggested that the state might establish a normal school for teachers.

X

This Committee of the Privy Council engaged, as its first secretary, a former Manchester physician, Dr Kay. At the same time the grants to the two voluntary societies were increased to £30,000 a year. Kay had experience of industrial slums in

Manchester, and as an assistant commissioner to the Poor Law Board (set up in 1834) had come to appreciate the redemptive potential of schooling.

Transferred to the Metropolitan District of London in 1838, he had established at Norwood a school on Pestalozzian lines, where children were 'led from the known to the unknown'.[1] He chose the more zealous and diligent boys and girls of 14 to act as assistant (or pupil) teachers. To help them improve he planned to set up a normal (or training) school. He approached the Home Secretary for financial aid for the workshops and a farm for Norwood, and obtained them.

When he became secretary of the Committee of Council, Kay still retained his responsibility for the metropolitan poor law schools. With his friend E. C. Tufnell, he set out on a three-month tour of Europe, taking in Holland, France, Prussia and Switzerland, all countries which had, by 1839, established state systems of education. As he saw it, there was 'no excuse' for 'the ignorance, nay the barbarism' of large numbers of Englishmen. On his return he set about putting what he had learned into practice.

In his ten years' tenure of the secretaryship of the Committee of the Privy Council on Education (from 1839 to 1849), Dr Kay worked through four media. The first was a training college. In a manor-house at Battersea (the first of many noble houses to be adapted to such a purpose) eight promising 13-year-old pupils of Norwood were indentured as apprentices, given clothes to wear and set upon a three-year course, culminating in the award of a certificate. Other students followed, sent by Leonard Horner, Lady Byron and Lord Chichester. Kay provided the money and, until his marriage in 1842 to Miss Shuttleworth (when he took the name of Kay-Shuttleworth) acted as its principal. His collaborator in this, E. C. Tufnell, could boast 32 years later 'We were pooh-poohed, then abused, then imitated; and now I have the satisfaction of seeing the establishment of forty training colleges all founded upon the principles first exemplified at Battersea.'[2] These principles were hard work (the students worked from five in the morning until nine or ten at night) and 'the spirit of Christian Charity' (which was enforced through student superintendents, or prefects who reported delinquents to the authorities). Satan was never allowed to find a pair of idle hands at Battersea. Since music was in the capable hands of J. P. Hullah (who taught singing by the 'fixed doh' method), their choir could frighten him away. The choir proved such a success that Hullah's techniques were adopted by the leading public schools. The choir gave vocal expression to the corporate, segregated life which, for good or evil, intending teachers were to lead in training colleges down to our own day.

Kay's second great adaptation of foreign practice was to appoint, in 1839, school inspectors with comprehensive roles as advisors and friends. He drew up no less than 174 minute and searching questions to guide them. The inspiration for their questions came from Holland, where inspectors were not 'a means of exercising control, but of affording assistance'. He described the inspectorate as the means 'by which information respecting all remarkable improvements may be diffused wherever it is sought'.[1]

His third response to the challenge of continental advance (voiced most loudly by Dr Hook, the Vicar of Leeds) was to provide a supply of recruits for the teaching profession. The *Minutes of the Committee of Council* for 1846 laid down that certain schools, approved by the inspectors, could become training centres for 'apprentices' or pupil teachers. Selected at the age of 13, these apprentices were to receive an hour and a half of instruction each day, £10 a year and annual increments of £2 10s. At the end of the apprentice period, they were to present themselves for a scholarship examination to a normal school or training college. If unsuccessful they were given minor clerical appointments in the Civil Service.

His last and biggest achievement was to sidestep the militant hostility of the Nonconformists, who in 1843 had wrecked the educational clauses of the Factory Bill, whereby district schools were to be established. This Bill, though in tune with the desires of Lord Brougham and Lord Ashley, was also intended as a check to Chartist agitations, riots and strikes. But the Dissenters objected to the Established Church controlling district schools and the Established Church liked the subsequent concessions less, as they virtually gave control of the schools to the Committee of the Privy Council.[1]

From this stemmed his fourth achievement: the harnessing of local enthusiasm for schools through local committees of managers established in 1847 not only for schools run by the National and British and Foreign Societies but for those run by Roman Catholics too.[2]

XI

The recognition of the Catholic Poor Schools Committee as the channel of communication between themselves and the committee of council[3] was a landmark. Its secretary T. W. Allies was to be a tower of strength for the next 30 years and play a conspicuous part in their advance. Catholic training colleges at Hammersmith and Liverpool were in operation by 1856 and their schools benefited generally from the re-establishment of the hierarchy in 1850.

Intellectually fortified by the Oxford Movement (Allies was a convert), English Catholics were numerically strengthened by the Irish. Beginning as a trickle of 'navvies' on the canals and railways, swelling to a flood after the potato famine of 1846, some half a million Irish people came to Great Britain between 1841 and 1851.[4] These immigrants were to add an unpredictable element to the northern English towns. 'I hear that the Roman Catholics are increasing fast amongst us,' wrote Dr Arnold. 'Lord Shrewsbury and other wealthier Catholics are devoting their whole incomes to the cause, while the tremendous influx of Irish labourers into Lancashire and the west of Scotland is tainting the whole population with a worse than barbarian element.'[5] Areas of concentrated Irish settlement, like Manchester, where Kay-Shuttleworth had obtained his early insights into the problems of poverty, were to witness some further experiments

116

like the Irish community of the Institute of the Blessed Virgin
Mary. Among them was Laurence Toole, who as parish priest of
St Wilfrid's was later to be elected top of poll in the first School
Board election in Manchester.

XII

It was the Catholic revival which convulsed Oxford. As geo-
logists pinned back the Old Testament story, 'new critics' (like
Arnold), tried to accommodate their findings within a Christian
framework.[1] Diverted from so doing by the counter-assault of the
Tractarians, dismayed by Newman's revelation that the Thirty-
nine Articles were inefficient as a screen against Roman Catholicism, and alarmed by Newman's own defection to Rome in 1845,
liberal opinion began to coalesce around the idea that both science
and dissent should be accommodated within the universities.

Dissent found friends at Oxford amongst Arnoldians like A. P.
Stanley and John Conington who, with Benjamin Jowett, urged
the importance of putting Oxford in order from within before
the pressures from without became too great to withstand. The
pressures from without had support at Cambridge where science
found champions in the persons of the chancellor (the Prince
Consort), Adam Sedgwick the geologist and William Whewell
the Master of Trinity.

It was a race against time. Adam Sedgwick's Unitarian friend,
James Heywood, was spoiling for a royal commission of inquiry
so Whewell moved quickly to forestall him by instituting tripos
examinations in moral and natural sciences at Cambridge. But
at Oxford the reformers found it more difficult to move against
Oxford's chancellor, the Duke of Wellington. So Heywood, with
the assistance of Bonamy Price (another Arnoldian), set his plans
and in 1850 moved for a royal commission into the universities
of Oxford, Cambridge and Dublin. After four months the names
of the commissioners were announced. Not surprisingly, the
secretary of the Oxford Commission was A. P. Stanley. Too late,

Oxford moved in 1850 to establish four final honours schools in litterae humaniores, mathematics and physical science, natural science and law and modern history.[1]

XIII

The findings of these commissions were, if anything, emphasised by the results of the Great Exhibition held in Hyde Park in 1851. The staging of such industrial exhibitions owed much to French example. In Paris, fairs in 1798, 1801 and 1802 led to the formation in that year of a society for the encouragement of the industrial arts and manufactures of France. Under its auspices and aided by the government, more national fairs of scientific inventions attracted an increasing number of exhibitors. By 1828 the value of these exhibitions stimulated a few 'progressively minded educationalists'[2] in England to stage one in the Royal Mews in Trafalgar Square. Provincial efforts in Manchester, Leeds and Birmingham, in 1837, 1839 and 1849 respectively, could not match the major displays in Paris in 1839, 1844 and 1849, for the latter of which the possibility of inviting foreign exhibitors was considered. English observers were impressed: the interest of the Prince Consort was roused and under his direction the Society of Arts took steps to stage the greatest (so far) of all exhibitions at Hyde Park in 1851.[3]

To thinking men, however, the great educational landmark of 1851 was not so much the exhibition in Hyde Park as the census. This showed that the population was now 17,927,609: an increase of 101.6% since 1801. The gloomy forebodings of Malthus seemed to be refuted. Special educational questions had been inserted in the census. These showed that the 2,144,378 children at 46,042 day schools in England and Wales represented a proportion of 1 to 8.36% of the total population. This was a great advance from 1818 when the proportion was 1 to 17.25%, the day scholars being 674,883, the day schools 19,230 and the total population 11,642,683.[4]

VII

FITNESS AND EFFICIENCY

1851–1868

I

'I am for the American system as it stands,' said Richard Cobden on 22 November 1851 at Manchester. As the hero of the repeal of the Corn Laws five years before, he was lending his voice to the National Public School Association, the successor of the Anti-Corn Law League, which had, since 1847, been campaigning for rate aid to education whether given in religious schools or not.

After the Great Exhibition, the campaign widened with the entry of the Prince Consort and his satellites, one of whom was Lyon Playfair, then probably England's leading chemist.[1] Whereas Cobden's eye was on American schools, Playfair's was on German universities. Cobden wanted local boards to sustain schools, Playfair envisaged a central industrial university with mechanics' institutes as its provincial outriders.

In 1856 the efforts of these two separate groups registered when two government departments were formed—joined, like Siamese twins, but separate in their operations—the Education Department at Whitehall, and the Science and Art Department at South Kensington.

Neither was exactly new. The Education Department was a recognition of the fact that the grants to voluntary schools had grown eighteenfold—from £30,000 to £541,233 a year—in the sixteen years that the committee of the Privy Council had been administering them.[2] The committee of the Privy Council still distributed the grants after the change, but it did so under a responsible officer of the Crown. This embryo Minister of Education was called the Vice-President of the Committee of the Privy Council on Education and his responsibilities included, as time went on, veterinary matters, like the control of rinderpest and trichinosis in imported livestock. The Science and Art Department had existed in embryo for the previous twenty years as the Council of the School of Design at the Board of Trade, formed in 1836 to encourage provincial schools of design. The £186,000 profit of the Great Exhibition and a further £150,000 from Parliament enabled three country estates in South Kensington to be purchased and here the Board of Trade established a Department of Practical Art in 1853, with Henry Cole, reputed originator of the Christmas card, as secretary, and a Department of Science in 1854 with Lyon Playfair as secretary.[1] When the Education Department was established at Whitehall in 1856, the two departments at South Kensington were amalgamated to form the Department of Science and Art and became the responsibility of the Vice-President of the Council.

II

Of the two, the Science and Art Department set the pattern.[2] Ignominiously housed in some huts known as the 'Brompton Boilers' in the grounds of the South Kensington estates, its initial attempts to promote science classes were poor. By 1859 only four 'science' schools, as such, existed, and Playfair left it for the chair of chemistry at Edinburgh.

Henry Cole then became secretary of the whole department. Helped by a young Crimean officer, Lieut. J. F. D. Donnelly, originally seconded to cut down trees on the estate, he promoted a scheme for paying teachers on the results of their pupils' success in examinations set by the department each May. One hundred and four candidates presented themselves in 1860, 1000 in 1861, 34,000 in 1870, and by 1895, its last year, 202,868.

Cheap, economical and, within limits, efficient, the Science and Art Department enlisted as examiners some of the best men of the day. Six of the eight first examiners were fellows of the Royal Society: A. W. Hofman, John Tyndall, Edwin Lankester, A. C.

Ramsay, W. W. Smythe and T. H. Huxley. Hofman, whose teaching at the Royal School of Mines was producing the first generation of British trained chemists, set the papers for the second generation till 1867. T. H. Huxley did the same for the biologists. Over them, like the good staff officer he might have been, Donnelly organised the examinations to cope with a steadily increasing number of candidates.[1] Rising in rank on this rising tide, he ended up as 'the very model of a modern major-general', a promotion joyfully anticipated in the person of Major-General Stanley in the *Pirates of Penzance* (1880):

> I am very well acquainted too with matters mathematical,
> I understand equations, both the simple and quadratical,
> About binomial theorem I'm teeming with a lot of news,
> With many cheerful facts about the square of the hypotenuse.

III

Examinations had long been kindling a spirit of emulation in the universities, eliminating charlatans amongst the apothecaries, and facilitating the division of labour. Adam Smith had pointed out that 'rivalship and emulation render excellency, even in mean professions, an object of ambition, and frequently occasion the very greatest exertion', whilst Jeremy Bentham supported them as a means of 'maximising aptitude', envisaging examinees questioning one another to gain places on a 'locable' list of civil service appointments. Both arguments were adopted by Macaulay who supported competitive examinations for staffing the Indian Civil Service in 1853 by assuring the House of Commons that 'the intellectual test which is about to be established will be found in practice to be the best moral test that can be devised'. In this spirit the Civil Service Commissioners were appointed in 1855 to make provision for examinations for the Home Civil Service as well, though not until 1870 was the competition actually thrown open.[2] Another selective examination, instituted in 1855, was for entry to the Royal Military Academy at Woolwich.

For hereditary officers facing the awful novelty of being examined, Dr Frost started a crammer's in 1864: prototype of modern institutions like 'Jimmy's', Davies, Laing and Dick and Unischol. To cater for those less able to avail themselves of such metropolitan facilities, correspondence schools began to emerge. It was a reciprocal process, examinations evoked institutions to cope with them, and other institutions, virtually in self-defence, set examinations. Thus the seven year old College of Preceptors organised examinations for boys and girls in 1853, and the Royal Society of Arts signalised its centenary by offering examinations to the mechanics institutes in 1854.

To tap 'the vast reservoir of unfriended talent' in the lower classes, examinations were enthusiastically promoted by the Rev. James Booth. Of the 23 separate virtues Booth saw in establishing such a system, two especially commended themselves to his generation: no capital would be expended in buildings, and no religious difficulty would occur. Indeed, he wrote, 'treating Churchman and Dissenter alike, it would calm down religious animosity'.[1]

The examinations of the Royal Society of Arts stimulated T. D. Acland, a doughty critic of the Committee of the Privy Council (whose establishment he had opposed on the ground that it would gravely prejudice the Church), to propose university examinations for middle-class schools. He wanted to tempt farmers' sons into them, in order to improve agriculture. For he was an enthusiastic agricultural reformer, having lost his seat for supporting the repeal of the Corn Laws and subsequently studying chemistry at King's College, London, with a view to its application to scientific farming. Through the *Journal* of the Bath and West of England Agricultural Society he tried to spread his ideas, and, as an example to others, he conducted experiments on his own estates.

With his friend Frederick Temple, formerly an examiner in the Education Department, he persuaded Oxford to offer its support to the examination of pupils from the middle-class schools at Exeter. His original idea was that some title like 'Associate in Arts' (A.A.) should be awarded to the successful candidates. Oxford agreed and established a delegacy to organise the examination (from now on known as 'the Oxford local'), and to award two certificates to successful candidates, one for those under 15 (junior), the other for candidates under 18 (senior). Cambridge followed suit in 1858, with two similar awards, one for pupils under 16, the other for those under 18. Since Cambridge refused to grant the title A.A. or A.C. (Associate of Cambridge), any hope that they might combine to hold the examination was scotched.[1]

Concomitantly, a former pupil of Thomas Arnold was working to establish county schools. He was the Reverend J. L. Brereton, and he conceived that they should be less expensive than public schools yet more scholastic than private academies. His first was established at West Buckland (where he was rector) in 1859. It influenced others at Cranleigh (1863), Framlingham (1865) and Barnard Castle (1883). To provide an outlet for their first pupils, he founded Cavendish College at Cambridge which lasted until 1892. Brereton also believed that education should be organised on a county basis: a belief to be justified in 1902.

By encouraging the spirit of self-help, examinations offered an outlet for the dissatisfied:

'Is it not a wise and conservative policy,' James Booth asked an evening class for young men in 1857, 'that promotion in the State should be sought by science rather than sedition, by competition rather than conspiracy, that men should endeavour to pass muster at the gate rather than clamber over the wall?'

Self-help was the title of a book published two years later by another favourite of evening classes, Samuel Smiles, who as a youth, had profited from the Haddington circulating library of Samuel Brown, and who subsequently provided a technological hagiography for this characteristic Victorian popular religion in the form of a series of lives of the engineers which illustrated the value of helping oneself to technical knowledge.

IV

As an instrument for securing efficiency in the public elementary schools, to stop four-fifths of their children attending irregularly, leaving early and learning little, examinations were advocated by inspectors with experience of both factories and schools, like H. S. Tremenheere in 1857.[1] For the cost of maintaining these schools was rising at the rate of £100,000 a year and by 1858 was £663,000.

In February of that year a Conservative M.P., Sir John Pakington, an advocate of such aid, asked for an enquiry. Four months later he got his wish when a Royal Commission was appointed under the Duke of Newcastle.

The Newcastle Commission surveyed elementary schools in Great Britain and abroad,[2] and after three years recommended, amongst other things, 'a searching examination by competent authority of every child in every school to which grants are to be paid with the view of ascertaining whether these indispensable elements of knowledge are thoroughly acquired, and to make the prospects and position of the teacher dependent to a considerable extent on the results of this examination'.

As conceived by Robert Lowe, the vice-president, this involved revising the Code of Grants in 1862. As a result, each child in the infant school earned 6s. 6d., and each older child 12s., for 'satisfactory' performance in an examination conducted by the H.M.I.s. Penalties for unsatisfactory attendance (4s. for each older child and 2s. 6d. for evening schools) and for unsatisfactory performance in reading, writing or arithmetic (2s. 8d. per subject and 5s. in evening schools), were imposed.

The Code extended principles already recognised: since 1846 the state had been examining teachers and pupil teachers and, since 1856, three-quarters of the pupils over 8 in any school applying for the capitation grant; whilst the Science and Art department had been paying science teachers by results since

1859. Its malevolent effect was to make (in the words of the Commission which preceded it), 'the prospects and position of the teacher dependent to a considerable degree, on the results of these examinations'.

Unhappily, this was only too necessary. Many teachers in the elementary schools had no qualifications at all, whilst those possessing them were often recruited for other than professional reasons. But the Pharaoh-like régime of the Revised Code did not immediately improve the quality of the teaching, and stories of the hardship and harshness it evoked were alternately to shock and amuse members of parliament for the next 28 years, as can be seen from the pages of *Hansard*.

Lowe's forecast that if it did not promote efficiency it would at least be cheap was right—for a time. The government grant fell by over twenty per cent in three years. Attendance rose. Children were tempted to remain at school longer. Books became less effusive and if anything more catechetical. But the unforeseen by-products of the Code when unimaginatively construed, led to many unfortunate practices. The cult of 'the register', acquiescence in large classes, the deliberate cultivation of rote-memory to defeat the inspectors; even, we are told, the presentment of sick children for the attendance grant could not, in many cases, be stopped.

Schoolmasters angrily flocked to swell the membership of their professional associations—the Association of British Church Schoolmasters and the United Association of Schoolmasters. Indeed, a central committee of the two organisations was formed to circumvent the operation of the Code. But Lowe was adamant. The principle of payment by results continued when in 1867 further grants were offered for performance in certain 'specific' subjects like history, geography and grammar. In the war of attrition against the Code, however, this minute of 1867 marked the first skirmish won. Matthew Arnold, from the point of view of an H.M.I., described its operation as a 'game of mechanical contrivance in which the teachers will and must more and more learn how to beat us.'[1]

But, in its long-term impact, the Revised Code reflected the secularising scientific outlook of the times, as more thoughtful contemporaries realised.[1]

v

The Newcastle Commission was the only one of four great Royal Commissions of this period to be concerned with the expenditure of public money on the education of the underprivileged. The three others, the Royal Commissions on the Universities (1850–2), the Clarendon Commission on the nine big public schools (1861–4), and the Taunton Commission on the endowed schools (1864–7), were preoccupied with endowments hitherto devoted to the education of the privileged. Here the same principle applied—a little free trade. Indeed, the traditional villain behind the Revised Code, Robert Lowe, was convinced that endowments led to incompetence, rigidity and shortage.[2]

The Royal Commissions on the Universities accelerated the derestriction of many collegiate endowments and their re-allocation to sustain a teaching and researching professoriate. Even more important, by insisting on the principle of open competition for fellowships and schoolmasterships, their increase in number and value, and the necessity of revising obsolete oaths, the Commissions opened the pores of Oxford and Cambridge to the world. After their reports appeared in 1852, subsequent Acts of Parliament on Oxford (1854) and Cambridge (1856) established executive commissions, which found it easier to implement the recommendations of the Royal Commissioners than they had found it to obtain evidence. These changes quickened the intellectual pace of the academic world. Entrants were now drawn from a wider and older circle of undergraduates, who read for new honours schools like natural science (established in 1851 at Cambridge and in 1853 at Oxford), law and history (established in Oxford in 1853 and at Cambridge in 1870). And when the last religious texts were abolished in 1871, the advancing tide surged in with unchecked vigour.[3]

London, having few endowments, opened its examinations instead, in 1858, to all comers (other than medical students). From now on an ever-lengthening file of 'external' students, encouraged by H.M.I.s like Matthew Arnold, began their nightly vigils, and to help them, correspondence colleges arose where local facilities were inadequate. King's College demurred, preferring to establish its own associateship (A.K.C.), which has never really caught on as a degree equivalent.

At Liverpool, the Mechanics' Institute sponsored Queen's College to help students to obtain instruction for a London degree, whilst other 'organised science schools' were established at Bristol and Birmingham by 1859. Certainly the Wigan Mining College (founded in 1858), the Royal Albert Memorial Institute at Exeter (opened in 1865) and science schools in Reading and Southampton were stretched by having this goal for their best students, so much in fact that the latter three developed into university colleges.

VI

By 1861, according to the Earl of Clarendon, the upper-classes were, educationally speaking, 'in a state of inferiority to the middle and lower'. He spoke as chairman of a Royal Commission appointed that year to examine the nine great public schools (Eton, Harrow, Winchester, Shrewsbury, Westminster, St Paul's, Merchant Taylors', Charterhouse and Rugby), on which he said the welfare of the Empire itself depended to 'the highest degree'.

The Clarendon Commission realised how necessary it was to provide suitable recruits for the universities, and the army, to both of which as we have seen, entry was by competitive examination. Moreover, the Duke of Wellington had instituted examinations for officers seeking promotion.

Though an impressive array of scientists pressed their case before Lord Clarendon they were no match for the headmasters, especially for B. H. Kennedy of Shrewsbury, who suavely observed that the natural sciences 'do not furnish a basis for education' as they were 'not synthetical enough for elementary instruction'. Synthesis was Benjamin Hall Kennedy's strength: his *Public School Latin Primer* (1866) was to be thankfully adopted by most schools aspiring to that name. His reluctance to yield to such contemporary pressures stemmed in part from the influence of his own schoolmaster-father, a friend of Coleridge. He voiced the old feeling that utilitarian studies were vulgar and banausic, but articulated a new argument to justify the teaching of classics: mental discipline. This was to be buttressed by the 'faculty psychology' then incubating in Germany.

The Clarendon Commission essayed to define a public school 'as it exists in England and in England alone', and said that it had grown up chiefly within the walls of these nine schools, 'and has been propagated from them; and though now surrounded by younger institutions, of a like character, and of great and increasing importance, they are still, in common estimation, its acknowledged types, as they have for several generations been its principal centres'. The middle-class evidently agreed, for as the commission was sitting, Beaumont (1861), Clifton (1862), Malvern (1862), Cranleigh (1863) and St Edward's Oxford (1863) were founded.

This powerful endorsement of their unwillingness 'to fritter away their power' as Kennedy put it, on providing a utilitarian curriculum for the children of local inhabitants, led to the 'local classes' established for that purpose becoming schools of their own. Thus the Lower School of John Lyon at Harrow came into being in 1875. Amputations had already been effected at Bedford (1764) and Dulwich (1857) to establish Bedford Modern and Alleyn's School. Similar institutions were now carved out of Oundle (the Laxton Grammar School), Rugby (the Lawrence Sheriff School), Repton (the Sir John Port School) and Whitgift (the 'Middle', now Trinity School).

VII

To round off inquisitions on the universities (1850–2), elementary education (1858–61) and the public schools (1861–4), a fourth commission was appointed to consider the endowed schools. It was provided, like its two immediate predecessors, with a memorandum on continental practice by Matthew Arnold, and indeed owed much in its conception to his influence.[1]

By classifying English endowed schools into three types according to the age at which their pupils left—18, 16 or 14—they have led some modern writers to see in this classification the germ of the tripartite system. The Commissioners deplored the poor distribution of schools, the inadequate provision for the teaching of science or modern languages and the almost total absence of secondary schools for girls (they only found thirteen). Unlike the Newcastle and the Clarendon Commissions, the Taunton Commission proposed that the whole system be remodelled with a triennial inspection by a district commission to ensure efficiency.

They also proposed more examinations by a national council composed of six Crown and six university representatives, which was to appoint examiners for schools, and issue certificates of competence to teach.

All four commissions believed in the virtue of examinations. In this they but reflected the views of their age, like John Stuart Mill who, in his inaugural address as rector of St Andrews in 1867 advocated the compulsory examination of children every year.[2]

VIII

Examination was even considered necessary for the custodians of the Victorian nursery—the governesses—whose ignorance and incompetence so appalled the Reverend David Laing (the honorary secretary of their Benevolent Institute and employment agency), that he proposed an examination to test their proficiency. Helped by some professors at King's College, like F. D. Maurice, his efforts, together with those of a maid of honour to Queen Victoria (the able Miss Amelia Murray, whose father had been director of the Admiralty telegraph system before becoming a bishop), resulted in the establishment in 1848 of Queen's College, London. A similar, if less ostensible connection, grew up between University College and a second women's college founded in 1849 in Bedford Square, which, eleven years later became the Bedford College for Women.

From Queen's College emerged a redoubtable pair.

> 'Miss Buss and Miss Beale
> Cupid's darts do not feel
> How different from us
> Miss Beale and Miss Buss.'

Miss Buss transformed her own private school in Camden Street into the North London Collegiate School for Ladies. A similar school, chartered in 1853 at Cheltenham, secured Miss Beale as headmistress in 1858. These two schools breached the examination wall, thanks to the help of one of F. D. Maurice's friends, Miss Emily Davies, who became secretary of a committee which by 1865 secured the assent of the Cambridge Local Examinations Syndicate to examine girls as well as boys.

Though some 24,770 ladies were registered as governesses in the 1851 census, there were many like Mrs Bodichon and Bessie Rayner Parkes who hoped to widen their professional horizons. In 1857 they started an association to promote the employment of women, with an employment bureau at Langham Place. To foster the desire of women to become independent, they also started *The Englishwoman's Journal*, and in the following year commenced their assault on that most privileged masculine citadel, the medical profession, fortified by the assistance of the American, Elizabeth Blackwell, who in 1859 became the first woman to have a place on the medical register—though the whole question was not resolved until 1877.

Another agency through which the middle-class mid-Victorian woman was trained, by participation in public work, was the National Association for the Promotion of Social Science. From its formation in 1857 to its demise in 1886, women played such a prominent part in its annual peripatetic meetings that the *Illustrated London News* describing a soirée of the Association on 21 June 1862, said 'one might almost imagine that "women's rights" had been ceded and that the feminine portion of creation had been admitted to full participation in the blessings of the representative system.'

The ruthless Miss Florence Nightingale, by founding a school for nurses in 1857, provided for others what she had been looking for all her life: 'a profession, a trade, a necessary occupation.' Her career showed that there was more toughness in the professional women than had been suspected.

For this was the age when much of the folk-lore and apparatus concerned with the physical education of girls was dissipated and discredited: tar water, taken internally to cure weakness of the eyes, hanging by the neck to increase height, boards strapped to the back to cure spinal deformity, iron collars to keep them at their books, stocks to ensure well turned-out toes. 'Care of the shape' was (and is) of deep-seated concern to the sex. To enlighten them the Ladies Sanitary Association was formed in 1857, largely as the result of the efforts of Mrs M. J. Roth, wife of Dr M. Roth, whose *Prevention and Cure of Chronic Diseases by Movements* (1851) was the first of a number of his books on the subject. From Roth's advocacy of Lingian gymnastics rose the Dress Reform Society, which played a great part in reforming women's fashions. For as Miss M. A. Chreimann said in one of the many tracts which the Association published: 'Persons who enjoy and reap benefits from such exercises will not readily submit to imprisonment in tight corsets, tight sleeves, weighty skirts, high heeled boots, tight stiff collars, ill adjusted braces and pointed toes.' Perhaps their most effective advocate was the muscular Christian, Charles Kingsley, who burst out at Winchester on 31 May 1869, with a scornful denunciation of 'stillness, silence and stays', and indicated that the unnatural limitation of feminine movements was contributing to the degeneration of the nation's stock.[1]

IX

While the raising of first-rate bullocks is an occupation on which educated men will willingly bestow much time and thought, the bringing up of fine human beings is an occupation tacitly voted unworthy of their attention.

An article written by Herbert Spencer containing these words was rejected by the editor of the *Quarterly Review* because he said 'it did not harmonise with his theological system or with the ideas which public school life had fostered in him'. For Spencer held that the physical development of children was an essential preliminary to educating their minds. In this physical development, the senses were the most important guides. With a metaphor which sprang from his earlier experience as an engineer (he worked for the designer of the Great Exhibition buildings), he wrote: 'A comparatively small and ill-made engine, worked at high pressure, will do more than a large and well-finished one working at low pressure.'[2]

Spencer emphasised that children should be trained 'not only to fit them mentally for the struggle before them, but also to make them physically fit to bear its excessive wear and tear'. He rejected gymnastics because they did not 'secure so equable a distribution of action to all parts of the body', and condemned the lack of interest they engendered. 'This comparative want of enjoyment,' he went on, 'is a cause of early desistance from artificial exercises, and is also a cause of inferiority in the effects they produce on the system'. To the question, 'What knowledge is of most worth?' his answer was science. Spencer's Nonconformist origins, by his own admission, also imbued him with an almost maniacal hatred of state power. Society itself, according to Spencer, was explicable in the same way as biology or physics, and the first volume of his *Synthetic Philosophy* (1864), exercised an enormous influence on emergent American pragmatists, and was to be reflected back to this country in the writings of William James and John Dewey. But perhaps his greatest influence in England was on young Beatrice Potter, later to marry Sidney Webb. But for Spencer's initiation into the life of the mind, she might have become a novelist.

By coining the phrase 'the survival of the fittest', Spencer indicated that the best competitors in a competitive society would win. In this, as in his emphasis on games, he voiced the feelings of his age.[1] For a veritable cult of organised games spread downwards from the universities and the public schools. From the impulsive act of a Rugby schoolboy, William Webb Ellis, who in 1823 picked up the ball to run to his opponents' goal, to 1846, when the rules of the game were established, Rugbeians had been spreading it in various schools.

Like examinations, games also fostered the spirit of emulation, as G. E. L. Cotton discovered at Marlborough in 1851.[2] Cotton appeared as the young master in *Tom Brown's Schooldays* (1857), the testament of that very muscular Christian, Thomas Hughes, who himself carried the spirit of 'fair play' into social affairs, promoting co-operation, trade unions and arbitration as well as pummelling dockers into a due appreciation of the Working Men's College.[3]

To the robust propaganda of Hughes were added the sturdy sentiments of Charles Kingsley whose *Westward Ho* (1855) and *Hereward the Wake* (1866)—challenging projections of the Carlylean hero-figure—showed what muscular forebears Tom Brown really had. Kingsley was a vigorous and effective crusader because he was abreast of the current teaching of natural science. As he told a friend in 1859, 'I have refused this winter to lecture on anything but the laws of health; and shall try henceforth to teach a sound theology through physics.'[4]

In the same year the first gymnasium and swimming bath in any public school was built by Edward Thring at Uppingham. Ever since becoming headmaster at Uppingham in 1853, at the age of 32, Thring had been fighting slummy conditions. By the 'almighty wall' (as he called such equipment), he hoped to shield boys against moral miasma; he also protected them against the miasma of the local drains by moving the school to Cardigan Bay for a year until the council improved them.

As well as opening the boys' pores by exercise, he widened their social outlook by introducing modern languages, craftwork and music into the curriculum, trimming the size of classes down to 25 to ensure more efficient teaching. Uppingham boys also showed how to help the under-privileged denizens of the social mudflats of London by adopting a poor East End parish in 1864.[1] Other public schoolboys followed, entering these metropolitan ghettoes, either as clergy or missioners, and bringing the code of the playing field with them. Later encouraged by Bishop Walsham How (who refused six colonial bishoprics before accepting responsibility for East London as Bishop of Bedford in 1879), they came in droves.

Even more obsessively concerned with fitness was H. H. Almond who worked on the maxim that 'the laws of physical well-being are the laws of God'. From 1862 to the end of the century, open windows, shorts, shirt-sleeves, cold baths and long runs in the rain were the order of the day at Loretto.[2] And Almond was, with variations, followed by many others who recognised that playing fields did more to extinguish hunting and shooting than any direct prohibition, whilst at the same time fostering personal self-discipline and team work.

The first Rugby football club, Blackheath, was formed in 1858 by the old boys of Rugby and Blackheath schools. The London Rugbeians flirted for a time with football enthusiasts at Cambridge and Sheffield with a view to establishing an Association, but since neither Cambridge nor Sheffield would consider handling the ball in the Rugby manner, withdrew. So the Football Association, formed in 1863, gave its name, characteristically abbreviated, to Soccer, whilst the old Rugbeians formed football clubs at Oxford and Cambridge in 1869. London clubs and Wellington College formed the Rugby Union in 1871.

Soccer rose to popularity as a means of combating the degeneracy of town life. The Football Association was formed the same year (1863) as William Booth's Salvation Army and Henry Solly's Union of Working Men's Clubs and Institutes. In the same year also some old Carthusian apprentices of the North Staffordshire Railway, one of whom singularly enough, was named Matthews, formed a football club later known as Stoke City: the first of many to be so founded.[1]

X

Three other factors sharpened the appreciation of physical fitness. The publication of Charles Darwin's *Origin of Species* (1859) seemed to endorse the doctrine that only the fittest survived.[2] The war scare of 1859 led to the volunteer movement and the formation of cadet corps at the public schools. Lastly, the efforts of the United Kingdom Alliance, founded in 1853, as a non-party organisation secured 'pledges' from its members to abstain from alcohol, and was so successful that the Church of England Temperance Society was founded in 1862.[3]

The *Origin of Species* also focused more sharply the dilemmas of the traditional Christians, like Frederick Temple, the head-master of Rugby, who in 1860 contributed to a volume called *Essays and Reviews*, the tone of which led the contributors to be known as the 'Seven against Christ'.[4] For their views indicated that Charles Darwin's *Origin of Species* was but one of a number of challenges. Another was Bishop Colenso's statistical inquiry into the arithmetic of the Pentateuch. Darwin's work emanated from the long search into man's past conducted by the natural scientists and amplified by the opening up of the world; Colenso's brought to a head the critical examination of Sacred Scriptures, averring that these books were post-exile forgeries. Around both books beat a tremendous controversy, for both weakened still further the documentary and mythological justification of Christianity.

Now Christian apologists were forced to look for new grounds on which to argue. No better ground could be found than human need, and so the more thoughtful began to stress spiritual and aesthetic values against the 'scientism' of Spencer and Huxley. Thus Quintin Hogg was led in 1864 to work with the lowest stratum of London life, and Matthew Arnold to take up his father's work for a truly national church based on a 'religionless' Christianity.

For Matthew Arnold was the intellectual anemometer of this age. He registered all the winds of change. From the time he became an Inspector of Schools in 1851 until he died 37 years later, he amplified his father's theme that the pressing need of the day was for the state to organise secondary education for the middle-classes, so that the embryonic working-class could have a model on which to form themselves. To this end he set himself (as he said), to 'rescue the middle class from the hands of their dissenting ministers,' whose bitter animosity to state education was fed by the tradition of the Clarendon Code. Ceaselessly he pointed out that the rising tide of agnosticism and positivism, no less than the growing demand for technical training for the lower classes, demanded action by the state. This made him the real opponent of the Nonconformist, anti-state positivism of Spencer.

Just as he wished the Nonconformists to be less Nonconformist, so he wished Christianity to be less theological. The 'extra-beliefs' that clustered round the Bible obscured its basic truths. Like his father, and indeed like Coleridge, he wished the schools to help their pupils to walk staunchly by the best light they had, and wanted not so much a national church as a national society for the promotion of goodness. God, to Arnold, was 'that stream of tendency by which all things strive to fulfil the laws of their being', and to help this, Arnold wished for a distillate of all the best that has been said and thought in the world to be available to the teacher. Arnold consistently refused to be intimidated by science. He told his mother on 8 December 1861, 'man shall not live by bunkum alone', and told the University of Cambridge that 'for the majority of mankind a little of mathematics, even, goes a long way'. In *Friendship's Garland* he poked fun at the curriculum of Dr Silverpump's academy:

None of your antiquated rubbish—all practical work—latest discoveries in science—mind constantly kept excited—lots of interesting experiments—lights of all colours—fizz, fizz, bang, bang. That's what I call forming a man.

But he was not opposed to science in the curriculum, only to the aridity of some of its champions. T. H. Huxley saw this when he told Arnold that the English middle-classes 'urgently stand in need of conversion by Extra-Christian missionaries'. This is what they both were—Huxley's mission to the scientists being 'something like' Arnold's to the Nonconformists.[1]

XI

'What influence may help us to prevent the English people from becoming, with the growth of democracy, *Americanised*?' asked Matthew Arnold, and replied, 'I confess I am disposed to answer: *nothing but* the influence of the *State*.'[2] By ensuring that schools were *respected* as well as *inspected*, the state, in Arnold's opinion, was doing its greatest service. State action on Arnoldian lines was evoked to cope with the avalanche of children being built up, partly by the increase in the population (another four millions were added in the two decades after 1851), and partly by the increasing rejection of juveniles from industry. In this rejection, the coercive power of the factory inspectorate was increasingly effective. Up to 1860 only the textile and allied trades were prohibited by law to take children unless they produced an educational voucher. A Royal Commission on Children's Employment appointed in 1861 recommended that children should be forbidden to enter the pottery, paper staining, fustian cutting, lucifer matchmaking, percussion cap and cartridge industries as well, and this became law in 1864. In 1867 other trades like copper, indiarubber, brickworks, printing, rope, glass, silk and papermaking were also brought under Factory Acts. Nor did it end here, for workshops and private houses which had hitherto escaped definition as 'factories' now came under the Workshops Regulation Act of 1867. Unfortunately, the administration of the Workshops Regulation Act came under the local authorities, not the factory inspectors, and, which made matters worse, they were not forced to act. The disincentive in most cases was strong: a genuine fear that the rates would rise if local inspectors were appointed.[1]

It was becoming increasingly clear, however, that the best Factory Act would be an Education Act, for if children were compelled to attend school, they could not go to work.

Almost annually such education Bills had been presented to Parliament during the fifties and sixties by private members like W. J. Fox and Sir John Pakington. Now, loss of face abroad and labour troubles at home precipitated Parliamentary action. The loss of face abroad was the poor show made by British exhibits at the Paris Exhibition of 1867. As interpreted by Lyon Playfair and John Scott Russell, this reflected inadequate technical training of the 'industrial classes'. So the government appointed a select committee under the great ironmaster Bernhard Samuelson. Its report on *The Provisions for giving Instruction in Theoretical and Applied Science to the Industrial Classes* showed conclusively that Paris was not the only centre where we were losing face, for American engineering products were making serious inroads in colonial markets.

Labour troubles at home were reflected in a series of outrages which prompted the appointment of a Royal Commission on Trades Unions. The unions' case was marshalled by an astute junta, whose leader Robert Applegarth shrewdly threw in his lot with the Birmingham manufacturers who had formed a League to promote rate-aided state education. He went on to record this, saying that:

opposition of masters and men does not arise from a desire of either to oppress the other, but rather from ignorance, from misunderstanding of each other's position, and failure to appreciate the others' point of view. I look to education to teach all parties better.

Labour support for Liberal causes was increasingly necessary after 1867 when the town artisans were given the vote. And labour criticism of Liberal measures (or Conservative ones for that matter), increased in volume as the Trades Union Congresses became, after 1868, national events. Face to face with the emergent populace, both Robert Lowe and Matthew Arnold (however much they might differ on details), agreed. 'It will be absolutely necessary,' Lowe told the House of Commons in 1867, 'that you should prevail on our future masters to learn their letters.' And letters, in the widest sense of the word, was what Arnold prescribed as the only antidote to the anarchic conflict of Barbarian, Philistine and Populace. 'Through the length and breadth of our nation a sense—vague and obscure as yet—of weariness with the old organisations, of desire for this transformation, works and grows,' he wrote in *Culture and Anarchy*, 'the centre of the movement is not in the House of Commons. It is in the fermenting mind of the nation; and his is for the next twenty years the real influence who can address himself to this.'

And this is precisely what he did. All who tried to impose technical education on the working classes at the expense of humanising them, found in him a persistent exposer of their slogan-mindedness, mechanistic outlook, and addiction to clap-trap.[1]

VIII

THE POLITICS OF THE BOARDS
1868–1889

I

Appointed Vice-President of the Council in 1868, W. E. Forster, as a member of the Taunton Commission, framed a Bill on lines recommended by that body whereby a state examining body was to certify secondary schoolmasters as efficient. But neither that proposal, nor others which would allow local rates to be applied by local authorities to secondary education, found favour. What did, and what emerged from parliament in the following year, was an executive commission of three commissioners armed for $3\frac{1}{2}$ years with power to revise schemes for endowed schools over 50 years old. Needless to say, the nine big public schools were not included.

Forster's brother-in-law, the H.M.I. Matthew Arnold put his finger on a reason 'why no effective remedy is applied to this serious evil'. 'It was,' he wrote, 'because the upper class amongst us do not want to be disturbed in their preponderance, or the middle class in their vulgarity. Even though these prejudices are unconscious, the result is just the same.'

Despite Arnold's pessimism, the three commissioners did get something done, indeed, G. A. N. Lowndes sees in them the real founders of our modern secondary school network.[1] With H. J. Roby as their secretary (he had served the Taunton Commission in a similar capacity), until 1872, and as their liveliest colleague until 1874, the commissioners established schemes for 235 schools: nearly a third of those examined by the Taunton Commission. These schemes created popular governing bodies, introduced science and modern languages and made special provision for girls.

By so doing the commissioners became very unpopular. Edward Thring, determined not to be bound and cast into 'a witches' cauldron', lamented to a correspondent, 'the future looks very dark and the present feels very cold, the bigotry of the Liberals is unspeakable.' He criticised the Endowed Schools Commission as an instrument for 'unchurching' schools, an embodiment of state power, 'advancing to crush him'.[1] It was a natural reaction, therefore, for him to organise his fellow-sufferers. So when Mitchinson of King's School Canterbury summoned a meeting of other headmasters of schools scheduled to be 'boiled down', Thring offered them the hospitality of Uppingham in December 1869.

By setting himself against all this, Thring inspired others. 'These powerful and practised red tapists,' he wrote, 'with nothing at stake, matched against poor me, with only my principles and experience.'[2] He underestimated himself. The Conference of Headmasters which Mitchinson of King's School Canterbury, Harper of Sherborne and he had called into being in 1869 became a permanent institution—the Headmasters' Conference. It was the first attempt to secure co-operation among leaders of the profession. Within two years, Eton, Winchester, and Shrewsbury had joined, and Thring was able to boast that the seven-school delusion was broken, and all the endowed schools were 'in the boat together'.

In 1873 the Headmasters' Conference urged Oxford and Cambridge to establish a joint board to inspect and examine schools and give certificates to successful pupils. This joint board enabled them to preserve their class nature while responding to the Taunton Commission's recommendation that a central examining council should be established to examine all pupils in the endowed schools.

Well might Roby remark that opposition to the work of the commissioners was 'exceeding fierce'. Even during the lifetime of the Liberal government their powers were pared and in 1873 an amending Act removed elementary schools from their jurisdiction, and transferred them to the Education Department.

When a Conservative government took office in 1874, it made haste to denationalise the schemes of the Endowed Schools Commissioners. Even *The Times* condemned them and wrote on 22 July 1874:

It is difficult to find a precedent for it—a bill proposing the wholesale redelivery to one religious body, of schools which, founded for national purposes and endowed with national property, have been set free for the use and education of all Englishmen,

while the *Economist* compared it to the sudden reversal of the engine of the ship of state: 'it makes everyone fear lest we are going rapidly towards our starting point instead of towards our goal.'

So, faced with a mauling debate, Disraeli dropped the denationalising clauses. The Bill transferred to the Charity Commissioners the functions previously discharged by the Endowed Schools Commissioners. The change decelerated the opening up of the endowments, and worse still, involved the dismissal of Lord Lyttelton and H. J. Roby. Roby lived to become a Liberal M.P., but Lyttelton, depressed beyond measure, committed suicide within months of relinquishing his office. But their work had not been in vain. Though the Charity Commissioners were slow, and were not directly under the Vice-President as their predecessors had been, their schemes did emerge to be discussed by the House of Commons. Moreover, the hubbub evoked by Disraeli had a salutary effect on his party and a Liberal could gloat 'nothing more has been heard of threats to occupy the dismantled fortress of educational exclusiveness'. Twenty years later 902 schemes had been framed and approved.

II

While his schemes for reconstructing the endowed schools were frightening the Headmasters' Conference into existence by their apparent radicalism, Forster was frightening the radical members of his own party by his very moderate suggestions that school boards (to be elected by town councils), were to provide schools in 'gaps' not already filled by the voluntary societies.

The radicals (organised in the National Education League), argued that the boards should be popularly elected, that their complexion should be secular, that they should be compelled to compel children to attend school and that the voluntary societies should not be allowed (as Forster proposed) a period of 'grace' to fill in the 'gaps' before boards were elected. The voluntaryists (organised in the National Education Union) reminded Forster that their schools had borne the heat and burden of the century without complaint and were willing to continue bearing it.

His Elementary Education Act of 1870 was a hard compromise, for it allowed the voluntary societies six months' grace before their districts were assessed for educational deficiencies. In return for this, he conceded to the radical groups their popularly elected school boards, and the exclusion of any sectarian religious teaching in the board schools. Compulsion to attend school was made optional for the school boards to exercise, in spite of persistent pressure from the Birmingham group of the National Educational League and moderate members of his own party.[1]

The spleen of the Nonconformists descended upon Forster. It was his misfortune to have broken the deadlock between them and the apostles of state education by uniting them both against himself. The Church, seeing him beset, supported him, and this further outraged the Nonconformists. They accused him of working the machine for the Church, and John Bright was loudly applauded when he declared that the 1870 Act was the worst passed since 1832.

A grand Nonconformist indictment was later drawn up by John Morley, the 34-year-old editor of the *Fortnightly Review*, roundly trouncing the 'holy army of misologists' whom Forster had subsidised from the public purse, and who were encouraged rather than extinguished by the permissive nature of the clauses dealing with the establishment of school boards and the enforcement of attendance at school. Pointing to the general trend to whittle away priestly power, he argued that in England it was being increased. Three counts in Morley's indictment were especially telling. First, the sects used the six months' grace to increase their schools by 30%. Second, the cumulative vote was working in their favour. Lastly, and most monstrous to the Nonconformists, the 25th clause of the Act allowed the school fees of children attending Church schools to be paid by the Boards of Guardians.[1]

That this last clause applied only to necessitous children was beside the point. It became the symbol of the whole struggle of the Church versus the Nonconformists. Those in favour of the clause favoured religious education. Those against it were the opponents of re-endowment of the Established Church. Dr Dale of Birmingham was blunter. He saw in it a fresh source of income for the Church of England and the Church of Rome.

In face of this mounting hostility, all Forster's subsequent administrative actions were exposed to fierce criticism. In 1871 he introduced a new Code, giving a number of new grants to leaven the soulless skills of tongue and pen which prevailed ever since the Revised Code nine years before. These grants (3s. for a pass in two specific subjects offered in standards 4 to 6) were an added encouragement to teachers. Moreover, schedules of ventilation, lighting and accommodation were published and the grants were increased to 6s. for attendance and 4s. for a pass in the Procrustean three Rs.

The Nonconformists were quick to seize on this. The additional grants were construed as making less onerous the expense of managing the sectarian schools. There was some ground for this complaint. Forster had extended the grants to efficient schools where the fees were not more than 9d., while the Board schools had their fees checked to ensure that there was no unfair competition with voluntary schools.

The doubling of the numbers supporting the National Education League's annual motion for compulsory education prompted Forster to draft a Bill not only to enforce compulsion but to repeal the 25th clause. The Cabinet agreed, but after a short interval out of office reconsidered the position, and the Bill was dropped. This left Forster caught between two fires, in the very year when the working of the Education Act was most difficult. For just as his department was having to force school boards on recalcitrant districts, John Bright damaged him at Birmingham on 22 October 1873 with a powerful speech. Its tone, coming from a colleague, was severe. The bad odour which lingered after similar Nonconformist attacks jeopardised the very real chances which Forster possessed of becoming leader of the Liberal Party.

He left office in 1874 having added 4,982 more schools to the 8,281 that existed when he took office. The average attendance had increased by over half a million. As he himself said, 'some education is now secured to all English children. Whether that some is enough to be of real value is now the question; but I do not think the work can stop.' He was right.

III

As a contributor to the first number of *The School Board Chronicle and Review*, a weekly which first appeared on 18 February 1871, remarked:

The three great principles at issue in the modern world of education—drill, compulsion, unsectarianism, were undecided by the bill; which left, and leaves, the public battle to be fought and won by the local Boards.

Called into life to levy local rates with which to build and administer schools, the sect-spiced elections to, and debates of, these school boards engaged some of the liveliest minds of the times. Each school board produced its great men. Birmingham had its Chamberlain, George Dixon and the Reverend E. F. M. McCarthy; Manchester its H. Birley; Bradford its James Hanson. In London, a galaxy of talent served at one time or another in the well-known board rooms on the Embankment. One of its chairmen, Lyulph Stanley was to Spanish liberals like Don Francisco Giner and Manuel Cossio the incarnation of liberal England.[1]

The vast accomplishment and scope of the London School Board made it a national institution. Its debates were reported in *The Times*, which had declared at the inception of the Board: 'no equally powerful body will exist in England outside Parliament if power be measured by influence for good or evil over masses of human beings.' Its buildings and its exemption ages for half-timers set standards. Men of the calibre of T. H. Huxley sat in its deliberations. As chairman of a committee on school organisation, he helped to draw up the scheme for junior schools for children between 7 and 10, and senior schools for older children: a pattern which exists to this day. London set the new methods of teaching on their feet. Other boards clung to the drill prescribed by the 1871 code, but London adopted P.T. under the supervision of Madame Bergman Osterberg. In Camden Town sloyd (or educational handwork) was put into practice under Miss Clarke.

London set precedents in all directions. Within three years of its establishment its architect, E. R. Robson, went to Germany to make a study of buildings. He returned with a pattern which became standard. Instead of a vast hall with tiered seats for classes, he built separate classrooms opening from the hall. This plan was adopted throughout the country. G. M. Young has immortalised 'those solid, large windowed blocks, which still rise everywhere above the slate roofs of mean suburbs which meant for hundreds of thousands their first glimpse of a life of cleanliness, order, light and air'.[2]

Later other boards set their own particular fashions. Nottingham set up the first 'organised science school', and with Sheffield and Bradford helped to create the model higher grade elementary school. Bradford towards the end of the century appointed the first medical officer of health to be concerned with the personal health of each child and encouraged the work of Margaret McMillan. Others were just as active. As soon as a school board was formed in Sheffield, the clerk, J. L. Moss, was sent to Germany to collect ideas. He reported in *Notes on National Education of the Continent* that the Prussian system 'by its cleanliness might well excite the admiration of the world'.

In this spirit the school boards forged ahead. At Bradford 25 schools were built in fifteen years, raising the average attendance to nearly 8,000. In Manchester 57 schools and 139 'departments' in other buildings were provided—so many that the chairman declared that they had been multiplied 'unnecessarily'. Leeds erected 43 new buildings. London far exceeded all others with 343 permanent schools, 22 schools made over by the denominations and 26 temporary schools. Only in large towns where the denominations were all-powerful—like Liverpool—was board progress less impressive, for Liverpool built only fifteen board schools in the same period.

Medical inspection began when the London School Board appointed in 1890 a medical officer, Dr W. R. Smith, to report on air space and the ventilation of rooms and, to examine mentally defective children. Bradford took a further step in 1893 when the medical inspection of children was organised under James Kerr, and for many years it was a pioneer of school medical services. School boards also acquired permissive powers to provide special schools for blind and deaf children (in 1893) and deaf and epileptic children (in 1899). Indeed, a Southsea physician-author, Dr Conan Doyle caught the general opinion. As Sherlock Holmes said to Dr Watson as they were travelling up to London (as recorded in *The Naval Treaty*):

'Look at those big isolated clumps of buildings rising above the slates, like brick islands in a lead coloured sea.'
'The Board Schools.'
'Light houses, my boy! Beacons of the future! Capsules, with hundreds of bright little seeds in each, out of which will spring the wiser better England of the future.'[1]

School board elections became pointers to national elections. The National Education League's organisation was transformed, once its objectives were attained, into the National Liberal

Federation, while Lord Sandon, son of the president of the National Education Union, became Vice-President of the Council in the Conservative administration of 1874. Sandon gave to the voluntary schools in the countryside grants of from £10 to £15, raised two years later to 17s. 6d. per child in average attendance. The controllers of these country schools (the squire and the clergyman) were suspected by radical Liberals (who had already encouraged the followers of Joseph Arch to form Trade Unions, and were shortly to demand that the agricultural labourers should be enfranchised) of being lukewarm over the education of future farm labourers. So the radicals claimed that only a system of universal school boards could bring about a system of universal compulsion to attend school. Conservative county members, on the other hand, had an equally rooted aversion to school boards.

This conflict of opinion reached a climax in 1876 when Lord Sandon introduced a Bill to establish school attendance committees in districts where no school boards had been erected. The Church fought back behind Disraeli.[1] The Bill itself was torn apart, clause by clause. But, as in 1870, the Minister, supported by the opposition, carried the measure against the members of his own party. Sandon vowed 'the government start from this position, they do not think the principle of direct compulsion would be a good thing in itself'. So the school attendance committees were merely empowered, like the boards, to make laws enforcing attendance at school. Sandon was accused by A. J. Mundella (who had introduced with G. Dixon of the League three private members' Bills in previous years, all of which aimed at direct compulsion, and who had only withdrawn them on Sandon's promise to legislate on the question), of being 'the mildest mannered man who ever scuttled a ship or cut a throat'. The ship was the promised content of the 1876 Bill and the throat that of the Dissenters. The contemporary historian of the fast dissolving National Education League agreed, describing it as 'an act for compelling attendance at denominational schools supported out of rates and taxes'.[2] Its leading spirit,

Joseph Chamberlain, in Parliament for the first time this year, wrote:

It is a tremendous blow to the dissenters and to the secular party . . . .
We shall have a kind of universal compulsion and universal education and there remains only two things:
  (i) free schools: for which this country is certainly not yet prepared.
 (ii) To wrest this education out of the hands of priests of all shades. This last is a branch of the disestablishment movement to which I am more and more convinced that the efforts of all radicals should now be directed.[1]

IV

In 1880 the swing of the pendulum carried the Liberals into office and A. J. Mundella became Vice-President of the Council in the Liberal administration of 1880–5. The farce of permissive compulsion was ended immediately. A short three-clause Act informed the school boards and school attendance committees who had not made bye-laws enforcing compulsion, that they must do so 'forthwith'. If they did not comply by the end of the year, the Education Department would do so for them. More-over, it made the employer of any child between the ages of 10 and 13 liable to a penalty if that child had not got a certificate of education as laid down by the bye-laws.

The Act caught quite a number who had not availed them-selves of the privilege of being able to frame bye-laws. Four hundred and fifty of the 2,000 school boards, twenty of the 109 school attendance committees, seven out of the 67 urban sanitary authorities, had not submitted bye-laws for approval, and 569 out of 584 unions had not got their parishes covered. A flood of bye-laws came in for sanction and within five months over 1,200 sets of them were sanctioned. The Bill became law on 26 August 1880, and by January 1881 only 28 Unions, 81 school boards, one school attendance committee and one urban sanitary authority had not complied. With such minute exemptions, the

F

entire population of England was obliged to send its children to school until they were 10 years old, when they could obtain an educational certificate entitling them to leave.

The Act also made it impossible for children to leave school at the age of 10 on the strength of 250 attendances: known generally as the 'dunce's certificate'. This was now restricted to children of 13, with the added obligation that such a child was required to attend as a half-timer until the age of 14. So incentives to work hard at school were strengthened, for the only way in which a child could evade this was by reaching Standard Five as soon as possible.

Three weeks before the Mundella Act became law, he announced his intention of bringing in a new Code. The Code itself was often completely incomprehensible to both managers and teachers, and attempts to alter it were treated with sceptical cynicism.

It was not only the changes which Mundella made in the Code, but the way that he made them, that was novel. For a Code committee was set up. This, as the Secretary of the Education Department confessed, was something new indeed. 'To have a committee sitting round a table and deliberating as a committee was a new departure as I understood it.' The committee consisted of Sandford, Cumin and Sykes (from the Department); Warburton Sharpe and Fitch (from the Inspectorate); and Matthew Arnold, Moncrieff, Oakeley and Blakiston (Inspectors for large towns). Mundella presided. Suggestions were received from all interested parties, and the draft report was hammered into a set of proposals which was laid before the House.

The Code marked a real breach in the system of payment by results, for a small part of the grant was made to depend upon discipline and organisation. 'Class Subjects'—grammar, geography, history and plain needlework, were brought in to the lower part of the school above Standard I. The teaching of these class subjects, as their name implied, was to be assessed by the ability of the class as an entity. So, taking the 1871 changes into account, the grants depended on the three obligatory subjects, the optional class subjects (which might be taken by the whole school), and the specific subjects taken by individual scholars above Standard IV.

New trails were blazed in the upper and lower ends of the elementary school. At the lower end, payment by results was moderated by a grant for play and manual work. The inspectors' reports from now on testify to the immense change that took place in the junior schools. At the upper end, Standard VII made its appearance. This made it possible to separate the new 'tops' into separate schools or 'higher grade schools'—a movement which had already begun in the large towns like Nottingham and Sheffield.

To make teaching more intelligent, a merit grant was introduced. Schools were to be classified as 'Fair,' 'Good,' or 'Excellent', and to guide the inspectors the following instructions were issued:

An excellent school is characterised by cheerful yet exact discipline, maintained without harshness or noisy demonstration of authority. Its premises are cleanly and well ordered, its timetable provides a proper variety of mental employment and of physical exercise; its organisation is such as to distribute the teaching power judiciously, and to secure for every scholar, whether he is likely to bring credit to the school or not, a fair share of instruction and attention.

Where circumstances permit, it has also got its lending library, its savings bank, and an orderly collection of simple objects and apparatus adapted to illustrate the school lessons, and formed in part by the co-operation of the scholars themselves.

The class and specific subjects were re-arranged. Heat, light, sound, chemistry and agriculture allowed the needs of the times to be catered for in the schools. The introduction of cookery as a grant-earning subject for the girls, and the teaching of elementary science throughout the school, were but two signs that the school was being regarded as a vestibule to adulthood.

The results of the Code were profound. For the first time the instructions to the inspectors and the requirements of the Department were bound in one volume. A permanent Code committee, modifying such articles as were harsh or misunderstood, enabled a more flexible system than hitherto to operate within the schools. New sub-inspectors of special qualifications and experience were appointed to cope with the extra work which followed on the re-organisation of the inspectorate into ten districts. Harshness was deprecated. By 1884 they were being urged to consider the 'health, age and mental capacity of the children' as well as 'their due progress in learning'.

It revealed the inadequacies of the existing methods of teacher training. Central instruction of pupil teachers, fought by the Department in the seventies, was now recognised as essential. Probationers were compelled to attend centres in the day-time, and within four years there were eleven such centres in operation. It bore heavily on the voluntary schools, where the pupil teacher often was the only other teacher on the staff besides the headmaster. It meant that in country districts 'the discipline and efficiency of the schools must inevitably be prejudiced'. That was the view of the Archbishop of Canterbury expressed in a letter to A. J. Mundella, and he added that he feared 'the proposed changes would lead to a diminution in the number of pupil teachers employed'.

A rallying cry against the provisions of the Code was not long in appearing. It was 'harsh' and caused 'overpressure'. The harshness fell, it is true, on the voluntary schools, and the 'overpressure' often bore heavily on the teachers whose inadequate training could not cope with the new requirements. A sensational report was printed, in which Dr Crichton Browne declared that overpressure was a fact, and it needed all the authority of the *Lancet* to declare that 'the educational system is not overworking children but demonstrating that they are underfed'. This was opening up a vast new field of school activity, which Mundella was not slow to realise. He urged all local authorities to follow the example of Rousden, a Devonshire village, and to provide cheap meals for the children. Mundella himself became president of the Central Council for Promoting Self-supporting Penny

Dinners, which circulated details of the Rousden experiment in the spring of 1885.

The army of school attendance officers thus created was the reconnaissance corps of social investigation. Their findings were exploited and utilised by a wealthy shipowner, Charles Booth. His results published between 1891 and 1903 under the general title of *Life and Labour of the People in London* massively proved that one-quarter of the people of London were living in poverty. By showing this in a dispassionate and scientific manner, he assisted the further extension of the protective hand of the state.[1]

V

By 1885 the rivalry between the school boards and the churches reached a climax. The churches resisted the secular advance of the state, as it had impinged on them since 1870 through the board school system. Most vocal were the Catholics and the Anglicans. The Catholics set up an education crisis fund, and began to mortgage their schools to meet increasing competition. The secretary of the Catholic Poor Schools Committee complained that since 1877 very real differences had arisen between the Education Department and his organisation, which had been refused 18 grants. In the name of all Catholics, he strongly protested against Catholics being forced into board schools, and asserted that they would suffer persecution rather than be so compelled. 'These schools,' he declared, 'will in the end overturn the whole system of religious teaching.'

With this point of view the National Society agreed. They claimed that voluntary schools were being supplanted, not supplemented, by the board schools, especially in view of the practice of board schools supplying accommodation when there was no provision for education being made.

The plight of the voluntary schools became more apparent with each new Code, which made demands upon their resources which it became increasingly difficult to meet. The teaching of science, drawing and manual training required smaller classes and better equipment than their falling subscriptions could provide. Moreover, the segregation of the 'higher tops' of the board schools became a grievance to those whose children were at private venture schools. They fulminated against it as 'middle class education by a side wind'. Significant in this connection was the formation of the Association of Independent Schools, formed for self-protection by the proprietors as they saw the higher-grade schools taking shape.

The acknowledged spokesman of the Anglicans was Canon Gregory, the treasurer of the National Society, and a quondam member of the London School Board. In the *Nineteenth Century* he openly charged the Education Department with unjust administration of the Act of 1870 in favour of the board schools. He demanded help for the voluntary schools in their distress, and suggested that it could most easily come from the rates. He found support from Lord Norton, a Liberal-Conservative who had introduced a Bill for rate aid to education twenty years before and now showed that the bluntness which had kept him out of Disraeli's cabinet had not deserted him. Norton accused the Liberal Ministry of 1880–5 of 'essaying a flight into continental bureaucracy,' and Mundella of 'having strongly avowed German preferences'. Ominously enough, he condemned the boards who had borrowed money to undertake 'independent educational experiments' far outside their authority.

This was a useful lever for the voluntaryists. For to accuse the school boards of acting *ultra vires* was very effective, especially since it was the multiplication of new subjects in the 'higher tops' which was causing the voluntary schools such great difficulties.

Voluntary schools were five times as numerous as the board schools. They were especially strong in the counties, where the squire built the school and the parson taught the catechism. Here the struggle was infected with politics, once the Liberals enfranchised the agricultural labourer in 1884. Memorials to Gladstone had no effect. So when the country went to the polls in 1885, the voluntaryists took good care that the full implications of the Liberal policy were laid before the electorate. The voluntary schools found a champion in Cardinal Manning, who in a speech on 24 June 1885 warned his audience against allowing their children to become state controlled, exhorting them 'to rise up and say they did not want board schools for their children'. Resolutions were adopted that the 1870 Act was 'unequal, unjust and dangerous to the voluntary schools of this country'.[1]

The Conservatives, returned to power in 1885, were once again quick to reward their supporters. This time a Royal Commission was appointed to examine the working of the Elementary Education Acts. The original chairman selected was the Bishop of London, but after the Conservative Vice-President had received protests against the denominational character of the commission, a new one was found in Lord Cross and five more members were added to the body as a whole.

The Cross Commission, as it was now called, had a galaxy of talent at its command. They fought the same battles as had been fought outside, and just as the voluntaryists had won outside, so they won on the Commission. The majority report was favourable to the voluntary schools and recommended that they should be supported from the rates and their resources increased. The minority, led by Lyulph Stanley of the London School Board bitterly opposed any such scheme, and formed themselves into a little pressure group to resist any attempt to carry the majority proposals into law. This group was known as the National Education Association, and it first met on 20 and 21 November 1888, resolving to promote a system of education 'which shall be efficient, progressive, unsectarian, and under popular control'.

But being composed mainly of Liberals, they could obtain nothing from a Conservative government. The Conservative leader, Lord Salisbury, had no wish to see the minority proposals of the Cross Commission magnified while the majority proposals were as yet unadopted. So in 1890 the majority report on 'payment by results' was used to modify and relax the system. At the same time Lord Salisbury told his followers that school fees must be abolished in elementary schools, 'for', said he, 'if our opponents should obtain a majority in a future parliament, they would deal with it in such a manner that the voluntary schools would be swept away.'

So, in 1891, to help the church schools and put a stop to the farce of uninvestigated necessity, elementary education was made free. A 10s. per head fee-grant was made to all schools, board and voluntary alike. The frankly political nature of this move was lamented by the *Economist*, which censured the government for 'yielding to the temptation to pose as benefactors of the working class'. The Liberals were at hand to extract the full pound of flesh offered by such a concession.

Perhaps the biggest testimony to the victory of the voluntaryists was the sight of Joseph Chamberlain, who twenty years before had tried to set the country on fire and consume them, now admitting that 'the extinction of the voluntary schools, painless or otherwise was not possible.' He was reduced to defending church schools in rural areas, stalking out majestically before the time came for a division. The voluntaryists did not rest with their victory.

VI

Disraeli, with his gift of prescience, saw that the 1870 Act would create 'a new sacerdotal class'. For the clamour surrounding the passage of Forster's Act led to the convening by J. W. Whitwell, M.P., of a conference of Liberal M.P.s on 9 April 1870, when various teachers were sounded on the religious question. The teachers unanimously gave their opinion that this was a 'platform difficulty' and suggested that a conscience clause should be introduced.[1] This conference led to the union of the various existing teachers' associations, which took place on 25 June 1870. On the same day they formed themselves into the National Union of Elementary School Teachers. As they expanded, they dropped the qualifying 'elementary'.

Within fifteen years of their incorporation, they numbered 11,000, a figure doubled by 1902. Their collective detachment (their first president was a churchman and their first secretary was not), and their organised strength (their annual conference came to be regarded as a pointer to progressive policy), gave them an increasingly powerful share in affairs. By combination, council, suggestion, promulgation and public action they helped remodel the teacher's status, and in helping to improve the standing of their schools, they improved their own. They established the strongest association of teachers in the world, and endowed it with one of the most lucrative organs of the educational press.

As teachers rose in status, so the clerics declined. Within a generation the Rev. A. C. Deane was lamenting *The Falling in quantity and quality of the Clergy* in the columns of the *Nineteenth Century*.[1] For the board schoolmaster, with his £120 a year, was rising in the social scale. The curate, with his £200 less and less augmented by a private income, was going down. Moreover, the teacher had not the crippling demands upon his purse which were the inevitable consequence of the curate's calling.

This new clerisy had its hierarchy. At its head both in seniority and status was the Headmasters' Conference—a veritable educational House of Lords, that stood for the traditional ways and slow internal change on individual lines. Standards were high and rigid. The godlike supremacy of the public school headmaster was so powerful that no assistant master was ever admitted to the conference, and when Oscar Browning was expelled from his assistant mastership at Eton, not even a question in Parliament could get him restored. Between Headmasters' Conference and the N.U.T. yawned a great gulf, which was spanned in the next decade by various associations of private schools (1883), the Teachers' Guild (1885) and the masters and mistresses in the endowed and higher grade schools. The proliferation of such associations enabled teachers of all kinds to exchange opinion, develop an outlook, and leaven the whole educational lump.

These professional groups began to think of professional training. Joshua Fitch had reported to the Taunton Commission that chairs of pedagogy and degrees in education should be established, and in 1872 the first of these suggestions was realised when the

College of Preceptors made Joseph Payne the first professor of education in England. Their example was followed four years later by similar appointments at Edinburgh and Aberdeen. In the meantime, Huxley lent powerful support to the advocates of teacher-training, as distinct from merely acquiring knowledge of subject matter. As witness and Commissioner before the Devonshire Commission, his views were made known. A deeper realisation of the problems at stake was displayed by Alexander Bain, whose *Mind and Body* (1872) called attention to the physiological nature of many of the so-called mental processes. In 1875 Bain and a few of the choicer spirits of the educational world formed the Education Society, which was intended to examine and criticise existing systems at home and abroad, and to collect, discuss and classify facts according to a definite plan. The following year he established the journal *Mind*, to serve him and his associates as a platform. *Mind* continued to wield its influence long after the Educational Society had been merged into the Teachers' Guild. Bain insisted that education was a science, and wrote a book with that title in 1879—the very year in which Wundt opened his psychological laboratory in Germany.

If Bain was laying the track for one line of educational philosophy, R. H. Quick was equally active in laying an other. Quick's *Educational Reformers*, published for the first time in 1868, was the most influential book on the history of education ever published in England. His inspiration came from America, and he himself maintained that American interest kept his book alive. Certainly Americans were primarily responsible for the publication of the revised second edition in 1890. Quick began to lecture to intending schoolmasters at Cambridge in 1879, four years after Compayré had delivered his lectures on the history of education at Toulouse. So, with Quick indicating the rich wells of inspiration that could be tapped, and Bain attempting to chart the frontiers of the mind, education was launched as a subject of serious academic study.

'It is,' wrote Huxley, 'a question of fact, not of metaphysic, theology or mere *a priori* reasoning: what education demands is a firmer scientific foundation.' Darwin's cousin Francis Galton first advocated the scientific study of the individual pupil and set up a small 'anthropometric laboratory' at the International Health Exhibition of 1884–5. This was subsequently moved to South Kensington. Mental testing, rating-scales, biographical schedules, record cards, the normal curve and statistical tools like Correlation and Factor Analysis came from him. Galton urged the school boards to establish laboratories.[1]

Teachers were quick to see the use of Galton's techniques. C. H. Lake in 1885 built up a record card based on Galtonian tests and Dr Sophie Bryant conducted a number of experiments 'Testing the character of Children',[2] while Professor F. Y. Edgeworth of Oxford, the half-nephew of Maria Edgeworth, suggested the application of rigorous statistical techniques to the marking of examination papers.

VII

Sophie Bryant represented both a product and a cause of these and other changes: she was an emancipated woman. Though John Stuart Mill was baulked in his attempt to include female franchise in the Reform Bill of 1867, women got the right to vote for and serve on school boards. Mill's arguments were reinforced by the spectacular agitation of Josephine Butler (wife of a Liverpool schoolmaster), who rocked public opinion by her campaign against the Contagious Diseases Act.[3] An Act of 1870 gave married women the right to keep their earnings (extended twelve years later to their own property).

As the number of congenial female occupations increased, so did the institutions for training them. University College London opened its classes to them in 1870. Agitation for examinations for women produced a standard higher than the Cambridge Local, later opened to men as well, with the title of the Higher Local Examination. Those who saw beyond examination projects joined Miss Emily Davies, and in October 1869 Girton opened its doors to six students at Hitchin. Three years later it moved to Cambridge. In Cambridge itself the women flocked to the lectures of James Stuart, a pioneer of university extension. By 1879, Oxford had followed suit with two halls of residence for women—Somerville and Lady Margaret Hall. The newer university colleges, needless to say, admitted women freely to their courses.

Girls' schools developed remarkably, thanks to Maria Grey and the National Union for Promoting the Higher Education of Women (1872). This in turn promoted the Girls' Public Day School Trust. Aided by business men and share certificates, it was expanded from three schools in Chelsea, Notting Hill and Croydon to a national network of 38 schools and 7,000 pupils. Maria Grey's enthusiasm was unabated. The Croydon school had a kindergarten department attached, and the Froebel Society, of which she and her sister were the moving spirits, revived interest in a writer who had been dead for more than twenty years. By 1878 she had also established her own training college for women. It is not surprising that co-education (a term popular in the United States after 1850), spread to England. Its merits lay in its expediency, but only isolated individual schools like Lady Barn saw its educational possibilities as early as 1873.[1]

At the instance of some women teachers anxious to hear lectures on the theory and practice of education, James Stuart came to Leeds, Liverpool, Sheffield and Manchester in 1867. But he did not talk on pedagogy, preferring instead the history of science. His auditors were enthusiastic and rallied to form the North of England Council for the Higher Education of Women. Stuart, a young Cambridge mathematician, was infected by their enthusiasm and two years later asked his university to set such work on a proper footing.

In this he was supported by others with experience of such efforts. Lancashire had provided audiences for similar lectures both during and after the cotton famine, so the Crewe Mechanics Institute and the Rochdale Pioneers supported his request. So did the working men's colleges of Leicester and Nottingham.

His university acceded, and in 1873 courses were arranged for those two towns and for Derby. In two years over 100 courses were in operation all over the country and by 1878 a Local Lectures Committee was in full swing. London followed suit in 1876 and Oxford in 1878 with A. H. D. Acland as secretary; but it was under Acland's successor, Michael Sadler, who took over in 1885, that the movement got under way. The Victoria University followed in 1886. By 1890 England was virtually covered by extra-mural teachers. In Wales and Scotland however the movement never took root, partly because universities took more students, and partly because their churches undertook more pastoral activities.

Pupil teachers as well as working men profited from this 'peripatetic university' as Stuart visualised it, and one later remarked 'the encouragement we received to read widely, to search and sift information for ourselves, was of the utmost value in our self development. . . . I feel that extra-mural lectures were a turning point in my life.'[1]

VIII

The school boards were kept virile by Whitehall, which could dissolve a board and appoint another in its place if necessary, and by the Science and Art Department at South Kensington, which made grants to every school or college which could satisfy its conditions, thereby encouraging the board schools to grow at the top. Spotlights were thrown on the intricate ramifications of the South Kensington system by the ten-part report of the Devonshire Commission on Scientific Instruction (1870–5). The power behind the scenes was undoubtedly Captain John Donnelly, who was in the department for 40 out of the 46 years of its existence.

As a close friend of Huxley, Donnelly urged upon the Privy Council the need for a college of general science in London to supplement the existing school of mines. Perhaps his greatest claim to fame, however, is his institution of the first technological examinations in the country. This was in 1871, three years before he became Director of Science. As the secretary of the Society of Arts recorded 'he not only proposed that the society should hold these examinations, but also planned the whole system on which they were carried out by the society'.

After overcoming opposition from the mining enthusiasts who virtually ruled the Royal School of Mines at South Kensington, the Normal School of Science was established and opened its doors in October 1881 under Huxley. Officially it was a single organisation, organised as a Royal School of Mines, and a Normal School of Science. But within the framework of each division a vigorous growth began which led to the Royal College of Science, and in turn, to the Imperial College of Science and Technology in 1907. The Normal School of Science trained not only the science teachers but interpreters, instigators, and inventors like H. G. Wells, Sir Richard Gregory and F. W. Lanchester.

Though it was a question of economic life or death to expand technical education, Donnelly was opposed by the very manufacturers who should have profited by his activity. For, fearing that their own secrets would be revealed, they refused to allow their workmen to discuss their own manufacturing processes. Far from assisting the scheme, they told him, they would do everything they could to stop it. In vain did Donnelly travel through the industrial north and east to persuade them. He never secured any co-operation from them, as he told a subsequent Royal Commission on Technical Education, which sat from 1882 to 1884. Fear of the revelation of trade secrets was the real stumbling block to any effective system of technical education.

The hitherto uneasy dichotomy which had prevailed between the Education Committee of the Privy Council at Whitehall and the Science and Art Department at South Kensington was resolved by the dual appointment of Sir Francis Sandford as permanent secretary, at Whitehall in 1870, then at South Kensington in 1874. In the interval he was also appointed to the secretaryship for Scotland in 1873. He possessed more administrative power over education than any other civil servant had ever done before or since in Great Britain. He was a close friend of Matthew Arnold, yet he genuinely deprecated the extension of the power of the state over national education—so much so, that after leaving office he devoted the remaining ten years of his life to being the most outspoken supporter of the voluntary schools. Sandford had joined the Education Department when it consisted of only three rooms at the Treasury. So great was his stature that even when he did not have the Vice-President in his pocket popular opinion supposed that he did.[1]

This was the golden age of the Inspector, then the real eyes and ears of the central authority, before their reports were muffled by stereotyped routine. Many of them were men of letters like Matthew Arnold, who worked from the Athenaeum rather than the Education Department. The administrative changes brought about an expansion in the inspectorate—from 98 to 244 in ten years—and a widening of the circle of recruitment. With the admission of ex-teachers to their ranks, many evils which the older inspectors had tolerated became less defensible than ever.[2]

IX

Huxley and Matthew Arnold both encouraged the movements that stirred, following the convulsive therapy of the 1867 Exhibition, to found local colleges. The older universities, already disturbed, had neither the capacity nor the intention of descending to the level of technical high schools.

So the florescence (the architectural style justifies the image), of the new university colleges began in the industrial towns. Some grew around the local mechanics' institute, or medical school; others were grafted on to existing literary and philosophic institutes. After 1870 their growth was accelerated by municipal pride and industrial munificence. Each college mirrored the technique of its town. Newcastle Royal College of Science (1871) had an initial obsession with mining; Yorkshire College, Leeds, with textiles (1874); and University College, Liverpool, with commerce (1881). The two latter emerged to full chartered status after a short period of affiliation to the University of Manchester. Firth College, Sheffield (1879), grew from the first people's college in Great Britain, but the foundation of Sir Josiah Mason at Birmingham excluded theology and mere 'literary study and education'. Yet even when they were admitted and Birmingham became a university in 1900, commerce was made a faculty and brewing set up as a department.

The financial help of South Kensington science grants and the protracted stimulus of the University of London examinations helped University Colleges at Nottingham (1881), Reading (1892), and Exeter (1893) to keep alive, foster the teaching of science and engineering and provide avenues of opportunity for their students.

Provincial colleges, especially one at Bristol (1876), found willing adjutants at the two older universities. At Oxford, Benjamin Jowett (elected Master of Balliol in 1870), did all he could to help them, using his many contacts to press for more scholarships, and later, as we shall see, pressing for state grants to support them.[1]

While they were taking shape, William James, a radical M.P., moved for an inquiry into the resources of the 89 city companies of London, and how much was devoted to 'technical education'. One of the sheriffs of the City of London said they only needed 'a little gentle persuasion' to make them give more. Huxley did his best, and the Progressive Party took up the cry in the elections to the London School Board in November 1876, informing the electorate of the relief from high educational rates which proper application of the resources of the city companies would afford them.

To their great credit, the companies did not shelter behind the doctrine that most of their resources were private property, but began to assist the local colleges. The Clothworkers gave help to Yorkshire College, Leeds, and also helped to form a City and Guilds Industrial University in London. One of their members, Sir Sidney Waterlow, aware of the rapid continental advances, had received reports from two commissioners who had been sent abroad for that purpose. With other companies, a committee was formed to take over the technological examinations which Donnelly had established for the Society of Arts. By 1880 this committee was incorporated as the City and Guilds of London Institute for the Advancement of Technical Education.

From the massive resources of London's City Guilds, Polytechnics were built on the German model in London. The first opened at Finsbury with W. E. Ayrton, John Perry and Sylvanus P. Thompson on the staff. Another—later called the Central Technical College—opened in 1883 at South Kensington, was paced by the development of the polytechnic at Charlottenburg, and was to become part of the Imperial College of Science and Technology.

Two further Welsh University Colleges at Cardiff (1883) and Bangor (1884), following that of Aberystwyth (1872), were established, and to supply them with students a select committee of 1881 recommended the fivefold expansion of secondary schools. This expansion was to be achieved by intermediate schools. Sustained by state grants, and rate aid, the intermediate schools were to channel ability from the existing elementary schools by means of scholarships.

But this ambitious 'ladder' scheme was deferred until 1889. Meanwhile, Welsh school boards were encouraged to set up 'advanced elementary schools for boys and girls', in which the instruction 'should be adapted as closely as possible to the characteristics of each place, and to the educational needs of the inhabitants'. These schools were modelled on the 'Higher Grade Schools' which the English school boards had also begun to establish in the late seventies.

x

As in Germany, research was to be the main role of these new civic colleges. This was partly due to the influence of those earlier professors who had been trained in Germany.

Pupils of Von Hofman taught at Mason's College, Birmingham (W. A. Tilden), Cambridge (S. Ruhemann), King's College, London (C. L. Bloxam) and Woolwich Military Academy (T. A. Abel). Pupils of Bunsen taught at University College, Bristol (William Ramsay), Yorkshire College, Leeds (T. E. Thorpe), Owens College, Manchester (H. E. Roscoe and Carl Schorlemmer). Pupils of other German professors like Rammelsberg (George D. Liveing) and Kolbe (H. E. Armstrong), were distributed around English colleges. A pupil of E. A. Frankland was to teach at Finsbury Technical College (R. Mendola).[1]

Men like Henry Roscoe and Lyon Playfair became politicians of science, and were supported by *Nature*, a new scientific journal established in England in 1869, whose editor Norman Lockyer argued 'the same method is necessary to raise, organise and equip a battalion as to perform a chemical operation'.[2] When the government instituted in 1870 a thorough inquisition, under the Duke of Devonshire, into the facilities for teaching science in England, Lockyer was appointed its secretary. The eight reports of the Devonshire Commission underlined the advances made by German and French scientific institutions, and the last actually suggested that a special ministry 'dealing with science and education as a public service' should be established.[3]

Roscoe brought over Carl Schorlemmer to Manchester to organise the first department of organic chemistry in the country. Roscoe's arts colleague A. W. Ward, who had spent his boyhood and adolescence in Germany, set the same research tradition in the humanities. The Manchester tradition was to predominate in the second half of the nineteenth century as the civic universities took shape.[4]

Manchester set the pattern for science departments in the new university colleges. It trained Sydney Young (1857–1937), who worked at University College, Bristol, from 1882 on hydrocarbons from petroleum; Arthur Smithells (1860–1939), who worked at Leeds from 1883 on improving coal gas, and the German-born Arthur Schuster (1851–1934), who went on to work under Weber at Göttingen, von Helmholtz at Berlin and at the Cavendish Laboratory at Cambridge. Schuster, returning to Manchester as Professor of Applied Mathematics and later Physics, was the first to show that cathode rays are gaseous ions accelerated in the strong field near the cathode.

A proposal, made in 1868, that the Cambridge colleges should contribute to the establishment of a laboratory (costing £5,000) and a temporary professorship of experimental physics met with strong opposition. 'A Prussian is a Prussian,' said Dr Phelps, the Master of Sidney Sussex, 'and an Englishman an Englishman, and God forbid it should be otherwise.' The scheme looked like foundering until the Duke of Devonshire, as Chancellor, offered to provide £6,300 if the University would maintain the teaching staff. As chairman of the Royal Commission on Scientific Instruction his offer carried weight and so the laboratory received the name of his illustrious forbear—the eighteenth-century chemist, Henry Cavendish.

The Cavendish Laboratory grew slowly: and not for 20 years did the research workers number 25. 'I have no place to erect my chair,' wrote J. Clerk Maxwell, the first professor, 'but move about like the cuckoo, depositing my notions in the Chemical Lecture Room in the First Term, in the Botanical in Lent and in the Comparative Anatomy in Easter.'[1] These 'notions' were delivered to a very small audience. Clerk Maxwell busied himself designing equipment from ideas picked up in William Thomson's laboratory at Glasgow and Clifton's at Oxford. The rest of his time he spent in editing the works of the great eighteenth-century scientist whose name the laboratory bore. Rayleigh, on succeeding to the chair in 1879, had to inaugurate an apparatus fund. He also secured the appointment of two able demonstrators, R. T. Glazebrook and W. N. Shaw, to take charge of the teaching. With increasing staff he redetermined electrical standards; his values were adopted by an international conference in 1893. By then Rayleigh had resigned his chair for one at the Royal Institution and J. J. Thomson had succeeded him in 1884. Under Thomson the Cavendish Laboratory became a nursery of physicists, concentrating on the conductivity of electricity through gases. Each step was stimulated by German detections, notably by Hertz's discovery of electromagnetic waves. Colloquia were instituted. The laboratory was enlarged. German practice was followed when in 1895 Cambridge allowed graduates of other universities to register as advanced students. There had recently been established a system of science scholarships supervised by the Commissioners of the 1851 Exhibition and from 1896 to 1921 no less than 60 of 103 such physics scholars came to the Cavendish. In addition a large number of workers came from the U.S.A., Germany, France, Russia and Poland. One of these 1851 Exhibitioners, Rutherford, was to succeed Thomson in 1919.

The Cavendish reinforced the enthusiasm for research in the new University Colleges, too. Four of their early principals were physicists: R. T. Glazebrook of the University College, Liverpool, Oliver Lodge of Birmingham, Hicks of Sheffield and E. H. Griffiths of Cardiff. In these new colleges the German-inspired chemists were as active as ever. At Leeds Dugald Clerk was directed by T. E. Thorpe (a pupil of Bunsen) to study the fractionation of petroleum oils and become a pioneer of the two-stroke engine, while Archibald Barr, another laboratory builder, was to make a name as a builder of range-finders.

Non-scientists like A. W. Ward of Manchester and Mark Pattison, Rector of Lincoln College, Oxford, caught the German fever. Pattison saw that 'There remains but one possible pattern on which a University, as an establishment for science, can be constructed, and that is the graduate Professoriate. This is sometimes called the German type. Education among us,' he lamented in his *Suggestions on Academical Organisation* (1868), 'has sunk into a trade, and, like trading sophists, we have not cared to keep on hand a larger stock than we could dispose of in the season.' Pattison took the chair on 16 November 1872 at a meeting of a short-lived association for the organisation of academical study which wished to establish research as a national object.[1] The same refrain was taken up by England's most distinguished inspector of schools, a poet and a professor of poetry at Oxford. 'It is in science that we most need to borrow from the German universities.

The French university has no liberty, and the English universities have no science; the German universities have both.'[1]

German superiority in matters of general educational practice had long impressed A. J. Mundella, whose business representative in Chemnitz, H. M. Felkin, made the first English translation of Herbart, the German educationist who was to exercise such an influence over training college techniques.[2] In 1882, during his Vice-Presidency of the Council, Mundella was responsible for the appointment of a Royal Commission to examine the nature of technical education offered abroad, and to compare it with what was offered in England. The great ironmaster Bernhard Samuelson was appointed as Chairman. To assist him, Professor Henry Roscoe examined the research work of foreign universities, and its bearing on industry; Philip Magnus visited and reported on the foreign schools; Swire Smith, a Keighley woollen manufacturer, reported on foreign methods of manufacture and the conditions under which they were conducted; and four other commissioners had special briefs.

After travelling both to Europe and America, the commissioners issued their final report in 1884. The kernel of their findings was that 'the best preparation for technical study is a good modern secondary school . . . unfortunately our middle classes are at a great disadvantage compared with those of the Continent for want of a sufficient number of such schools'. The commissioners 'looked to some public measure to supply this the greatest defect of our educational system'. That measure might have been taken had not the gigantic red herring of Ireland been drawn across the path the following year.

The Commission raised the pregnant issue of decentralisation. They stressed the desirability of empowering 'important local bodies like the proposed County Boards and municipal corporations to originate and support secondary and technical schools in conformity with the public opinion for the time being of their constituents'. Here was to be the embryo of a new system.[3]

IX

COLLECTIVISM AND THE
COUNTY COUNCILS

1889–1911

I

Moulders of responsible opinion were beginning to feel the imperative necessity of what became known as collectivism in education. Matthew Arnold (who died in 1888), had consistently pointed to the necessity of public secondary schools as 'the first practicable of those great democratic reforms to which we must, I believe, one day come'. To his long sustained and now silent voice, was added another—that of T. H. Green, who at Oxford helped to breed a new race of guardians: civil servants, recruited by competitive examination from the public schools, who had learned from him that the essence of human life lay in the deep, deliberate pursuit of an ideal of its own betterment. This will, for Green, was the real basis of the state,[1] which could enable citizens to make 'the most and best of themselves' by affording regular labour and educational facilities.

External circumstances reinforced their case. A Royal Commission appointed in 1886 by a short-lived Conservative administration to examine the causes of the depression in trade admitted that American and German industrial techniques were surpassing those of Britain. The year of jubilee prompted Huxley to warn readers of *The Times* on 21 March 1887:

We are entering, indeed we have already entered, upon the most serious struggle for existence to which this country was ever committed. The latter years of the century promise to see us in an industrial war of far more serious import than the military wars of its opening years.

Since he envisaged this industrial war being waged against America and Germany, he urged that victory should be 'organised'.

Huxley's metaphor of an industrial army fired the imagination of some forty M.P.s who met in the Society of Arts (home of earlier efforts to promote industrial education), together with delegates from school boards, trade unions, chambers of commerce and other interested parties to form a society to awaken public opinion. Huxley himself came, together with A. J. Mundella, Sir Bernhard Samuelson and Tyndall.

The government acted, and in 1887 introduced a Bill allowing local authorities to decide whether they would have technical education or not. But so many amendments were tacked on to this Bill that it was dropped within two months. It was at this point that the society became the National Association for the Promotion of Technical Education, with Sir Henry Roscoe, the famous chemist, and Arthur Acland as co-secretaries. Both introduced Bills to keep the question before Parliament. Both failed for lack of a suitable authority to which such a function could be entrusted.

That authority was now increasingly agreed to be the county. All sides saw this. Liberal-Unionist members of the Conservative administration like Goschen and Chamberlain were anxious to reform local government: Goschen having condemned the sprawling *ad hoc* authorities in the seventies, and Chamberlain having put elected county councils on his 'unauthorised programme' in the eighties. Then again, the extension of the franchise to $1\frac{3}{4}$ million country voters in 1884 implied that at some time or other they would be able to elect their own councils as well as their own parliament.

The National Association for the Promotion of Technical Education supported the idea of county councils' undertaking educational work, and publicised the Samuelson Commission's report to that effect. Administrators openly acknowledged the administrative convenience of the county, whereby the devolution of returns, the introduction of block grants and the provision of rate aid both to voluntary and to board schools would be greatly facilitated. Indeed, the secretary of the Education Department, Patric Cumin, said so before the Cross Commission of 1886–8.

A. H. D. Acland argued that county boards would have yet another function—they would bridge the gap between the elementary school and the university, a gap unknown in Prussia or Scotland.

And so, by the Local Government Act of 1888, 62 county councils were created, and county boroughs were set up in towns of more than 50,000 population. To them was transferred the old business of the quarter sessions. But as Gladstone observed, the Act was an outline map, the details of which had yet to be filled in.

II

By exploiting powers given them by three apparently unimportant Acts of parliament passed in successive years, the county councils filled in the map. In 1889 they were empowered to levy a penny rate for technical education. Twenty-one M.P.s saw that this foreshadowed the end of the school boards, and, in a hot August afternoon, fought the measure. It was left for an Irish M.P. to comment:

when we consider the character of the poverty in this country, which is different from the poverty of other countries in its aimlessness and helplessness through want of technical education, I marvel that any Englishman should throw any difficulty or obstacle in the way of such instruction.

In the following session (1890) they acquired 'whisky money,' almost by accident. A proposal that a tax on spirits (to conciliate the temperance interest) should be credited to the newly formed county and county borough councils, partly for police superannuation, partly for the purchase of publicans' licences in order to get rid of redundant public houses, was fought by Sir William Mather, the great Manchester electrical engineer and A. H. D. Acland. They argued that the proceeds of the tax should be allocated to technical education in England and Wales. After three days the government agreed to their proposals and handed the money to the county councils to expend as they thought necessary. Mather's part in this victory illustrates the impact which electrical engineering was having in education and politics by the last decade of the nineteenth century. *The Times* was disgusted at the government's surrender, and commented, 'it seems as if ministers are following the line of least resistance.' Whisky money was a real stimulant to the new authorities, enabling counties to build laboratories and qualify for South Kensington grants. Within five years, 93 out of the 129 borough councils were spending the whole of their whisky money on technical education, although only in thirteen cases was a rate levied.

A third measure was an enabling Act allowing the county councils to provide scholarships. To administer all these functions the county councils set up technical education committees, and by October 1891 an association of organising secretaries for technical and secondary education was established, which agreed that the moneys they administered should be equally divided between technical and secondary education. One of Acland's friends, the organising secretary to the county council of Surrey, argued that if his council were to be given a free hand over the endowed schools, 'we might deal with secondary education in a much more comprehensive manner than we do at present'.

Here Wales afforded a fruitful example. In 1889 the Welsh Intermediate Education Act transferred to education committees (the majority of whose members were elected by the county councils), the control over secondary education hitherto vested in the Charity Commission. With the 'Celtic Fringe' already adorning so many departments of national life, it is not surprising that they led in the sphere of education also. But the focus of events centred on London, where in the last decade of the century the struggle of board versus voluntary schools was to be resolved by creation of a fresh authority and a new pattern for state education as a whole.

III

But, argued a contributor to *Fabian Essays in Socialism* (1889),[1] county councils would not be of much use unless enough public-spirited councillors could be persuaded to serve on them. This contributor was Sidney Webb, who also wrote *Facts for Londoners* (1889) as propaganda for the Progressive Party in the elections for the London County Council. He was also elected as representative for Deptford.

Webb's contribution to *Fabian Essays* was singled out by one of Charles Booth's assistants, Beatrice Potter, as 'by far the most significant and interesting essay'. The eighth of nine daughters of a wealthy Lancashire business man, her passionate interest in the co-operative movement led her to approach Sidney Webb for material on the condition of the working class in the eighteenth century. She was impressed by his polymath factual knowledge and touched by his belief that 'collective administration and collective control' would 'diminish if not abolish poverty', They became engaged and in 1892 were married.

Beatrice's private income and Sidney's industry produced a unique social intelligence service. In a series of volumes as authoritative and influential as Blue books, they incised the outlines of the collective administration through which poverty would be eliminated. Their scheme for an educationally sifted meritocracy was itself an impetus to collectivism. Beatrice Webb formulated the creed as 'essentially collective ownership wherever practicable; collective regulation everywhere else; collective provision according to need for all the impotent and sufferers; and collective taxation in proportion to wealth, especially surplus wealth.'[2] Above all, as Fabians, they believed in 'the inevitability of gradualness'.

All was now ready to Sidney Webb's hand in London. In 1892 he became chairman of the L.C.C.'s Technical Education Board of 35 members, and during his eight years in office he made it the most important committee of the London County Council. From its first meeting, thanks to his energy and industry, the fifteen co-opted professional teachers and the twenty London County Councillors had a development plan, and were not deflected from it. Sidney Webb habitually wrote out the exact words of resolutions to be passed at each meeting, and personally signed every cheque to make sure that there was no danger of a surcharge. With this minute industry went real largeness of vision. He set H. Llewellyn Smith (who had assisted Charles Booth and A. H. D. Acland), to survey the field of effort, and his report, submitted in January 1893, adumbrated policy. An elaborate scholarship system was constructed, large in extent, elaborate in organisation and diversified in its ramifications, taking pupils from the lowest elementary school to the most distinguished institutions of university standing. The basis was the county scholarships system which articulated elementary, higher grade and endowed schools and, from them, fed the higher institutions. Through this the Technical Education Board was brought into contact with all the schools in London, whereas the London School Board only controlled elementary and higher grade schools, with an occasional pupil-teacher centre. From Webb's board the languishing endowed schools received some much-needed help. Polytechnics rose from 8 to 26. Technologically and pedagogically London once more began to set the pace with a Central School of Arts and Crafts and the London Day Training College. All this was done in eight years. As he said,

We have endeavoured to build up here the greatest capacity-catching machine that the world has ever seen. Time has yet to show to what extent we shall be successful in discovering hidden treasures of genius and ability and practical wisdom which, as we believe, exist in almost as large a proportion among the children of the poorer sections of the community, as among those more favoured in pecuniary fortune.[1]

IV

In all this Webb was helped by the tapper of whisky money, A. H. D. Acland, who became in 1892 the Vice-President of the Committee of Council. Acland enjoyed great independence in this office, for unlike his predecessors, he was not fettered by the Prime Minister. 'Each man manages his own department,' he wrote. 'We have not had a cabinet for weeks. I do not think we have had more than three for the last three months of the Parliamentary session.'[1] He advised Sidney Webb to appoint a highly paid expert physicist, the 42-year-old Dr William Garnett, a product of the Cavendish Laboratory and a former professor at the civic university colleges of Nottingham and Newcastle, as secretary and adviser. Dr Kimmins became chief inspector.

South Kensington aid was forthcoming for a special list of subjects to be taught in London schools. Thus modern history, economics, geography and commercial education were added to those already subsidised by the Science and Art Department, and Sidney Webb could say with some satisfaction, 'we can now lawfully teach anything under the sun except ancient Greek and theology.'

Acland established an Office of Special Inquiries and Reports under Michael Sadler, who had succeeded him as secretary to the Oxford University Extension Delegacy. Sadler chose as his assistant Robert Morant, who had been an educational adviser in Siam, and had recently been working at Toynbee Hall in the East End.

To encourage further education in the evening schools, Acland personally drafted the syllabus on the life and duties of a citizen. Well he might, for he had written a history of England which was proving a best-seller. He wrote in his diary with some pardonable satisfaction, 'I have really made it [the syllabus] an intelligible document, with memorandum, contents etc. One must compare the evening code of 1892 which did not become law to understand the difference.' From now on, every person who attended an evening school was eligible for a grant. Elementary subjects were no longer compulsory. Grants were assessed not on the mechanical principle of attainment, but on the aggregate number of hours of instruction which were given. As Acland confessed, 'at South Kensington I have had to fight Donnelly a good deal'. The clash of the young radical reformer and the old soldier who believed in his own system of payment by results ended, as it should, in Acland's victory.

Payment by results was abolished in other branches of South Kensington's work: grants became available for practical work, and the variable element in the main grant now depended on the inspectors' report in which the literary as well as the scientific element in the curriculum would be considered. Most remarkable was the introduction of compulsory literary subjects into all organised science day schools and the reduction of the minimum of scientific instruction from fifteen to thirteen hours a week. (These organised science schools had grown rapidly in the past ten years from 3 to 125.) To supervise the new dispensation Acland wrote: 'I have selected what I hope will be a really good set of men as *permanent inspectors*.' These, he hoped, would settle in the provinces and become the nucleus of a permanent staff.

In other ways, Acland pursued a policy of 'collectivism'. He extended the period of compulsory education for blind and deaf children to sixteen years. For normal children at elementary schools, he raised the age to twelve—and thus redeemed a pledge made two years previously at a conference in Berlin by Sir John Gorst.

The most controversial of Acland's operations was his famous Circular 321. This laid down certain sanitary and building conditions to which grant-earning schools had to conform. On its appearance, *The Times* wrote: 'the blow which has been long suspended has at length fallen . . . it marks a new departure in the action of the Education Department . . . the friends of the voluntary schools must rally round these institutions, and by prompt and large sacrifices secure them against every attack on their position.' The two Archbishops set up a committee to examine the position, consisting mainly of those who had made their opinions heard on the Cross Commission eight years before. Cross was on this committee too, together with such firm friends as Lords Cranbrook and Cranbourne, the Bishop of London, and the vehement Canon Gregory. After circularising the voluntary schools, they reported that the worst pressure existed in the urban districts, Lancashire, Yorkshire and South Wales, all places where fees were already too high yet rates were heavy. Their melancholy conclusion was that the Church schools would not be able to hold their ground in any national system, 'unless churchmen bear the burden of contributing largely to their support'. The only alternative was rate aid.

Though compared to Julian the Apostate and to a Bengal Tiger menacing the Christians (references to his one-time position as a curate in Northumberland), and criticised by Sandford, ex-secretary of the Education Department, now in the Lords, Acland pursued his collectivist way. A conference on secondary education was held at Oxford in 1893, at which for the first time all institutions affording secondary education were represented. Though Acland was not able to attend, he was aware of the opinions expressed and noted in his diary: 'I think I shall appoint a Royal Commission.' This was perhaps the best thing he ever did. It sat under the chairmanship of James Bryce, a man of the most varied educational experience and achievement. He had been an assistant commissioner for the Taunton Commission nearly 30 years before, and had published the authoritative interpretation of the American Commonwealth for his generation. Among the sixteen commissioners who sat with Bryce were, for the first time, three women. The scope of the commission was nothing less than:

to consider what are the best methods of establishing a well-organised system of secondary education in England, taking into account existing deficiencies, and having regard to such local sources of revenue from endowments and otherwise as are available or may be made available for this purpose and to make recommendations accordingly.

The Bryce Commission endorsed the growing collectivist trend of the times. Secondary education as they defined it was:

a process of intellectual training and personal discipline conducted with special regard to the profession or trade to be followed . . . . All secondary schools, then, partake more or less in the character of institutes that educate craftsmen.

Culture itself had no intrinsic end save that of making 'the private person of more value to society and the state'.

The recommendations of the Bryce Commission envisaged yet more collectivism. A central authority, under a responsible minister, was to replace the three hitherto independent authorities; the Education Department, the Science Department (at South Kensington) and the Charity Commission (at Gwydyr House, Whitehall). It was to be advised by an educational council of twelve (with powers of co-option). Local authorities, in the shape of county and county borough councils, were to recognise secondary schools for grants under certain sanitary and educational conditions to be confirmed by inspection. A register of teachers, based upon their degrees or certificates of competence was to be kept.

v

Before these recommendations were published, the Liberals went out of office in 1895, deserted by the Irish Catholics, who thought more of their schools than they did of Home Rule for Ireland. The Catholics and the Church of England joined to put a Conservative government in power in 1895. Even the Fabians had thought that 'With the exception of Acland, none of the Liberals are doing any work,' and they sat by at the elections with their hands in their laps, wishing for the Liberals to be beaten. 'Our only hope,' wrote Beatrice Webb at the time, 'is in permeating the young middle class man—catching them for collectivism before they have enlisted on the other side.' In this the Fabians were to be singularly successful.

'The question of further aid to denominational schools is now the one which seems likely to be raised first of all in the new Parliament,' wrote Lyulph Stanley. For, he argued, the clergy 'write, speak and preach as if School Boards and Board Schools were places organised for the purpose of uprooting Christianity'. He went so far as to prophesy a virtual re-establishment of the Test Act, not by law but by 'abuse of patronage'.[1] For the Archbishop of Canterbury was really in action against the school boards, publishing a statement on 15 January 1895 that in 316 board areas no religious instruction whatsoever was given whilst in 50 districts no religious observances were taking place. Voluntaryists, continued the Archbishop, had so far spent 73 million pounds in helping to provide the instruction which the boards were jettisoning.

In November 1895, less than four months after the Conservatives came to power, the Primate personally led a deputation to the Premier asking for relief, and in March 1896 Sir John Gorst, the new Vice-President, tried to give it in a Bill which proposed that the new county authorities should make additional grants to voluntary schools (the 17s. 6d. limit was abolished); that educational institutions should be exempted from the rates; and that religious instruction should be determined by the majority, with the option that any parent could withdraw his child for special instruction into another part of the school building. Confusion could not have been worse confounded. The overlap which the Bryce Commission had just condemned was to be itself overlaid by another: for the school boards were to be retained as a sop to the virtual co-premier, Joseph Chamberlain. It was little wonder, therefore, that 1,238 amendments to the Bill were tabled and that the Duke of Devonshire could complacently and succinctly inform his Vice-President, 'Gorst, your damned Bill's dead!'

> Here lies consigned whether via Styx
> The Education Bill of ninety-six
> And, done to death by over-vivisection
> Sleeps without faintest hope of resurrection.[2]

From this 'discreditable failure', Beatrice Webb drew a moral:

It is only another instance of how impossible it is nowadays to succeed in politics without technical knowledge of the great democratic machine . . . . Who could trust the building of a bridge to a man who started with such infinitesimal knowledge of engineering as Balfour or Gorst have, of national education and its machinery?[1]

Its failure did not help the voluntary schools. To help them, another Bill was drafted which passed in the following session. This gave them an additional capitation grant of 5s. (a shilling more than the proposed rise of a year before). But the question as to which authority should distribute this grant was again burked. The Bill recognised yet another body—this time 'associations of voluntary schools'. So this fearful reaction into the arms of the voluntaryists was eagerly seized upon by the Liberal opposition, who were bought off by a similar grant to poor board schools. In the end, this 1897 Act merely afforded a free gift of £615,000 to the voluntary schools and £514,000 to the board schools. The overlap and waste of effort in secondary education still remained.

VI

Gorst began to consult Sidney Webb in 1896, and so did the Department of Special Inquiries and Reports. Every day, as Beatrice records in her diary, they 'were becoming more connected with the superior rank of civil servants', among whom she lists Sir George Kekewich, the successor of Patric Cumin at the Education Department. Gorst invited the Webbs to dinner at the House of Commons and confided to them his dislike of Balfour. For Gorst had himself, fifteen years before, been a member of the famous Fourth Party, a 'ginger' group of Conservatives. So it was in character when he kicked over the party traces and made a speech on 17 June 1898 which caused surprise among Conservatives. For he actually attacked the prevailing standards, exposing the low age-limits for school attendance, the pupil-teacher system, the irregular attendance, the injustice of the half-time system. He quoted from a report, with great gusto, the reason why a child of over 12 was rarely found in a country school:

the farmer and the squire are no friends to elementary education. They associate agricultural depression and high rents with compulsory education, and they grudge to pay for that teaching which deprives them of servants and furnishes their labourers with wings to fly from the parish. On the other hand, the labourer has not learned the value of education. The earnings of his children are important to him and the present shilling obscures the future pound.

When a private member introduced a Bill to raise the compulsory school-leaving age to 12, Gorst gave it hearty support.

Another government consultant at this time was R. B. Haldane, a Liberal by inclination, whose advice was often sought on non-party questions. Haldane had the advantage of a German as well as a Scottish education, and believed in learning and research for its own sake. He and Sidney Webb took charge of a Bill to establish a teaching University of London. After they had besieged a great number of people, they succeeded. Balfour agreed to allow Gorst to sponsor the Bill, which was carried in the face of fierce attacks. In this new university, an important part was played by one of the Webbs' own creations—the London School of Economics.

In 1899 the first instalment of the Bryce recommendations was made law when the Board of Education was established by Act of Parliament, merging the old Education Department and the Science and Art Department under a responsible President who received a salary of £2,000 a year. Provision was also made for the gradual merger of the functions of the Charity Commission (which controlled the Endowed Schools), with the new Board. A consultative council was also set up, and the register of teachers commenced.

As an adjutant in piloting this Act through the House of Commons, Gorst chose on 3 July 1899 Robert Morant of the Department of Special Inquiries and Reports. Morant had recently written a report on Swiss education in which he had obliquely dealt a blow to the boards. Morant was even more meritocratically minded than the Webbs, and advocated, in a paper read to a civil service club, that each nation should have 'directive brain centres', constantly watching developments and planning changes. He asked:

is not the only hope for the continued existence of a democratic state to be found in an increasing recognition, *by* the democracy, of the increasing need of voluntarily submitting the impulses of the many ignorant to the guidance and control of the few wise, and thus to the willing establishment and maintenance, *by* the democracy, of special expert governors or guides or leaders, deliberately appointed by itself for the purpose, and to the subordination of the individual (and therefore limited) notions to the wider and deeper knowledge of specialised experts in the science of national life and growth, having their outlook over the whole field of national growth?[1]

VII

An 'expert governor' was certainly needed to mitigate the passionate quarrel now raging between the London School Board and the Technical Education Board of the L.C.C. The school boards, claimed Lyulph Stanley in a letter to *The Times* in 1898, had not only 'statutory authority to give instruction in evening schools without limit to cost, range of subjects and age of scholars', but they were 'the only bodies with full statutory powers to do this'. Morant, on the other hand, had said in his report on Swiss education that though the English school boards extended the scope of elementary education by providing day schools of a higher grade, 'they have frequently been told by the Central Authority that they cannot take any such steps . . . in as much as they were only empowered by the Act of 1870 to use the rates to provide Elementary Education'. Gorst held that it 'was little use lamenting that there should be two because neither one nor the other can by any possibility be got rid of'.

On Sidney Webb's retirement from the chairmanship of the Technical Education Board, Dr Garnett, its secretary, became its prime mover. Garnett now suggested to the London Technical Education Board that they should apply for grants under an administrative minute issued by the Science and Art Department in 1898. But the representatives from the London School Board (who, it will be remembered, were members of the technical education board by co-option), showed ,such determined opposition that the debate had to be postponed. The school board wrote a letter to the London County Council asking for a discussion with London County Council representatives of both the bodies (school board and technical education board) over the question. This discussion was duly held by the London County Council, but it only resulted in their endorsement of their own technical education board's application to the Science and Art Department for grants under the new minute.

Again the school boards appealed. Sir John Donnelly decided to hear both sides of the question and representatives of the school board and the technical education board went before him. For the school board, Lyulph Stanley opposed the London County Council's application on the ground that it would virtually stop their operations. He was supported by Dr Macnamara (also on the school board), who threatened that if the London County Council's application were granted, the school board would deliberately open new classes and schools to compete with them. Once more the case went against the school board.

To obtain a ruling on the legality of the school board's expenditure on higher education, Dr Garnett arranged with the headmaster of the Camden School of Art to query such expenditure with the auditor, T. B. Cockerton. On 26 July 1899, Cockerton charged the members of the school board for certain moneys expended by them in the teaching of science and art. Naturally, the school board took the matter to the High Court, and enlisted H. H. Asquith to appear for them. Lord Robert Cecil represented the auditor. After a year, judgement was given. On 20 December 1900 the wings of the school boards were very severely clipped by the judgement of Mr Justice Wills. He opined that the idea that school boards were

free to teach at the expense of the ratepayers to adults and children indiscriminately the higher mathematics, advanced chemistry both theoretical and practical, political economy, art of a kind wholly beyond anything that can be taught to children, French, German, History and I know not what, appears to me to be the *ne plus ultra* of extravagance.[1]

From this judgement the school boards appealed in vain. Their essays in secondary education were now illegal, and 150,000 children were concerned.

VIII

Into the area of secondary education which the school boards would have to vacate, the government were fearful to tread. But they were urged on, both by the voluntaryists and the Fabians. Bishop Talbot, of Rochester, personally appealed to Lord Salisbury on 4 December 1901: 'This is not a case of "Wolf!" The cry has no doubt been heard before: but it has been louder each time: in 1896–7 it expressed what was already, as Balfour owned, intolerable: the palliative of 1897 is exhausted (in many places), and the strain is now at *breaking point*.' The Bishop was not exaggerating. Many of the voluntary schools, he confessed, only held out in the hope that 'this government would give relief'.

The Fabians were enthusiastic that the government should pass a comprehensive measure, and 50 copies of Sidney Webb's pamphlet *The Education Muddle and the Way Out* (1901) were ordered by Sir John Gorst for distribution to his permanent officials. In it Sidney Webb advocated a state secondary school system; public elementary education removed from the school boards and put under the local authorities; and the strengthening of the dual system by allowing grants to Church of England schools. The latter would preserve variety in the schools. Supporting Sidney Webb was Haldane, who broke from his Liberal political friends to support a government Bill drafted along these lines.

The 1902 Education Act embodied both the Fabian and clerical views.[1] The Fabian element was administrative efficiency: 2,568 school boards were supplanted by 328 local education authorities. County councils or county boroughs now dealt with education as they dealt with other public services, aiding voluntary schools from the rates, as well as the former board schools. Balfour, who piloted the 1902 Education Act through the Commons, afterwards confessed: 'I did not realise that the act would mean more expense and more bureaucracy.'

The clerical element—whereby voluntary schools received rate aid—outraged the Nonconformists. David Lloyd George won himself a public reputation by his slogan that 'Rome had been put on the rates'. Some 70,000 Nonconformists were subsequently prosecuted for refusal to pay the rates after the Act had been passed. The teachers' organisations plumped for the Bill, and Joseph Chamberlain, the voice of Nonconformity within the Cabinet, was prostrated by a cab accident. During the stormy passage of the Bill Lord Londonderry became the first President of the Board of Education. Morant, its real author, who had coached Balfour in his parliamentary part, was made Permanent Secretary of the Board of Education from 1 November 1902. Balfour himself became Prime Minister.

The 1902 Act was a tardy statutory attempt to cope with an increasing flood of children who, though the school-leaving age was not raised to 11 until 1893 or to 12 until 1899, had been 'staying on' at the elementary school, going on either to 'higher grade' schools or 'higher tops'. In 1895 no less than 470,876 children in the elementary schools were above the age of 12 and 252,026 were above the age of 13. At the same time only four or five in a thousand of the pupils registered in elementary schools at this time had any hope of passing to a grammar school.[2]

This is the real reason why 'grammar-type' municipal

secondary schools grew after 1902, when the L.E.A.s were empowered to establish such schools, helped by grant and by a direct capitation grant by the board. When the Liberal government ruled in 1907, for political reasons, that any secondary school accepting a capitation had to reserve at least 25% of its intake for non-paying pupils from elementary schools, the older grammar schools were also opened to pupils of ability. And when 'pupil teachers' were allowed to stay at a secondary school for an additional year as 'bursars' the numbers of elementary school pupils in grammar schools was increased still further, and a body of direct-entry recruits for the training colleges thereby built up.

The short-comings of the old higher grade schools, with their excessive emphasis on scientific studies, was condemned by H.M.I.s and professional associations of teachers as one-sided, and detrimental to more humanistic and literary studies. Moreover, there was a growing demand for clerks, pupil-teachers and commercial recruits. So, after a Commons debate in July 1903, new regulations were issued to ensure that such an imbalance should not recur.[1]

This trend was strengthened by the local efforts of Michael Sadler, whose unfortunate departure from the Office of Special Inquiries and Reports for a specially created chair of the History and Administration of Education at Manchester University enabled him to serve as a 'consultant' to many northern local authorities.[2] 'Premature specialisation,' he argued, 'is dangerous' and his views won support from many directors of education. In this, as in perhaps nothing else, he and Morant had a sentiment in common. For Morant undertook the dismantling of the old unimaginative subject-code of the Science and Art Department because it did not assess school work as a whole but subject by subject.

The formation of a federal council in 1906 by the professional associations concerned with secondary education continued the diffusion, throughout the country, of academic standards. The leading members of the Federal Council were the Association of Headmistresses (founded by Miss Beale and Miss Buss in 1874), the Association of Headmasters (1890), the Association of Assistant

Mistresses (1884) and the Association of Assistant Masters (1891) and the College of Preceptors (1848). They stayed together, speaking for secondary education until 1917, when a joint committee of the first four was formed, now popularly known as the Joint Four, still (1963) the active champion of the 'grammar school' tradition.

The competence that comes from specialist teaching was also fostered by the newly formed associations like the Modern Languages Association (1892), the Geographical Association (1893), the Mathematical Association (1897, from the Association for the Improvement of Geometrical Drawing, founded in 1871), the Association of Public School Science Masters (later the Science Masters' Association (1900)), the Art Teachers' Guild (1900), the Classical Association (1903), the Historical Association (1906) and the English Association (1907). These groups were professional versions of the old learned societies. Each fed its particular nutrient into the educational garden.[1]

The growing autonomy of the teacher under the new dispensation can be seen in the elementary schools also. It is perhaps best illustrated by the meaningful title of a publication issued by the Board in 1905: *Suggestions for the Use of Teachers and others concerned in the work of Elementary Schools*. This stressed that:

each teacher shall think for himself and work out for himself such methods of teaching as may use his powers to the best advantage and be best suited to the particular needs and conditions of the school.

The cumulative result of all this was that grammar schools trebled in number, from 491 (in 1904) to 1,616 (in 1925), while the pupils attending them nearly quadrupled from 85,358 (in 1904) to 334,194 (in 1925). By 1925, as we shall see in the next chapter, other circumstances necessitated a closer look at secondary education.

IX

All this had implications for the 'civic' universities (as Haldane was to call them), which, thanks to the pertinacity of the Principals of Sheffield and Bristol, received their first grant—£15,000 —from the government in 1889. A small committee was appointed to advise on its distribution:[1] this was the embryo of the modern University Grants Committee. In the same year the Board of Agriculture was established with, amongst other duties, the obligation of inspecting and aiding any higher schools which fostered expenditure in this field. Agricultural departments grew up at Leeds (1890), Newcastle (1892), Nottingham (1894), Reading (1894) and London (Wye College, 1896), each with a grant of £800 a year. Two further accretions, one to their exiguous funds and the other to their student body, in the form of 'whisky money' and day training colleges were forthcoming in 1890. The latter virtually saved their faculties of arts and science from extinction.

The cultivation of science was especially the concern of the British Association, which at the turn of the century became a sounding board for men like Oliver Lodge, who warned the annual meeting in Cardiff in 1891 that 'the further progress of physical science in the somewhat haphazard and amateur fashion in which it has hitherto been pursued in this country is becoming increasingly difficult.' He continued, 'the quantitative portion especially should be undertaken in a permanent and publicly supported physical laboratory on a large scale'.[2]

Lodge wished to strengthen existing private laboratories by establishing an English counterpart to the German Physikalische Technische Reichsanstalt. But not until ten years later was the National Physical Laboratory established in London 'to bring scientific knowledge to bear practically upon our everyday industrial and commercial life, to break down the barrier between theory and practice, to effect a union between Science and Commerce'. Its first director, R. T. Glazebrook was a 'Cavendish man'. Experiments on aviation, helped by government support, made possible the superiority of British aircraft in the 1914–18 war. The director of its Chemical Research Laboratory was a 'Finsbury man', G. T. Morgan (1872–1942) who condensed phenol with formaldehyde leaving it to Baekeland in America to exploit this and make plastics. With £13,000 for buildings and equipment and a five-year subvention from the government of £4,000 a year under the beneficent control of the Royal Society, the National Physical Laboratory was an apt institution to found in the twentieth century.

A continuous descant on German and American superiority in the provision of universities was sustained. In a characteristically eloquent presidential address to the British Association at Southport in 1903 on the Influence of Brain Power on History, Sir Norman Lockyer contrasted the 22 state-subsidised universities in Germany and 134 state and private universities in America with the thirteen in Great Britain. He urged that Britain should organise its scientific effort as the Germans organised their navy, found eight new universities and establish a scientific national council.[1] He asked the British Association to serve as a pressure group for science. Since it was unwilling, he founded the British Science Guild. At its inaugural meeting in 1905, R. B. Haldane called for a permanent commission to advise the government on the development and application of scientific knowledge.

Haldane was greatly impressed by the industrial progress of Germany which he attributed to the partnership between the universities and industry. His favourite example of this partnership was Charlottenburg. He joined forces with Sidney Webb to work for a similar institution in England. Two South African millionaires, Sir Julius Wernher and Sir Ernest Cassell, together with Rothschild, helped to raise an endowment of £500,000. The 1851 Commission was persuaded to give a four-acre site at South Kensington and Webb bent his manifold energies to persuading the London County Council to give an annual grant. In face of the opposition of Ramsay MacDonald and John Burns this was secured. Sir Francis Mowatt, head of the Treasury, was prepared to transfer control of the Royal College of Science and the Royal School of Mines to the British Charlottenburg. So it received its charter in 1907 as the Imperial College of Science and Technology.

Haldane devoted more time and energy to the promotion of the welfare and status of universities than any other politician of his day. As J. F. Lockwood observed:

In what he knew to be the urgent national interest, from 1889 onwards he put his shoulder to a great wheel, which turned in time so well that, if we look now at the Universities of Bristol, Liverpool, London, Wales, Belfast and the National University of Ireland (not to mention several others which might be regarded as his posthumous offspring), we can see the marks of his handwork.[1]

To this end, he had worked to secure the University of London Act in 1898, and his speech in the House of Commons undoubtedly secured its passage. With Webb, he was also one of the founders of the London School of Economics and later presided over Birkbeck College. It was he who in 1904 presided over a small committee which recommended the establishment of the University Grants Committee. It was this committee which was to exercise the decisive influence over the development of universities in the twentieth century.

The status of the universities was vastly improved. Birmingham received its charter in 1900, followed by Liverpool (1903), Leeds (1904), Sheffield (1905) and Bristol (1909). Birmingham, which had already created a university with much help from the American steel millionaire Carnegie, also imported from Harvard Professor W. J. Ashley to organise its faculty of commerce, some say to enable the manufacturers there to be schooled in the operation of American tariff laws.

Sidney Webb was retained by Liverpool as its counsel when it applied for a university charter in 1903. He wrote in the *Cornhill* in April of that year:

it is exactly true, however much the term may be disliked, that the new universities will, apart from their higher purpose of being centres of scientific investigation and research, inevitably take on the character of technical schools for all the brain-working professors of the time.

By establishing examining boards, the University of London in 1902, and the Northern Universities Joint Matriculation Board in 1903, strengthened relationships with schools.[1] Exit channels from the schools were also provided by municipal training colleges which began to grow after 1904 as a result of the newly acquired power of their founders—the local education authorities. These colleges, which numbered twenty by 1913, set new patterns in professional training and fed new ideas to the schools.

x

Outside the catchment area of grammar school and university was a large element considered by many as potential fodder for agitators like Henry George, or General Booth: one the advocate of the single tax, the other of controlled emigration. In his tireless lectures against Henry George, Arnold Toynbee virtually wore himself out, and to honour him members of his old college, Balliol, founded a settlement in his name in Whitechapel, under the guidance of the local incumbent, the Reverend S. A. Barnett.[2] Scenting 'socialist autocracy' in General Booth's Darkest England scheme, T. H. Huxley roundly asserted that the Science and Art Department was a better instrument of salvation than the Salvation Army. But it was Toynbee Hall that the churches hastened to emulate with Oxford House in Bethnal Green (1884) and the Oxford Medical Mission in Bermondsey (1897). Oxford House began, aptly enough, in a disused national school, to provide club life for boys and men. A home was established at Limpsfield to give them a little fresh air. Cambridge followed with collegiate missions: St John's at Walworth (1884), Trinity at Camberwell (1885), Corpus Christi in the Old Kent Road (1887) and Caius at Battersea (1887) set the pace for others which worked for men and boys, with gymnasia. Cambridge House (1896) then developed as a university mission, and the movement was in full swing.[1] Nonconformists followed with Mansfield House in Canning Town (1890), the Bermondsey Settlement (1891) and the Robert Barry Settlement in Walworth (1890). Settlements were also established by Manchester University (1895), by Liverpool and Bristol (1907).

The impact of settlement work on those undertaking it was almost more important than upon those for whom settlements were intended. Much valuable sociological research was done in them, notably by E. J. Urwick and R. A. Bray. Equally valuable was the experience it gave to future bishops like Hensley Henson and Winnington Ingram, to social reformers and administrators like W. H. (later Lord) Beveridge and W. J. Braithwaite and to commercial pioneers like F. J. Marquis (later Lord Woolton), the warden of the Liverpool University Settlement.[2]

In these social laboratories many experiments were made. The first children's play centre and the first non-residential school for crippled children took shape, one founded in 1897 by Mary Ward with the help of money from Passmore Edwards.[3] Similarly, the Industrial Welfare Society was founded by R. R. (later Sir Robert) Hyde of the Maurice Hostel at Hoxton. Other pioneers hoped that the settlement movement would provide a people's university.

This was an unfulfilled dream until Albert Mansbridge suggested that co-operatives, trade unions and universities should combine to provide it. Mansbridge, a clerk with the C.W.S., also edited the magazine of the Junior Civil Service Prayer Union. Anglican clergy like Charles Gore (founder of the Community of the Resurrection) and university teachers like J. Holland Rose (editor of the *University Extension Journal*) supported him. Rose published Mansbridge's plea and circulated it in pamphlet form.

In spite of initial discouraging noises from Canon Barnett of Toynbee Hall, Mansbridge founded in 1903 his Association to Promote the Higher Education of Working Men. He found support at Reading where what became the first W.E.A. branch took shape as a result of joint effort by the Reading University College, the local education authority and the co-operative society.[1] By the end of 1905 seven more branches were established, including one at Rochdale, William Temple had joined the association and Mansbridge had become its full-time secretary.

With the accession of R. H. Tawney, one of the greatest twentieth-century teachers and scholars, the movement got under way. For Tawney, then part-time lecturer at Glasgow, started tutorial classes at Longton and Rochdale in 1908, during the week-ends. For many years these classes were the life of the movement. To spread them, committees of universities and the W.E.A. were formed—first at Oxford in 1907, then in the following year at Cambridge, Manchester, London, Liverpool, Leeds and Sheffield.

As a 'people's university' the W.E.A. was unpopular in several quarters. Suspected (by Mrs Bridges Adams) of diverting the working classes from seeking entry to the universities and (by Catholic working men like John Scurr) of diffuse theology, its success in diverting the working class from taking action to solve material problems annoyed George Lansbury, and outraged the more militant crusaders of the Labour movement, who seceded *en masse* from Ruskin College, Oxford, to form Labour Colleges.

In spite of, or perhaps because of, such opposition, the W.E.A. enlisted in ten years the support of 11,430 members organised in 179 branches with full-time district organisers, linked to fourteen university joint committees. Financial help for their 145 tutorial classes (3,343 students), had been obtained from the Board of Education and from the local education authorities. Summer schools had become an accepted feature of their work.[2]

By co-operating with the W.E.A. the universities drew still further together for closer consultation; while their staffs kept contact with the outside world (and often supplemented meagre salaries) by taking classes. A generation of graduates found in adult education a stepping-stone to political and academic life. But perhaps the most beneficial by-product of the movement was that steps were taken which led eventually to the establishment of the National Central Library in 1916.

Chautauqua, which brought culture, education and entertainment through many media to millions of Americans, inspired the Rev. J. B. Paton, president of the Congregational Institute, Nottingham, to found the National Home Reading Union in 1889: it was one of his many voluntary schemes for social regeneration.[1] This later merged (1897) with the Co-operative Holidays Association, holding 'summer assemblies' in Blackpool and the Lake District. Two years later, in 1899, two Americans, Carl Vrooman and Charles Beard established Ruskin College, Oxford. When Vrooman appealed to that eminent English educationist Herbert Spencer for books, Spencer haughtily replied that he had 'a profound aversion to the teachings of Mr Ruskin, to Socialism and to Free Libraries'. Bernard Shaw, at the same time, refused to lecture there on the grounds that the 'real business of Oxford was to make a few scholars and a great many gentlemen'.[2]

Another 'angel' was the dynamic little American soap-manufacturer Joseph Fels who gave much needed early support to George Lansbury and Margaret McMillan.

XI

American influence was increasingly visible in the Office of Special Inquiries and Reports, a branch of the Education Department established by A. H. D. Acland in 1893 with Michael Sadler as its director. For it was modelled on the intelligence service of the United States National Bureau of Education.[3]

The Elmira Reformatory in New York under Z. R. Brockway much impressed Sir Evelyn Ruggles-Brise, who started a modified counterpart at Borstal in Kent. Here the youthful prisoners above the age of 16 were to be 'individualised' morally, physically and mentally. By 1906 Sir Evelyn was so convinced that the scheme was working that he advised the Home Secretary to introduce legislation which would empower the courts to commit offenders between the ages of 16 and 21 to other 'Borstals'. Thus the place gave its name to institutions at Portland and Feltham (for boys) and Aylesbury (for girls).[1]

Meanwhile the *Daily Mail* began to publish in June 1901 a series of articles by F. A. McKenzie which were subsequently gathered up as a book with the revealing title *American Invaders* (1902). In the same month the *Saturday Review* (no friend of the United States of America), commented:

The full force of the present American commercial concentration falls on us. What we have to do is by harder work, more scientific method, fiscal readjustment and imperial consolidation, to prevent the Americans getting so far ahead of us.

Excluding food, drink and tobacco, American exports to the United Kingdom doubled from £10,279,669 in 1890 to £21,317,471 in 1900, and in that total, iron and steel exports had quadrupled, from £500,000 to £2,000,000. American locomotives and carriages were being used on the underground railways in Glasgow and London and were known as Yerkes's Jerkers from the name of Charles Tyson Yerkes, the American engineer who built them. In self-protection, and partly in imitation, British manufacturers were forming trusts on the American model to resist being taken over by Americans: thus the Imperial Tobacco Company was formed by Player's, Wills' and Ogden's. A typical case of American economic infiltration was that of shoes. In 1902 three-quarters of a million people in the United Kingdom were wearing American boots, and the Northamptonshire Education Committee were so perturbed that they sent Mr E. Swaysland to report on the American shoe industry.

America was Britain's most potent trade rival in the Empire too. In New Zealand American exports jumped from £200,000 in 1896 to £1,000,000 in 1901, and as a result special commissioners were sent from Britain to investigate conditions in 1905–6. Another commissioner, sent to South Africa in 1903, declared that 'America is undoubtedly our most formidable rival, present and future'.[2]

What the newspapers, the Office of Special Inquiries and

Reports and English travellers could not do was to bring home the seriousness of the lag in the English educational system. This was attempted by Alfred Mosely, who while mining in South Africa had come to appreciate American technological skills through his friendships with Gardner Williams, the famous Californian mining engineer who did so much for De Beers, and with Louis Seymour, who built bridges for the British Army so successfully during the Boer War. Mosely returned to England and gathered together two groups of experts: one from the English trade unions, the other from British universities and schools. He sent them both to America on fact-finding missions. These two Mosely Commissions, the first of 23 representatives of the labour world and the second of 25 representatives of the educational world each produced a report that had a considerable influence in the years before the first world war. The Labour Commission reported that: 'One of the principal reasons why the American workman is better than the Britisher is that he has received a senior and better education, whereby he has been more thoroughly fitted for the struggles of after life.' The Education Commission numbered among them the president of the N.U.T., and Professor Henry E. Armstrong, who had founded Section L (Education) of the British Association in 1901. Though their individual reports varied, their joint opinion was:

We are satisfied that, in years to come, in competing with American commerce we shall be called upon to face trained men, gifted with both enterprise and knowledge. We desire to impress on the British public the absolute need of immediate preparation on our part to meet such competition.[1]

Eleven representatives of the new local education authorities created in 1902 went to America on the Mosely Commission, and other authorities not so represented soon took steps to remedy this. Thus Leicester sent a deputation which reported in 1907, while Reading (backed by L. Sutton the seed merchant and Alfred Palmer the biscuit manufacturer) sent a fact-finding group to examine American agricultural colleges which reported back in favour of a similar establishment at Reading.[2]

Such visits dissolved more prejudices than they formed, and H. B. Gray, the Warden of Bradfield, another Mosely commissioner, moved at the Headmasters' Conference of 1908 that there should be a closer relationship between the Board of Education and the public schools. Mosely was responsible for initiating in 1906–7 the visit of several hundred school children to the United States and Canada, a project mooted by Choate, the U.S. Ambassador in 1901. In 1909 the then Vice-Chancellor of Sheffield conceived the notion that a twentieth-century 'grand tour' should embrace the New World, and a movement was set on foot to promote it. In 1910 the Central Bureau for the International Exchange of Students opened to increase British efficiency as citizens.

Having to cope with the thousands that funnelled out into the west America became the first nation to face the problem of educating everybody. To help the schools to change such a mixed population into Americans and to feed the optimistic and enthusiastic belief in educational environment, an intense study of the developing child began. G. Stanley Hall gave the new movement a mouthpiece when his *Pedagogical Seminary* began to appear in 1891 with its studies on children's ideas and aptitudes that were to lead to his great work on *Adolescence*. Psychiatrists who met him at the World Fair in 1893 caught his enthusiasm.

In England James Sully founded the British Association of Child Study in 1895, while another Englishman, J. J. Findlay, the headmaster of Wesley College, Sheffield, and later professor of education at Manchester, introduced English readers to the ideas of John Dewey, in whose laboratory school at Chicago projects like cooking became the basis of the curriculum.

XII

Similar ideas had been stirring in English public schools. In 1892 two years before Dewey went to Chicago, the 35-year-old F. W. Sanderson had been called in by the Grocers' Company to reorganise Oundle. A product of the new age (he had first graduated at Durham), he built engineering laboratories and workshops at Oundle and introduced co-operative methods of study, and a wholly new approach to a synthesised curriculum. H. G. Wells (who had suffered an education on the South Kensington model), thought him 'beyond question, the greatest man I have ever known with any degree of intimacy'. According to Wells, Sanderson 'soft-pedalled the fall of man',[1] and, being no athlete himself, frowned on the fetish of games. Sanderson tried to get boys working together in a free adventurous community school. 'Real live education—boys marched up to the frontier of the unknown—to go into the world as pioneers—Darwins—Listers' was his justification for establishing gardens and farms where boys could learn in a purposeful way.[2]

Gardens and farms were even more in evidence at Abbotsholme, which was founded in 1889 under Dr Reddie, a chemist who had studied at Göttingen. 'The New School Movement' really began under him in the unspoilt Staffordshire countryside where boys helped to organise and superintend work as well as working themselves. Their diet and growth were under Reddie's constant scrutiny. The liturgy of a non-dogmatic, non-sectarian religion suited to the young was written by Reddie himself, who also in chapel introduced readings from the works of the great masters of English literature.[3]

One of Reddie's assistants, J. H. Badley migrated to Petersfield in Hampshire to start Bedales in 1893. This, unlike Abbotsholme, was co-educational. Similar 'colonies' (to quote Reddie) sprang up in Germany, where Dr Lietz, another Abbotsholme master, opened a school at Ilsenberg in 1898, and in France where M. Edmond Desmolins, who had met Reddie in 1894, started the École des Roches.[4]

Nor was Bedales the only new type of school of the period. From Bishop Wordworth's, Salisbury (1890), Leighton Park (1890), Worksop (1895), Arnold, Blackpool (1896), Clayesmore (1896), St Benedict's, Ealing (1902), Douai (1903), the Royal Naval College, Dartmouth (1905) to St George's, Harpenden

(1907), others in diverse ways were to show the same realistic influence at work. Schools like these helped the older schools to adapt themselves to an ever more rapidly changing world.[1] It is also worth noticing that preparatory schools formed themselves into an association in 1892.

By 1909 a number of reforms were suggested for public schools, like the institution of a common leaving certificate, in a book edited by the headmaster of Bristol Grammar School. One of the contributors was the secretary of the Mosely Commission, and several of the others quoted William James and G. Stanley Hall in support of their various arguments.[2]

XIII

By 1909 C. F. G. Masterman could remark that teachers were 'taking up the position in urban districts which for many years was occupied by clergy in rural districts'.[3] For the balance of educated intelligence had reacted against one of its chief supports —evangelicalism. The new evangelist of their age was H. G. Wells, in whose writings we can trace the flow of thought. Energetically and virulently in over a hundred books and several hundred articles, he set himself 'to rescue human society from the net of tradition in which it is entangled', and to kindle a reverence and enthusiasm for the achievements and possibilities of science. Science, socialism and education, could, according to Wells, enable man to direct the course of his own evolution.[4]

Besides his *Anticipations of the Reaction of Mechanical and Scientific Progress upon Human Life and Thought* (1902), the shadow boxing of the sects seems very unreal, and certainly anti-climacteric. The Nonconformists rallied to the National Passive Resistance League, drummed up by Dr Clifford, who played on their fears that Sunday chapel teaching would be undermined in the day-schools if the preferential treatment accorded by the 1902 Act to Anglican teachers was allowed to continue. On the other hand, Anglicans, fearing that lay prescription of religion would become proscription, banded together in the Church Schools' Emergency League. The only really satisfied group were the Roman Catholics, who founded the Catholic Education Council the better to implement the 1902 Act.

Following the election of a Liberal government in 1905 various attempts were made by Birrell (1906), McKenna (1907) and Runciman (1908) to placate these fears, and compromises like 'right of entry' (or 'universal facilities'), and general religious education plus supplementary facilities and 'local option', stirred the sectarian journals to wheel in attack and support. The issue was further confused by divisions within the ranks of the Nonconformists, who were blamed by the secularists for perpetuating the dual system. So the Secular Education League was formed in 1907 to work for the exclusion of all religious teaching from state-supported schools.[1]

The real issue of the first decade of the twentieth century was not over rate aid to the voluntary schools (now a fact), but whether the country could afford to neglect any longer the more material aspects of child welfare. For, since 1880, a growing volume of evidence had been accumulating to show that children were actually underfed. Seebohm Rowntree had shown in 1901 that over a quarter of the population of York were too poor to buy 'the minimum necessaries for the maintenance of merely physical efficiency.'[2] Striking confirmation of his findings was provided by an Interdepartmental Committee on Physical Deterioration which recommended in 1904 that 'definite provision should be made by the various Local Authorities for dealing with the question of underfed children', and that they should also be medically inspected.[3]

These issues were brought to the House of Commons by the 40-strong phalanx of Labour members who had entered the House of Commons in 1905. Though none of them owed what education they had to board schools, one of them introduced the motion which ultimately led to the Provision of Meals Act of 1906. This gave L.E.A.s the authority to provide premises for the provision of meals: if such meals could not be provided by voluntary associations the Act empowered L.E.A.s to do so from the rates. This was the earliest example of relief from public funds to a specific section of the population by an agency other than the poor law.[1]

Another member of the Labour Party, but not of the House of Commons, began in 1904 to work for a system of health centres in London to inspect and treat school children, on the lines of those she had previously established in Bradford. Her name was Margaret McMillan. She enlisted the support of numerous medical men (including Dr J. Crichton Browne), for a national scheme compulsorily inspected, reported on and administered from Whitehall. After several deputations she got her way when an Act of 1907 empowered local education authorities to provide medical treatment: treatment which eleven years later they were obliged to give. She later started a clinic at Bow with support from Joseph Fels.[2] By 1912 there were a hundred clinics in the country, 25 years later there were 2,000.

Draftsman of the Act which thus started the School Health Service was Dr (later Sir) George Newman, who also became in 1908 the first medical officer of the Board of Education. A former medical officer to the poor and overcrowded metropolitan borough of Finsbury, Newman brought persuasiveness to his task: his 26 annual reports to the board were propaganda for open-air schools for the delicate, and for new techniques in physical education. From this experience at the board he went on to help build the new Ministry of Health.[3]

A third innovation was the establishment of juvenile employment bureaux by the L.E.A.s. These were recognised by the Education (Choice of Employment) Act of 1910 and empowered to advise boys and girls under 17 as to their choice of a career.

With the state offering such services, its schools increased, after 1902 in proportion to those of the voluntary bodies. By 1911 the number of children in the latter had declined from 3,790,000 to 2,826,000, whereas in the former it had risen from 2,880,000 to 3,980,000. This shift in the centre of gravity is more impressive in that, when one adds to the former total those in the Methodist

(60,000) and British and Foreign Schools (109,000), the impressive total of 4,160,000 pupils is obtained, compared to the 2,648,000 in Anglican, Roman Catholic and Jewish schools.

XIV

The last eruption of feeling took place in 1911, when E. G. A. Holmes, the chief inspector of elementary schools since 1905, expressed himself rather trenchantly, and probably with much justification on the local authority inspectorate, whose members he described 'as a rule, uncultured and imperfectly educated', and whose work as 'a hindrance rather than aid to educational progress'. Unfortunately, however, he elaborated them in a document circulated with the approval of Robert Morant, and to make matters worse the newspapers got hold of it. This released much pent-up feeling against the board. A question was asked in the House of Commons on 14 March 1911 by Mr Samuel Hoare (later Lord Templewood) and only turned aside as a joke. But no joke could turn aside the wrath of many Liberal and the Labour back-benchers. Here was a stick with which to beat the assassin of the boards and the man who had subsequently prevented them from redeeming their election pledges that 'Rome would come off the rates'. Having killed the boards in 1902, Morant was now insulting their living heirs, the local authority inspectors. The 'pernicious fruit' of the Morant régime was bitterly denounced by the veteran campaigner, Dr Clifford, but to no avail. Lloyd George was deaf this time and solved the problem by appointing Morant to the chairmanship of the new National Insurance Commission, where his drive and experience were needed. As Margaret McMillan told Morant: 'This agitation *appears* what it is not. It is sectional and inspired by partisans. Besides what did you say? What everyone thinks!'[1]

Morant's removal left the way clear for the local authorities to flex their sinews.

X

CHANGE THROUGH CONSULTATION

1911–1944

I

The circumstances surrounding Morant's departure showed how strong local authorities were becoming, especially when led by imaginative and resourceful officers.[1] From being virtually agents of the board they became partners, a role enhanced by increased powers and financial aid acquired during two major wars and a long depression. As Morant's successor, Lewis Amherst Selby-Bigge[2] (who held office from 1911 to 1925) acknowledged, 'the value of liberal consultation, and of the personal discussions to which it gives rise, is very great, and indeed is essential to the easy and effective working of the English system.'[3]

The focus of this 'liberal consultation' was the Consultative Committee. Created out of the 'Code Committee' in 1902, this now became a design centre of development. The board also made increasing use of advisory bodies and interdepartmental committees and was cited as worthy of emulation for so doing by the Machinery of Government Committee in 1918.[4] The Consultative Committee suggested in 1911 that examinations should be reduced in number.[5] Under the chairmanship of A. H. D. Acland six years of negotiation followed. As a result the Secondary School Examinations Council was established in 1917, and it was decided that first school certificate examinations (of a general character) should be established for pupils of about the age of 16 and a second school examination (more specialist) for pupils of about 18.[6] It was hoped (ironically enough in the outcome) that these examinations would follow the curriculum rather than determine it.[7]

Following this, the Consultative Committee examined the

scholarship ladder from 1914 to 1916. As a result of the encouragement of advanced study and of the reorganisation of examinations,
a system of state scholarships to the universities was instituted in
1920, which (though suspended for economy reasons in 1922 and
1923) tapped a steadily increasing stream of first and second class
honours students for the universities.

Reconstituted after the war under the chairmanship first of Sir
Henry Hadow (until 1934), then of Sir Will Spens, the Consultative Committee continued its enquiring way, reporting on seven
inter-war problems, and influencing (as we might expect), local
authorities to take action. These seven problems were the subject
of *Differentiation of Curricula between the Sexes in Secondary Schools*
(1922); *Psychological Tests of Educable Capacity* (1924); *The Education of the Adolescent* (1926) (the 'Hadow Report'); *Books in
Public Elementary Schools* (1928); *The Primary School* (1932); *Infant
and Nursery Schools* (1933) and *Secondary Education* (*Grammar
Schools and Technical High Schools*) (1938) (the 'Spens Report').

II

That the Consultative Committee should carefully consider the
utility of psychological tests was a tribute to the great progress
made since 1911. In that year the special committee, appointed
by Section L of the British Association to inquire into the
tests used (and proposed to be used) in the diagnosis of feeble-
mindedness, organised a number of investigations in which
an experimental and statistical procedure was evolved (now
known as 'factor analysis'). The secretary of this committee
was J. A. Green, who the year before had founded *The Journal
of Experimental Pedagogy* (now the *British Journal of Educational
Psychology*).

In 1913 an even more important step was taken when the
L.C.C. formed what was for a long time the only scheme for
child guidance in the country by appointing its own psychologist
Dr (now Sir) Cyril Burt,[1] a pupil of McDougall. By case study

and statistical analysis of the dull, defective, delinquent and neurotic, Burt showed how the study of these types of children could enrich the nature of the learning process. During the first world war other group tests were exploited by the American Army in order to sort some two million recruits. Afterwards their value in the 'junior scholarship examination' for grammar schools became apparent. They were adopted by Bradford in 1919, and, as sifting instruments, by the Civil Service for recruiting clerks in 1920.

In 1923 the Northumberland Education Committee, concerned that nearly one-third of the children in their area were not presented as candidates for junior schools examination, asked Professor Godfrey Thomson to devise a set of group tests for all the children in the area. The success of these tests in bringing to light ability in country districts encouraged the Committee to make them a permanent part of the selection process. Other authorities followed, like Blackpool. So, too, did certain schools like Rugby and Cheltenham Grammar School.

Institutional momentum to the testing movement came from the establishment of the Industrial Health Research Board during the war and that of the National Institute of Industrial Psychology in 1920. The latter employed Burt from 1921 as Director of its section for vocational guidance.

The use of these tests not only facilitated the investigation of backwardness and delinquency, but enabled the educational ladder to be improved. 'Guidance' tests became 'classifying tests', based on the mental ratio, or intelligence quotient, of children, designed to make 'the ladder' more ascendible by merit.

As the secondary system developed, two other English psychologists (in addition to Burt) left their mark upon it: Charles Spearman (a member of the British Association Committee of 1911 and propounder of the g and s theory) and Godfrey Thomson (whose subsequent work at Moray House was to provide L.E.A.s with tests for what became known as the 11+ examination).

But as psychological techniques of selection developed, a

contrapuntal sociological criticism began to make itself heard. Kenneth Lindsay showed that not more than 9·5 per cent of the primary school children passed into grammar schools, that the percentage varied from one district to another by as many as 27·1 (Bradford) to 6·4 (London), and that the social background of the parents determined its size. Thus in London the proportion of children from well-to-do boroughs winning scholarships was four times as high as that in seven smaller boroughs.[1] Lord Haldane was much impressed by the evidence and, in deploring the highly competitive nature of the examination, suggested that the provision of more schools, larger maintenance allowances and the abolition of fees at municipal secondary schools was overdue.[2]

III

The growing insistence on proper conditions of entry for the grammar schools was due to their steady expansion, which was remarkably and unexpectedly accelerated by the first world war. The number of children attending them rose from 4·4 to 11·3 per cent between 1910 and 1935. Advanced courses in them were accelerated by a grant in 1917. The percentage of graduate teachers increased from 5·4 to 7·8 between 1910 and 1935, attracted first by increased status and remuneration offered by the Superannuation Act and the Burnham Salary Scales, and later by the depression.

Meanwhile, from the pruned stock of the elementary schools, other types of para-secondary schools had been sprouting in the north and in London. 'Higher elementary schools' (from 1906), 'central schools' (from 1911) or junior technical schools (from 1913), appeared sometimes even under the shade of the technical colleges, since the necessary incentives to elementary-school pupils to attend day technical classes had been given by the 1905 regulations of the board. One hundred and eleven institutions had such day technical classes by 1912, so the board recognised some of them as junior technical schools and, later, others as junior commercial schools. Thus recognised, 37 were in existence by the time the first world war broke out.

After the first world war, high hopes were roused when the Fisher Act of 1918 empowered local authorities to raise the school-leaving age to 15, and endowed them with increased powers to develop a comprehensive system of public education in their areas. These hopes, though dashed by economies after 1921, were raised again when the Labour government in 1924 referred to the Consultative Committee the whole question as to what education children up to the age of 15 should receive.

The moving spirit in the subsequent report of the Consultative Committee was Professor R. H. Tawney, the Labour Party's spokesman for education.[1] For *The Education of the Adolescent* (1926) recommended the establishment of secondary modern schools for the other 90% of the population not actually being catered for by 'secondary' schools.

The Hadow Report, as it was called, was the major breakthrough, and acquired added force because the part-time continuation schools envisaged by the Fisher Act of 1918 had been virtually suspended. The impact of the report was reinforced by pamphlet No. 60, *The New Prospect in Education*, explaining how the proposals could best be implemented.

Anxious as many of the local authorities were to implement the Hadow proposals, they were handicapped by continuing financial stringency. The great strike of 1926 and the subsequent difficulty of raising the school-leaving age to 15 further handicapped them. When a Bill was actually introduced in 1931 to raise it, the anxiety of the voluntary (or, as they were called, 'non-provided') schools to obtain adequate grants to enable them to cope with the extra year torpedoed it. The voluntary schools did eventually obtain these grants (up to 75% of the cost of implementing the raising of the school-leaving age) in 1936, when the school-leaving age was finally raised with effect from September 1939. But once more external events interfered, this time the threat of war, and again action was deferred.

In spite of all this, many schools were 'reorganised' (as the term went), for by 1937, 72·6 per cent of all children in council schools and 32 per cent of those in voluntary schools were enjoying some form of 'secondary' education.

IV

Architecturally, the new schools set new standards. The old stereotype of board school, with central hall having classrooms opening out from it had the virtue of compactness. Rapid movement of classes and headmasterly supervision were assets far outweighed by its conservation of the odours of its pupils, of their meals and of its laboratories. Nor was its setting (usually in a desert of asphalt) attractive. The new type as outlined to the Board of Education by Dr Reid, the Medical Officer of Health for Derbyshire, let fresh air into the classrooms by placing windows on both sides. As developed by George Widdows, the Derbyshire county architect, these new schools did not place all the classrooms under the headmaster's eye, thus giving greater freedom to the classroom teacher. So, in single-storey quadrangular blocks, they sprang up in suburban areas, fostered and encouraged by Sir Felix Clay,[1] the chief architect of the Board of Education from 1904 to 1927. For Clay had issued the first building regulations in 1907 which had laid down new principles in lighting, hygiene and ancillary accommodation (gymnasia, practical rooms and laboratories), as well as establishing the standard size and height of classrooms.

By 1939, nearly 30% of school accommodation dated from after 1902.[2]

V

A new approach to youth work outside the schools is also visible. As H. G. Wells said in his anti-Fabian novel, *The New Macchiavelli* (1910):

There suddenly appeared in my world a new sort of boy—a most agreeable development of the slouching, cunning, cigarette smoking town youngster—a boy in a khaki hat and bare knees and athletic bearing earnestly engaged in wholesome and invigorating games— the Boy Scout. I like the Boy Scout.

This was written three years after Colonel R. S. Baden-Powell's experimental camp on Brownsea Island in 1907; by that time no less than 109,000 Boy Scouts had been enrolled in the United Kingdom alone. By drawing boys right outside their mean streets and schools, trusting them with positions of responsibility, setting before them a positive standard of conduct in the Scout Law and capturing their sense of adventure by camps and 'do-it-yourself' activities, Baden-Powell tapped hidden springs in the youth of the day, even to the extent of satisfying their gangster instincts by letting them work in patrols, each under a leader. He imposed no religious catechisms or duties other than practising the good life in the open air. Unlike the Boys' Brigade (to which he owed a great deal), the Scout movement had no 'physical drill' and the minimum of centralised administration. True, a central office with J. Archibald Kyle as secretary existed from 1909 and the movement obtained a charter of incorporation in 1912, but it worked outside the educational system, doing for boys what the 'educational' system was powerless to do except in small measure, for it took them while still at school and carried them past the school-leaving age up to the beginning of adult life.[1]

From the scouts the movement spread to Girl Guides (1910), Wolf Cubs (1916) and Rover Scouts (1918). At his jamborees (the first of which was held in 1920) Baden-Powell looked out on society with the eye of a crusader. At Gilwell he founded (in 1919) a virtual college for training Scoutmasters; the first real attempt to train youth leaders.

The para-military activities of the Boy Scouts during the first world war, however, led to three defections. Edward Westlake, a Cambridge naturalist, founded in 1916 at Sidcot School the Order of Woodcraft Chivalry—a co-educational movement based on self-government. John Hargrave, even more anti-imperialist and non-militarist, founded the Kibbo Kift Kindred in 1920 which looked like becoming the Boy Scout movement of the Labour Party. This role was eventually discharged by a third group, the Woodcraft Folk, founded in 1925 with the support of the Co-operative movement. All these three splinter groups derived much inspiration from the American Ernest Thompson Seton, whom Baden-Powell had appointed Chief Scout in the U.S.A., a post from which Seton resigned in 1915 to devote himself to his own movement, based on his *Book of Woodcraft*. His pantheistic gospel, with its echoes of Hiawatha and Daniel Boone, made it very popular.[1]

The first world war also posed, at a national level, the problem of juvenile delinquency. A central juvenile organisation committee was set up with local J.O.C.s to organise diversions, like games leagues. Though these J.O.C.s were the recipients, in 1921, of the first grants to voluntary organisations, they did not survive, fifteen years later only 36 of them existed in any recognisable form.

More helpful (since it was more representative), was the National Council for Social Service, another war-time product. Inaugurated in 1919 and incorporated in 1923, it played a major role in convening the conference which led to the foundation of the National Association of Boys' Clubs, the National Federation of Young Farmers' Clubs and the Youth Hostels Association. Boys' Clubs were, as we have seen, a characteristically English creation, but Young Farmers' Clubs were American, imported to England by Lord Northcliffe during the first world war, much publicised afterwards in the *Daily Mail* and adopted by the National Farmers' Union. They obtained, on Northcliffe's death, the support of the Ministry of Agriculture and federated in 1932. Youth Hostels owed much to the German *Jugendherbergen*, and the convention of the meeting that led to the foundation of the Y.H.A. in 1930 was decisive, for the movement acquired the driving power of a good secretary, E. St John Catchpool, and by 1939 had 83,417 members and 297 hostels.[2]

Through convening national conferences of this kind the

National Council of Social Service built up good relations with most of the leading voluntary youth organisations, and it was from one such meeting, convened in 1931 to discuss the allocation of grants for camping, that a standing conference of youth organisations took shape in 1936. This proved so useful that its membership was later extended with a view to co-ordinating a policy for youth in war-time.

Camping, hostels, youth centres and clubs, all need money. So, on the jubilee of King George V in 1935, an appeal was launched for a trust of that name to provide it. From the money collected, some £425,000 was given to youth organisations in eight years. The trust did more than this, for it commissioned Dr A. E. Morgan to survey the needs of the 14–18 age group and the means by which they were being, or ought to be, met.[1]

When the second world war broke out, the youth service was put on a level with other educational services. The preliminary rumblings of change had been heralded by the establishment of a National Fitness Council. As a result two famous memoranda, 1486, *In the Service of Youth*, and 1516, *The Challenge of Youth*, a National Youth Committee, with local counterparts, was established to devise activities for the 14–20 age group. To help them local authorities were assured of a 50% grant from the Board of Education. Further war-time expedients like the Youth Service Corps, the Air Training Corps, the Army Cadets, the Sea Cadets and the Girls Training Corps provided the local authorities with further experience in fostering youth activities. The result was that when the McNair Committee was appointed to consider the training and recruitment of teachers, their terms of reference significantly included youth leaders too.[2]

VI

The threshold to employment was being raised so rapidly that more sophisticated firms, especially those concerned with the electrical and chemical industry, had started schools where boy entrants could continue their education.[1] These day (as opposed to evening) continuation schools were generally admired, if not emulated, and L.E.A.s were recommended by the Consultative Committee in 1909 to provide them for young people in employment until they reached the age of seventeen.[2]

Though many of them were closed in the feverish mood of the 1914 war, a Departmental Committee appointed under H. Lewis in 1916 considered juvenile employment when the war was over and recommended that all half-time labour before the age of 14 should be abolished, and further, that continuation classes for children lasting not less than eight hours a week should be established for those from 14 to 18.[3]

This idea was incorporated into the Fisher Act of 1918. But soon after, the wintry atmosphere of economy forced all the continuation schools run by local authorities to close down. A shining exception was Rugby—a town dependent on new industries.[4] In other places industry, having a direct interest in the technical efficiency of boys, sustained schools of its own.[5]

One county, however, faced by the progressive emaciation of its rural life, began to provide a system of village colleges where such continuation education could continue side by side with primary, secondary and adult education. The scheme as adumbrated by Henry Morris, the Secretary for Education for Cambridgeshire, and accepted by the Education Committee, provided for eleven such colleges, to be community centres of the neighbourhood where 'a child would enter at three and leave the college only in extreme old age'. The four opened before the war—Sawston (1930), Bottisham (1937), Linton (1938) and Impington (1939)—exerted such a powerful influence on thought that when the concept of continuation schools was revived during the second world war, it bore the name 'county college'.[6]

The mutiple problems arising from the technical readjustments of the economy in the inter-war years led to the establishment of 'Regional Councils' for further education. Those, in three such vital areas as Yorkshire (1928), South Wales (1935) and the West Midlands (1935), helped to cope with the preparation of young employees in sectors of the economy hit hardest by technological change.

There was an obverse (and adverse) side to this urgent problem of technical competence, namely that of the young who, for one reason or another, could not obtain employment. So prophylactic measures to prevent them from degenerating had to be devised by the Ministry of Labour. Beginning in 1918, no less than five schemes for juvenile unemployment centres were tried out by L.E.A.s with varying amounts of Exchequer support, until a joint committee of the Ministry of Labour and the Board of Education under D. O. Malcolm recommended that they should be put on a more permanent basis. After the General Strike and coal stoppage of that year (1926), further centres were organised in the depressed areas of Durham, Northumberland, South Wales and Southern Scotland and a National Advisory Council for Juvenile Unemployment was established. These juvenile unemployment centres were endowed with a more positive role in 1929 as Junior Instruction Centres and many were set up in the cotton areas of Lancashire. By 1934 they had coped with over a million 'teen-agers'. The principal of a day continuation school expressed the hope that the Junior Instruction Centres would become 'Leisure Colleges', analogous to the Mechanics' Institutions and the Polytechnics of the previous century.[1]

VII

'Leisure' of an enforced and demoralising kind was the overriding problem in the inter-war years, and here the residential colleges and settlements for adult education were to give some help. The first of these was Woodbrooke, housed in the former Cadbury home at Selly Oak, Birmingham, which was made over as an educational settlement for short-term study in 1903 and became the nucleus of a number of others like Fircroft (1909). Like the Danish Folk High Schools, other settlements like Leeds (Swarthmore, 1909), Newcastle (Leamington, 1913), Wakefield (the Homestead, 1913), Scarborough (Rowancroft, 1918) and Sheffield (1918) helped the English unemployed to comprehend (and sometimes conquer) the forces that threw them on the social scrap heap. The formation of the Educational Settlements Association in 1920 provided the movement with some central direction.[1]

A mutant of the residential settlements were the Educational Settlements which also formed an association in 1920. They provided a focus through which the W.E.A. and the schools could reach the unemployed through drama, craft work, history and philosophy. In South Wales after 1929 they were launched by the Carnegie Trust and sustained by the South Wales and Monmouthshire Council of Service to keep many of the unemployed at least sane.[2]

These settlements did more. The idea of short-term courses in residential colleges like Coleg Harlech (1927) spread ten years later to Manchester where Holly Royde took shape. The colleges became such a popular method of training during the second world war that after 1945 a number of business firms started them too.

Yet another segment of the population to whom leisure was a problem were the women, whose progressive enfranchisement (those over 30 received the vote in 1918 and those over twenty-one in 1928) deprived their pressure groups of a goal. So their crusading spirit was channelled into Townswomen's Guilds, which did yeomen work in the distressed areas. The Townswomen's Guilds owed much to an earlier war-time importation, the Women's Institutes. Introduced from Canada by Mrs Arthur Watt, and helped by the Development Fund, by 1933 they numbered 5,000.[3]

The focus of much voluntary and statutory effort in this field was provided by the National Council of Social Service. From its foundation in 1919 it began to enrich village life (through village halls), to humanise new housing estates in the towns (through community committees), and (working with the Commissioners for Special Areas) salvage the derelict areas (by establishing three training centres for unemployed welfare workers—King's Standing near Burton, Hardwick Hall in County Durham and Wineham Hall in Lancashire).[1]

A more variegated pattern of adult education, one to spring from increased financial help, was the theme of the Final Report of the Reconstruction Committee in 1919, which recommended that universities should establish extra-mural departments and that local education authorities should develop evening institutes.[2] These, too, helped in their respective ways, to alleviate the tedium of unemployment.

Nor, in the evaluation of leisure-consuming organisations should the most pervasive and persuasive force of the age be forgotten: the B.B.C. Its creator, 33-year-old J. C. W. Reith, was determined that it should 'not be used for entertainment purposes alone . . . [but] . . . should bring into the greatest possible number of homes . . . all that is best in every department of human knowledge, endeavour and achievement'.[3] Formed at the end of 1922 and chartered in 1926, it adopted a regional structure in 1927. A Council for Adult Education was established in 1929 to promote wireless discussion groups and, to help them, the B.B.C. started *The Listener*. A Central Council for school broadcasting, established at the same time, enlisted the help of lively teachers such as Ann Driver, whose Music and Movement programme is still popular.[4]

The cinema was perhaps even more of an absorbent of leisure in the inter-war years. There were 4,967 cinemas in Great Britain in 1938, with an attendance of some 990 million: 1,635 million by 1946.[5] Thanks to experiments initiated by the American Charles Urban and his associate Percy Smith, and mounted by H. Bruce Woolfe, it became one of the first instruments in educational technology, opening up great tracts in nature study, geography, science and industrial processes.

VIII

The creeping malaise affecting the work force was attacked by siting new technical colleges to boost new industries or to cultivate adaptability in areas where the old ones were dying. From 1909, when the first of these colleges was established at Loughborough, through the years which brought into operation Workington (1912) and Cardiff (1916), to 1936 and 1938 when the magnificent institutions at Dagenham and Walthamstow were opened, local authorities and local industries in various forms of partnership helped colleges to rise above the prevailing slough of apathy and misunderstanding.

These developments were underpinned by the progressive multiplication of secondary schools, and by the ever-increasing vocational needs of adolescents. Moreover, the abolition of the old science and art examinations at the lower grade in 1911 enabled a more flexible system of awards, based on regional examining boards to develop.[1] Indeed, so many institutions applied to join the Union of Lancashire and Cheshire Institutes that it had to refuse them; so the disappointed parties formed the East Midland Educational Union in 1911. When the advanced science and art examinations were in turn discontinued in 1918 yet another regional union was formed in 1921; this was the Northern Counties Technical Examinations Council. These regional examining unions enabled courses to be adapted to local needs, and afforded opportunities for both teachers and industrial representatives to meet in mutual consultation. Not unnaturally, they were increasingly utilised both in the new secondary schools then taking shape and in the technical colleges.

The growth of technical colleges after 1911 was marked. In that very year the permanent officials of the authorities (whom we would now refer to as their directors of education) sent a deputation to America, which warmly endorsed American training.[2] By 1918 local authorities were so well primed with transatlantic practice that when the Fisher Act of that year empowered them to levy more than a twopenny rate to finance such colleges they went ahead, prodded by the various professional associations, to emulate what they had seen.

A third ingredient of their growth was the establishment of a new award of high standing, the 'National Certificate', granted jointly by the professions and the board after the completion of a five-year part-time course. Since the prime mover in this scheme was H. S. Hele-Shaw, an engineer of distinction as well as a teacher of engineering, the first national certificate scheme was established, in mechanical engineering, in 1921.[1] It was followed by other schemes; chemistry (1921), electrical engineering (1923), naval architecture (1926), building (1929), textiles (1934), commerce (1939), showed the inter-war pattern. Production engineering (1941) and civil engineering (1943) indicated war-time needs. The trend continued after the war with applied physics (1945), metallurgy (1945) and applied chemistry (1947), chemical engineering (1951) and mining (1952).

Industry pressed forward with increasing unanimity, on their side. Forty-nine firms who were carrying out educational schemes for the benefit of their employees formed the Association for the Advancement of Education in Industry and Commerce (AEIC) on 28 May 1919. This later joined the British Association for Commercial Education (formed on 14 July 1931) to form the British Association for Commercial and Industrial Education (BACIE) on 27 April 1934. This, and other industrial groups prompted the board to appoint committees of industrialists, teachers and local education authorities. The specific problem of education and industry occupied the Malcolm Committee (1926 and 1928), that of education for the engineering industry, the Clerk Committee (1929) and that of education for salesmanship the Goodenough Committee (1931).

All this was as music to the ears of Lord Eustace Percy, President of the Board of Education from 1924 to 1929, who regarded the neglect of the technical colleges as 'one of the worst examples of waste in all educational history', urged that they should federate with schools of commerce and art, and, what is more, said so in his aptly named *Education at the Crossroads* (1930). By 1939 a government scheme of capital expenditure of some £12 million was agreed, and it seemed as if these efforts of the enthusiasts had succeeded. Unfortunately, however, less than a sixth of this was actually spent, for the war intervened.[1]

IX

The pace of all this advance was severely regulated by the Treasury, which in 1911 appointed a departmental committee under Sir John Kempe to examine whether its grants should be on an *ad hoc* or percentage basis. The Kempe report came down heavily in 1914 on the side of block grants for all local services (including education) as most likely to reduce existing inequalities of rate and allow the central authority to prime the pump. But war broke out and not until 1917 was elementary education aided by a block grant, one calculated at 36s. per child, plus three-fifths of teachers' salaries, plus one-third of other expenditure, and minus the product of a 7d. rate.[2]

Treasury grants to local education authorities were further simplified by the Fisher Act of 1918, which merged seventeen separate grants for elementary and 40 for higher education into two annual grants for elementary and higher education. The former was to be on the basis of the supplementary grants of 1917, the latter at a flat rate of 50%. The Act, when passed, also provided for the submission of 'schedules of development' to the board by the local authorities. The grant system was now virtually based on the percentage of money spent on education by the local authorities and this encouraged them to spend more.

This system no sooner came into operation in April 1919 than the wintry climate of economy set in. Public expenditure was checked by the board virtually rationing any new activities on the part of the L.E.A.s going beyond the provision of minimal statutory services.[1] If this was not enough, a committee under Sir Eric Geddes recommended economies of such severity in all branches of public expenditure that it was known as 'the Geddes axe'.[2] He castigated the Kempe-Fisher formula as a 'money-spending device',[3] because it left the Board of Education 'impotent . . . in either controlling expenditure, or effecting economies, once the policy has been determined'. This the board strongly denied in a subsequent White Paper. Fortunately, the advent of a Labour government, though brief, stopped the pruning process.

But the need to phase programmes of development so to make possible an estimate of its future commitments led the board to consider seriously the possibility of emulating the proposals of the Ministry of Health, that all grants should be rolled up in a block. This suggestion excited such opposition that the board dropped the idea only to find it taken up under the Local Government Act of 1929 as an aid to L.E.A. expenditure.[4] Though subsequent committees in search of economies repeated the suggestion that the board should adopt the block-grant system, the board side-stepped them by citing the existence of two types of local education authority, one administering only elementary education and the other including higher education.

The local education authorities themselves were unhappy as grants on the Kempe-Fisher line for elementary education were decreasing in proportion to their total expenditure, as the Local Government Act of 1929 had cut the amount of money they could obtain from the rates. They demanded an inquiry. This was not conceded, but the board helped them to reorganise their secondary schools by raising grants for new buildings and equipment from 20 to 50%. When war broke out in 1939 further increased grants were made for air raid precautions (up to 100%), school meals, milk and youth services.

Figures are a poor guide in times of rising prices, but assuming the purchasing value of £1 to have been twice as great before the first world war as it was at the end of the second, the following are not quite so impressive as they appear:

	Local authority expenditure	Exchequer grant
1913–14	£30,011,000	£13,828,000
1919–20	£52,730,000	£28,568,000
1938–39	£93,815,000	£45,500,000
1944–45	£113,745,000	£58,290,000

The low prestige of the Presidency of the Board of Education during this period was a great handicap to the permanent officials. When Fisher told A. J. Balfour that he had accepted the office, Balfour 'raised his eyebrows and expressed misgiving that a man of ability should go to the Board of Education.'[1]

X

The emergence of the Treasury as the major patron of universities was indicated by the appointment in 1911 of an advisory committee under Sir William McCormick to advise on the distribution of grants to English colleges and universities. These then amounted to some £149,000. This committee was under the Board of Education until 1919, when, reorganised as the University Grants Committee, it was empowered 'to enquire into the financial needs of University education in the United Kingdom and to advise the Government as to the application of any grants that may be made by Parliament towards meeting them.' Oxford and Cambridge were now admitted to its grant list.[2]

Two other bodies began to pipe other Treasury grants into the universities. The newly appointed Development Commissioners (established as a result of Acts of Parliament in 1909 and 1910) fostered biological research affecting agriculture and fisheries, the former bulking so largely that by 1931 an Agricultural Research Council was established to deal with it. The second was a Medical Research Committee, which as a result of the Insurance Act of 1911, was endowed with contributions from insured persons, and became by 1919 the Medical Research Council.

Enrolments in the newer foundations began to rise as a result of further legislation and administrative action. The Coal Mines Act of 1911, by demanding higher qualifications for mining engineers, enlarged the clientèle for courses in geology and the allied sciences. Postulant teachers (who kept the faculties of arts and pure sciences alive), were from 1911 allowed by the Board of Education to pursue a four-year as opposed to a three-year course, for the profession. Hitherto their three-year course had embraced both academic and professional studies; now academic studies were to occupy the first three years, leaving professional studies for the fourth.

Within three weeks of the outbreak of the first world war, a special committee under Lord Haldane was appointed to consider how chemical products and dyestuffs, hitherto imported from Germany, could be best obtained. Nine months later, on 23 July 1915, the President of the Board of Education outlined a scheme whereby a special department (the Department of Scientific and Industrial Research), working under a committee of the Privy Council, with an advisory council of eminent men of science under the chairmanship of Sir William McCormick (already chairman of the Board of Education Advisory Committee on University Grants), would foster research and help found special institutions or departments. Accommodated and serviced by the Board of Education, D.S.I.R. grew so rapidly that in December 1916 it became a separate department with Sir Frank Heath as its first permanent secretary.[1]

Student numbers rose after the war from 22,234 (in 1913–14), to 36,424 (in 1919–20), and to 41,749 (in 1924–5). By 1932 they reached the 50,000 level, but fell between 1937 and 1939. The second world war saw them drop below 40,000. It is interesting to note that the numbers of students from grant-aided secondary schools increased from less than a thousand in 1910 to more than 4,000 by 1939.

Another significant policy group affecting universities was the

Committee of Vice-Chancellors and Principals which, thanks to the establishment of the Universities Bureau of the British Empire in 1912, was equipped with a secretarial staff. It was through them that the Foreign Office suggested that universities might consider awarding Ph.D. degrees to attract students who normally went to Germany. Most universities adopted the suggestion. The Committee of Vice-Chancellors and Principals became increasingly concerned with policy as universities themselves were integrated into the national educational grid. For, through the Secondary School Examinations Council (established in 1917), they were linked to the schools; through their extra-mural departments (established after 1918), they were linked to the W.E.A., and they also began to play an increasing role in training college affairs.[1]

Indeed, the universities' relations with the training colleges were significant. As the result of a departmental committee report in 1925, examinations for the teacher's certificate in training colleges, hitherto under the Board of Education, were delegated to eleven regional boards organised round various universities and university colleges. Although these boards began to operate after 1928 they did not satisfy the N.U.T., which pressed for the increasing integration of the training colleges with the universities. The drastic reconstruction envisaged during the second world war strengthened the N.U.T.'s case. A special committee under Sir Arnold McNair was appointed in March 1942 'to investigate the present sources of supply and the methods of training of teachers and youth leaders and to report what principles should guide the Board in these matters in the future.' From its deliberations emerged an integrated system of training with a central training council based on area training organisations. The conscript army of intending teachers ceased to sour the undergraduate course and the 'pledge' to teach (which began in 1890) was abolished as a condition for obtaining a university grant. A three-year course was recommended in all training colleges, which were to be even more closely associated with the universities through institutes of education.[2]

XI

Collateral financial aid, especially for new enterprises, was forthcoming in ever-increasing amounts from American foundations.[1] Here the pioneer was Andrew Carnegie, the American steel magnate, who up to 1913 had given local education authorities some £1,770,000 and promised some £174,970 more with which to establish public libraries. As applications increased, Carnegie placed the future administration of such grants in the hands of the Carnegie United Kingdom Trust. Founded on 3 October 1913, with an income of £100,000 a year this was intended 'to promote the well being of the masses of the people of Great Britain and Ireland'. It was the fifth of his foundations from which the people of Great Britain benefited directly.[2]

One of its first acts was to commission Professor W. G. S. Adams of Oxford to survey the existing state of public library provision. He found that 329 places in the United Kingdom had already received a Carnegie library grant and recommended that more assistance should be given to libraries in rural areas and that all of them should be linked to a national central library. His suggestion flowered in the County Library Scheme and the National Central Library. Carnegie generosity pointed the way to legislation in 1919 which gave County Councils in England and Wales the statutory powers to undertake and sustain such enterprises.[3] He also gave a generous grant to the London Library of Political Science and that of the W.E.A. Carnegie money also helped to purchase playing fields, and establish Cambridgeshire village colleges and museums.

New institutions like the pioneer adult college at Harlech in North Wales (1927), or the Carnegie College of Physical Education at Leeds (1930), junior instruction centres (1934), a schools museum service, and wireless discussion groups, owed much to grants from the Carnegie Trust. Moreover, the voluntary agencies and the statutory authorities were able to co-ordinate their services under the aegis of the National Council of Social Service by establishing autonomous county agencies. By providing establishment grants for the first three years, the Carnegie Trust enabled rural community councils to be set up in most counties. These rural community councils provided village halls and services for rural industries. By the time (1937) the Carnegie Trust discontinued their grants to rural community councils the Development Commission stepped in (until 1953).

The Rockefeller Foundation gave another helping hand to higher education. Its first gift was of £835,000 for clinical units at University College Hospital Medical School: £400,000 of this was for buildings and equipment alone and grants for similar units at St Bartholomew's, St Thomas's, London, Middlesex and the University College Hospitals were supplemented by the U.G.C.[1]

A further half million dollars was given to the University of Edinburgh to improve teaching and research facilities in medicine. As an overall stimulus, a system of fellowships was instituted to send the leaders of medical education to the United States or Germany, indeed to anywhere where new ideas were germinating.

London University was able to build its present administrative headquarters in Bloomsbury thanks to £400,000 from the Rockefeller Foundation, coupled with a Parliamentary supplementary estimate of £212,500. Similarly, both Oxford and Cambridge obtained a substantial sum towards new university libraries. The Rockefeller Foundation gave advice with its money. Thus Abraham Flexner, the secretary of its General Education Board asked his English audience in 1930 whether the national debt could not be reduced relatively to the national wealth by developing physics and chemistry in the same way as steam, coal and iron were developed to reduce the relative burden at the close of the Napoleonic war.[2]

For 30 years the Rockefeller Foundation enabled the British Medical Research Council (established in 1919), to dispatch a picked nucleus of research workers to study overseas. Half a million dollars have been expended in this way, and the names of the Fellows include Sir Howard Florey, Sir John Conybeare, Professor A. A. Moncrieff and Professor C. H. Waddington. Then again, during the second world war, when British facilities for medical training were stretched to breaking point, the Foundation enabled many promising young medical trainees to spend two-year periods at 23 medical schools in the United States and Canada. Promising individuals have also been helped, in their own institutions, to obtain vital apparatus at a time when the calls on university finances have been unusually heavy.

Individual grants to the civic universities enabled many new lines of research to extend. Thus X-ray studies of the biomolecular structure of wool, keratin and other proteins by W. T. Astbury at Leeds were helped, providing the foundation on which was based all later knowledge of wool-textile processes, of all present-day methods of cold permanent waving in the hairdressing trade and even of the production of Ardil from the protein of ground-nuts by Imperial Chemical Industries. A similar story could be told at Sheffield of their help to Professor H. A. Krebs, the Nobel prize biochemist. Other projects so assisted include the re-stocking of the National Central Library at London (itself owing much to Carnegie generosity). Up to 1956 no less than 28,761,453 dollars were spent in Britain by Rockefeller trustees.[1]

Equally influential was the Commonwealth Fund, which provided fellowships for post-graduate study in America. It was this fund which, in response to Mrs St Loe Strachey's appeal, set up child guidance clinics in Great Britain. A cadre of child guidance workers trained in America was built up and by 1939 50 clinics were in operation.[2]

XII

American influence (as opposed to affluence), is visible in educational practice, even to the very texture of the consultative committee's reports.[3] True, it came after sympathy for 'progressive' ideas involving free expression, activity through hand-work and dramatisation had been courageously expressed by

E. G. A. Holmes,[1] the author of the circular which had led to Morant's departure from the board.

Holmes issued what might be called the manifesto of the English progressives in *What Is and What Might Be* (1911). Around him gathered a body of disciples who also found inspiration in the ideas of Madame Montessori, an account of whose work in the *Casa dei Bambini* appeared in English in 1912, when a society was formed to adapt her ideas in England. In the following year, Dr Montessori held a training course for 83 students from Great Britain and the U.S.A., mainly for intending infant teachers and social workers.[2]

Holmes represented responsibility and continuity; responsibility in that he had been an inspector since 1874, continuity in that he had been so influenced by Matthew Arnold that after reading *Literature and Dogma* he 'finally broke with the hypothesis of the supernatural and with the dualism of the human and the divine'. Holmes castigated the 'codes' he had administered as 'monuments of bureaucratic ignorance and imbecility', and after his retirement confessed himself a 'sinner' for helping to enforce them.[3] His New Ideals Group, meeting annually from 1914 onwards, also attracted Lord Lytton, the sponsor of a powerful and imaginative American, Homer Lane, who, eighteen years before, had established a therapeutic self-governing junior republic in America.[4] Speaking at Gresham's School, Holt, in 1913 (where the headmaster Howson had reduced formal discipline and regimentation to a minimum), Homer Lane in turn impressed J. H. Simpson, one of the staff, who remarked 'Lane shrank from the ecclesiastical mentality that insisted on the doctrine of original sin and from the religious temperament that accentuated the supernatural character of Christ'. Simpson began himself to experiment on a form of boys along lines of self-government following Lane but found the unit too small.[5]

Another, influenced both by Lane and Montessori, was Norman MacMunn who before the war had been teaching modern languages by activity methods at King Edward VI School, Stratford-on-Avon, leaving a record of his work in *A Path to*

Freedom in The School (1914). Perhaps the best known was H. Caldwell Cook, whose *Play Way* (1917) showed that activity work was not the prerogative of experimental schools. The New Ideals Group was strengthened by the surge of idealism liberated by the peace. *The New Era*, a recently established journal of education, convened an international conference at Calais in 1921, where the New Education Fellowship was founded by Beatrice Ensor and Dr Adolphe Ferrière,[1] then secretary of the International Bureau of New Schools. Comprising administrators, teachers, educationists and even governments, the New Education Fellowship rapidly increased its membership, becoming, as one of its members wrote, the 'most highly vitalised body which exists in the world for the investigation of new methods of teaching and for the recording of experience gained in all lands in the fascinating and urgently needed task of adapting education to new social ideals.'[2] Its journal, *The New Era*, not only featured continental activity-schools like *L'école des Roches* in France and the *Landerziehungsheime* in Germany, but also the work of Dr Decroly in Belgium, Dr Claparède in Switzerland, Cousinet and Profit in France and Rabindranath Tagore in India. The transatlantic corps of Dewey's disciples, like Professor C. H. Judd and Carleton Washburne, attached themselves to it with enthusiasm.

Meanwhile, English teachers were themselves opening up new vistas. At Prestolee, a L.E.A. school in Lancashire, from 1918 onwards, E. F. O'Neill established under great difficulties a community centre for youth.[3] Susan Isaacs used the opportunities provided at Malting House, Cambridge (from 1924 to 1927) to apply psychoanalytic techniques to children,[4] and published her work in *Intellectual Growth in Young Children* (1930) and the *Social Development of Young Children* (1933).[5] Also at Malting House the 36-year-old S. R. Slavson worked on theories of group psychotherapy which he was later to improve by work in New York.[6]

More in the Homer Lane tradition, A. S. Neill started a community school at Hellerau near Salzburg which, after some migrations, settled at Leiston in Suffolk in 1921 as Summerhill

School. This tended, if anything, to overemphasise Freud and reject theological assumptions. 'Some day,' Neill wrote, 'a new generation will not accept the obsolete religion and myths of today. When the new religion comes, it will refute the idea of man being born in sin.' The co-educational Summerhill still takes some 45 children from 5 up to 15, keeping them generally until they are 16 years old, housed in age-groups with a house-mother for each group. Apart from this the children are free. 'It began,' Neill wrote, 'as an experiment and became a demonstration.'[1]

Other experiments added variety to the progressive education movement. There was the Caldecot Community, founded in 1911 in Cartwright Gardens; the Uplands Association founded in 1914; the theosophical schools, which took root in the garden city of Letchworth in 1915; the anthroposophical schools of Rudolph Steiner specialising in severely handicapped children, the Community of War Orphans at Tiptree Hall; Dauntsey's school at Wiltshire, with its school council and farming interests; Alex Devine at the Clayesmore school, Winchester; Bertrand and Dora Russell's experiment on the wind-swept Sussex Downs at Beacon Hill in 1927; Priory Gate in Suffolk, a laboratory for testing the psychological theories of its founder Major Theodore Faithful; King Alfred's school at Hampstead under Joseph Wicksteed, an enthusiastic disciple of William Blake; and, perhaps most ambitious of all, the experiment in rural reconstruction begun at Dartington Hall by Leonard and Dorothy Elmhirst in 1925 with a view to effecting a regeneration of country life, with a school under W. B. Curry forming part of the scheme.[2]

The polyglot inspiration of these experiments—rationalist radical thought, the 'non-interference' pacifism of Tolstoy exemplified in Yasnaya Polyana and the ever-increasing volume of exegesis and exhortation from the disciples of Dewey—should, however, not blind us to the fact that a native tradition of such experiment had been growing steadily articulate since Cecil Reddie established Abbotsholme in 1889. Abbotsholme, and even more its offshoot Bedales (founded by J. H. Badley in 1893), bore, in fact, the 'progressive' label with distinction. Bedales, a co-educational boarding school, had become by 1923 (in the words of the American C. W. Washburne) 'perhaps the most progressive and alive of all the "New Schools"', and 'apart from an orphanage in Czechoslovakia Bedales was the finest school . . . in all Europe'.[1] That its pupils included the children or wards of such men as Ramsay MacDonald, A. N. Whitehead, Bernard Shaw, Sir William Rothenstein, Roger Fry and Sir Arthur Schuster showed how respectable the movement had become.

All this busy experiment was not lost. Much of it filtered down into the most unlikely quarters. In 1930 a fourth boys' Borstal at Lowdham Grange in Nottingham was begun. Built by the boys themselves, it had none of the external symbols of penal discipline such as walls, locks and bars. It was followed by two other open Borstals, Hollesley Bay, which began to breed sheep and Suffolk punch horses, and North Sea Camp, begun in 1938 as a land reclamation and farming unit on the shores of the Wash.

At the Board of Education these ideas were so congenial that a jubilee review of educational development published in 1935 described them as characterising the 'New Humanism'.[2] This new humanism was carried forward on a tide of child studies, in which scientifically trained women were outstanding. Melanie Klein's use of play techniques in 1922 and 1923, to verify certain Freudian speculations on the importance of early family life (as outlined in his analysis of 'little Hans' in 1909),[3] led to her being invited to London by Dr Ernest Jones in 1925, thus opening the way to child-analysis. Charlotte Bühler's *Testing Children's Development from Birth to School-Age* (1935), followed up Gesell's hope of plotting norms for various stages of development. A similar but more complex attempt to distinguish stages in child-development was initiated by the Swiss Jean Piaget, whose *Language and Thought of the Child* (1923) has been followed by a series of studies that have had an increasing impact on English teachers.

The therapeutic value of community clubs was demonstrated

by Joshua Bierer. David Wills in 1941, declaring the need for 'shared responsibility' in his experimental community for emotionally disturbed adolescents, likened himself to a matron of a hospital whose purpose is to provide the atmosphere in which doctors and nurses work.[1]

XIII

All these changes reverberated in the public schools which had been subjected, by H. B. Gray, warden of Bradfield and a former member of the Mosely Commission, to 'the bitterest and most thorough criticism' they had ever received, in his *Public Schools and the Empire* (1913).[2] Gray argued for parity of educational opportunity, for a sufficient leaven of manual and practical work, for non-competitive scholarships and (despite his own holy orders), the soft-pedalling of religion as a controlling influence in the school. Three years later in *Eclipse or Empire* (written with Samuel Turner), he proposed that the school-leaving age should be raised, and that science replace the classics for some professions. Revisiting America at the close of 1916 he reported in *America at School and at Work* (1918) that progress made there since his previous visit in 1903 was greater than that made in the public schools of England since 1861. Gray was not alone. 'It must be frankly admitted,' wrote A. C. Benson, 'that the intellectual standard maintained at the English public school is low, and what is more serious, I do not see any evidence that it is tending to become higher.'[3]

Yet others were at work quietly leavening the curriculum of the schools. For instance, Percy Ingham, a public-school master, invited Jaques-Dalcroze and his team to London in 1912 to demonstrate the music and movement system of eurhythmics devised and improved at Hellerau. Ingham's subsequent enthusiasm was matched by that of Miss Salt, who at a G.P.D.S.T. School in Streatham Hill worked on similar lines with a percussion band. By 1919 it was adopted by the board in its physical exercises for children under 7.[1] Even more important, the Dalton plan of individual work was modified to suit English habits and spread with great rapidity in many schools.

As the smaller public schools could not provide pensions comparable with those of state-aided schools under the Teachers' Superannuation Act, a conference was held in 1919 between representatives of the Headmasters' Conference and the Board of Education. At a subsequent meeting the Headmasters' Conference not only offered 'as a voluntary service', but claimed . . . 'as a privilege that share in the education of ex-elementary school-boys which was demanded by the State from other schools'.[2] The reply of the president of the board spoke of allowing them to take boys aged 15 or over. Later other state benefits became available to public school-boys like state scholarships (1936) and cheap milk (1942).

In spite of sustained and heavy criticism from their own products,[3] public schools weathered the storm. They were saved by three things: the institution of 'educational policies' by the insurance companies, the consistent support from the Established Church (which recruited many of its leading bishops from head-masters), and the increasing use of interview techniques in public appointments. Indeed, by a strange paradox, the availability of large country houses stimulated the formation of new schools. Thus the Reverend Percy Warrington, Vicar of Monkton Combe, with the support of a syndicate of Low Churchmen and the Legal and General Assurance Company, bought the Adam mansion that once housed the Dukes of Buckingham and Chandos for Stowe School, to start in 1923. In the same year, he bought Lord Wimborne's house and opened Canford School. Having already founded Wrekin College in 1921 from an earlier school at Wellington, his syndicate went on to refound Seaford College in 1927 and later resold it. They also took over five girls' schools: Lowther College in North Wales, St Monica's in Surrey (1927), Westonbirt (1928), Felixstowe College (1929), and Harrogate College (1929). When Warrington over-reached himself finan-cially by founding an evangelical theological college at Clifton, the Legal and General Assurance Company virtually took over the schools in 1934.

To these caste-factories H. G. Wells attributed Britain's imitative imperialism and solemn puerility'. Their teachers he described as having the 'mentality of residual men', their outlook as 'ignorance classically adorned'.[1]

As he spoke yet more new public schools were growing to rebut this charge. Rencomb was founded in 1919 by Noel Wills to take 50% of its boys from the public elementary schools and, under its headmaster, J. H. Simpson, it became very progressive.[2] Even more notable was the regrafting of the English public-school idea of fitness by Kurt Hahn, whose own school at Castle Salem in Germany was virtually liquidated by his arrest in 1933. Thanks to Ramsay MacDonald he came to England in 1934 and started Gordonstoun in Morayshire. Here by leisurely athletic training in the middle of the morning, by allowing boys complete freedom of movement, and by giving them opportunities for self-discovery through practical tasks, the school built up a fine reputation.[3]

Yet by 1939 the attacks were so strong and the economic position of some of the less-well-endowed schools was so weak, that suggestions were made that they be converted to 'junior universities',[4] that 90% of them would need public assistance[5] and that a Royal Commission should be appointed to consider how they could be incorporated into the public system. That this last suggestion should have been made by Cyril Norwood, a former headmaster of Harrow, was a significant measure of the pressure directed against them.[6]

The economies and difficulties of the second world war led to the creation of the Governing Bodies Association in 1941, which in concert with the Headmasters' Conference approached the Board of Education to work out a plan whereby 'the facilities of their schools could be extended to those who desire to profit by them, irrespective of their means'. The government's response was to set up the Fleming Committee in 1942 'to consider means whereby the association between the Public Schools . . . and the general educational system of the country could be developed and extended'. Here at last was a recognition of the fact that both sides were anxious to draw together.

XIV

Illusions as to the efficacy of all this educational progress at the lowest levels were rapidly dispelled when the avalanches of evacuees descended on non-vulnerable areas at the outbreak of war in 1939. Their noisy barbarity so afflicted their hosts that the correspondence columns of *The Times* began to swell with complaints that they were 'little heathens'.[1] The leaders of the churches responded with a call for some drastic action, and in January 1941 the President of the Board of Education (Mr Ramsbottom), indicated that plans for educational reconstruction were being drafted. For the next two years all the pressure groups were in action. The National Union of Teachers wanted the elimination of the non-reorganised schools, the abolition of fees and the strengthening of local authorities. The churches (more united than before) fought to prevent the relentless pressure of secularism.

The new president of the board, Mr R. A. Butler, issued a 'Green Book', a confidential memorandum of proposals for reconstruction, in October 1941. This was eagerly conned by all parties, especially by those most interested in the maintained schools (the Association of Education Committees, the N.U.T. and the Free Churchmen), who refuted the accusation that religious instruction in such schools was not Christian. After numerous discussions with various parties, the president then issued in 1943 a revised edition of the 'green book', this time a 'white memorandum'. Stern opposition to religious tests for teachers in non-provided schools was offered by the N.U.T., which, joined by the W.E.A., the T.U.C. and the Co-operative Union formed a 'Council for Educational Advance' under the chairmanship of R. H. Tawney. This council was in turn opposed by the Roman Catholics, and a lively battle raged until the president issued a *White Paper on Educational Reconstruction* in 1943, which formed the basis of a Bill which was presented to Parliament on 15 December 1943.[1]

By the Act (which became law on 3 August 1944) voluntary schools could opt to become 'controlled' (and obtain 100% grant), or 'aided' (and obtain 50%) or 'special agreement' (and obtain from 50 to 75%). The grant was in inverse ratio to their freedom to provide denominational instruction.

Meanwhile a committee appointed in 1941 under Sir Cyril Norwood to consider 'suggested changes in the Secondary Schools Curriculum and the question of School Examinations' had strayed far beyond its terms of reference, and their report, when it appeared in 1943, contained a blueprint for 'the main features of a new secondary education which will cover the whole child population of the country and carry them on to part-time education'. It was pre-eminently a work of ingestion and synthesis for the blueprint was a tripartite system of secondary schools composed of grammar schools together with secondary modern schools (as proposed in the Hadow Report of 1926), and the secondary technical schools (as proposed in the Spens Report of 1938). All three types were to 'be accorded all the parity which amenities and condition can bestow'. Thus the implicit assumption of the Taunton commission, three-quarters of a century before, still prevailed.

In a cosy psychological gloss, the Norwood Committee recognised three 'types' of pupil for whom the schools would cater. Grammar schools would cater for 'those interested in learning for its own sake', technical schools for those 'whose interests and abilities lie markedly in the field of applied science or applied art', and modern schools for those 'who deal more easily with concrete things than with ideas'. Allocation to each type was to be based on teachers' reports, supplemented, where necessary, by objective tests. And, for justice' sake, transfer up to the age of 13 between the types was recommended. So that this transfer should be as easy as possible, a common curriculum from 11 to 13 in each of the three types of school was envisaged. This report was to affect many of the development plans put up to the Ministry by the local education authorities after the 1944 Act.

That Minister was given, not only his title, but enhanced powers by the 1944 Act. All schemes put up by local authorities now required his approval; all private schools were obliged to qualify for position on his register.

The untidy practice of public education being divided into two separate fields, elementary and higher, administered in many areas by different local authorities, and in other areas by different committees of the same authority was replaced by a unitary system of primary, secondary and further education. Local Education Authorities, reduced in number from 315 to 146, now found that their 'powers' of providing facilities for secondary, technical and adult education were converted by the Act into 'duties', whilst the stages of the new system they were to administer were clearly defined. Primary education was to begin at 5; secondary at between the age of $10\frac{1}{2}$ and 12, ending at 15 and as soon as practicable at 16. All fees were abolished in these two stages, as in the third—part-time education up to the age of 18 in county colleges.

They were to convene conferences to agree syllabuses of religious education, and where such agreement was impossible, the Minister himself was to ensure it. They were also to provide extramural facilities of a medical and recreational kind, and even clothes, where necessary. To help them do this, further grants were forthcoming from the Ministry of Health as well as more compounded grants from the Ministry of Education.

This Act marks the apogee of the age of consultation, for its provisions were the result of consecutive airings of three plans: The Green Book and the White Memoranda I and II. The stage was now set for the era of long-range plans.

XI

LONG-RANGE PLANS

1944–1964

I

A vehement assault on the upper class Englishman's philosophical breviary—*Plato's Republic*—was launched by K. R. Popper in 1945. Challenging the conviction that it was useless for men to try to shape their ends (historicism) and the dogma that it was wicked to do so (the closed society), he argued for 'a social technology' which could be tested by 'social engineering'. Popper's conviction was that 'we can influence or change the history of man just as we have changed the face of the earth'.[1]

Earlier versions of the case had been put just before, and convincingly demonstrated by others during, the war. The British Association heard Sir Frederick Gowland Hopkins in 1933 and Sir Josiah Stamp in 1936 argue that the government should utilise planning techniques. Supported by Sir Richard Gregory of *Nature*, the movement secured the adhesion of, amongst others, Sir Henry Tizard and F. A. Lindemann (later Lord Cherwell), as well as Harold Laski and Julian Huxley. In a series of articles and books C. H. Waddington[2] developed the case for applying objective, empirical and *ad hoc* methods to put the world to rights, while J. D. Bernal, a war-time scientific adviser to Lord Louis Mountbatten, indicated that the best guarantee of democracy lay in applying operational research techniques developed during the war.

Such ideas evoked strong criticism from religious thinkers. C. S. Lewis[3] in the *Abolition of Man* (1946) foresaw that this would result in 'men without chests'. T. S. Eliot in his *Notes towards the Definition of Culture* (1948) saw that they would have a cramping effect on education. Defending 'the happy combination of

237

privilege and opportunity' represented by existing public schools and the older universities 'of which no Education Act will find the secret', Eliot urged that the 'one thing to avoid' was 'a *universalised* planning, one thing to ascertain is a limit of the plannable'. Education could not, he argued, be the instrument for realising the social ideals of the planners, as it was a moot point whether more of it made people happier, or that everyone wanted it, or that it could, or should, be organised to give 'equality of opportunity'. The last, he continued, 'would tend to both restrict education to what will lead to success in the world, and to restrict success in the world to those persons who have been good pupils of the system'.[1] Eliot was followed by the former chairman of the University Grants Committee, who named the 'religion' of the planners as 'scientific humanism' and described it as a blend of 'Francis Bacon and Karl Marx'.[2]

But the case for planning was skilfully put in the cloudiest sociological prose by Karl Mannheim, whose ideas, as T. S. Eliot remarked, 'deserve the closest attention, both for their own value and because of the influence they exert'.[3] Mannheim conceived of an educationally selected élite, free-floating and un-anchored by social ties, and looked to the re-organisation of education to produce it.[4]

The Ministry of Education, as created by the 1944 Act, adopted the principle of operational research with the advice and help of four advisory councils. The first and most important of these was the Central Advisory Council, which unlike its predecessor, the Consultative Committee, had the powers of initiating its own investigations. Its first chairman, Sir Fred Clarke, a disciple of Mannheim, looked forward to a 'much more thoroughly collectivist' order of society in which schools were to be unified, and considered that 'developments seem to be moving towards the creation of some kind of Ministry of Culture, not indeed to reduce the natural jungle to a trim totalitarian garden, but to minimise wasted effort, to increase effectiveness, and above all to interpret and direct institutional action of whatever kind that has a distinct educational bearing so that it may contribute towards the ends of a genuine common culture'.[1]

The three other councils were concerned with specialist arms of the educational service: the National Advisory Council for the Training and Supply of Teachers, the Secondary Schools Examinations Council was reconstituted, and the National Advisory Council on Education for Industry and Commerce. Like the first, these three were work groups exchanging ideas, advice and criticism. Their first task was to discharge war-time legacies and in doing so they evolved new techniques for coping with further change.

II

A shortage of teachers and school places had first to be overcome. Fifty-five country houses or military encampments (the terms were often synonymous) were rapidly adapted between January 1945 and January 1948 as emergency training colleges. By 1951 they had produced 35,000 teachers. Five thousand destroyed or damaged schools had to be replaced or repaired. The raising of the school-leaving age by April 1947 meant that 168,000 new places had to be provided. A Hut Operation for the Raising of the School Age raised and furnished 6,838 H.O.R.S.A. classrooms equipped with S.F.O.R.S.A. 'utility' furniture by 1949.

These crash programmes led the Ministry to establish a development group which, in adopting three key ideas—annual building programmes, minimum physical and educational standards and a limit of costs per place—built schools cheaply, rapidly and well. The group's activities were justified as fresh problems loomed in the 1950s: the high birth-rate of 1944-9 (which involved a 40% increase of the school population), and the housing boom. Taken together this involved raising the target set in 1949 for 1961 of two million extra places by another 600,000.[2]

Haste and urgency bred further innovations. Following research by the London and Hertfordshire County Councils, the Nottinghamshire County Council showed how even in areas affected by mining subsidence, schools could be rapidly built from standardised light prefabricated metal and wood classrooms riding on concrete platforms, joined by spring loaded joists enabling buildings to settle without cracks fissuring the structure. On 24 July 1957, the Ministry convened a meeting of authorities affected by subsidence at which the Consortium of Local Authorities Special Programme (C.L.A.S.P.) was launched. C.L.A.S.P. enabled six local authorities to build schools rapidly and well: so well that one of the Nottinghamshire schools won the prize at the Twelfth Milan Triennale. A second consortium, known as S.C.O.L.A. was formed on the initiative of Shropshire. Groups in Yorkshire and Lancashire followed, whilst in October 1960 West Germany adopted the C.L.A.S.P. system for fifteen years.[1]

The sustained high level of the birth-rate elicited, in 1958, a five-year plan for expanding secondary schools, costing £300 million. By 1 February 1959, L.E.A.s had settled details of the first two years of this programme—the first time since the war that this was done so quickly.

The voluntary schools were also called in to help. Their 'aided' schools which had hitherto received only 50% of their costs of maintenance from the state were now offered 75% by the Education Act of 1959 for new secondary schools to accommodate children from their own existing primary schools.

The Roman Catholics planned to raise numbers from 547,000 (in 1960) to 750,000 (in 1970) and established a National Catholic Building Office in Manchester for this purpose. The Church of England, hitherto preoccupied with the stipends of its clergy, was also stimulated by the Act to raise its building programme to £80 million.[2] To provide teachers for these voluntary schools was also necessary, so the government raised the grant to voluntary colleges from 25 to 75%. The voluntary colleges rallied so rapidly that by 1961 they had provided 41% (6,914) of the extra places in that year.

Other targets for the teaching force were raised. That for the secondary schools was raised to 24,000 by 1966, that for technical teachers (set at 700 a year up to 1961 by the Willis Jackson Committee in 1956) was raised to 1,000 a year up to 1963–4. Day training colleges were also set up near the great towns, while the three existing colleges for training technical teachers were rebuilt and enlarged, and supplemented by a fourth in the midlands.[1]

A three-year course was introduced for training colleges. Those having more than 400 students rose from 3 to 56, whilst those with less than 200 students decreased from 77 to 34. The National Advisory Council for the Training and Supply of Teachers forecast in 1962 that the number of teachers in maintained primary and secondary schools (264,000 in 1960) would have to increase to 372,000 by 1980, and, if the school-leaving age was to be raised to 16 and junior school classes reduced to 30, to 496,000.[2] The immediate target for training colleges, set in January 1963, was 80,000 students by 1970.

III

Though no mention of types of secondary school was made in the 1944 Act,[3] most local authorities worked to the tripartite formula allocating pupils to grammar, technical or modern schools on varying systems of selection.

Though the provision of grammar school places varied from 10 to over 40% in England and in parts of Wales reached 60%,[4] the national average was, by 1956, just over 20%. They were the target of ambitious parents. On the day allocation results were published, they sat, as Professor D. V. Glass remarked, 'like King Aegeus . . . on the cliffs, waiting to see if the returning sails are black or white'.[5] A similar nautical metaphor was employed by A. J. P. Taylor, whose advice was 'run away to sea rather than go to a secondary modern'.[6] Non-selection to grammar school at 11 was doubly unfair to working-class children, for not only was it shown largely to depend on social and class factors, but it demanded 'decisions critical for vocational choice' with no possibility of challenge, except transfer at 13+.[1]

It was to anticipate such objections that other schemes for secondary education were adopted. Comprehensive schools were endorsed by the L.C.C. as early as 19 July 1944, and later by Birmingham, Coventry and the West Riding.[2] 'School bases,' embodying grammar, technical and modern schools with separate headmasters but shared facilities on one site were built by Bolton, Derby, Brighton and the Isle of Wight.[3] Bilateral (i.e. grammar-technical or technical-modern) schools were established in the East and North Riding, Barrow-in-Furness and St Helens and Berkshire.[4] Even more experimental were the junior non-selective high schools established from 1956 onwards by Leicestershire, for children whose parents promised to keep them at school until 16 years of age.[5] A junior college was (and is being), actively canvassed by Croydon to cope with the shortage of teachers, the earlier puberty of children and the increasing size of the 15 to 18 age range requiring further education.[6]

The 'tripartheid' system (as it was now nicknamed) was further weakened by socio-medical evidence advanced by researchers like J. W. B. Douglas in The Home and the School (1964), while the election of a Labour government later in the year galvanised most of the 146 local authorities to prepare schemes for comprehensive schools.

Supporters claimed that they would overcome the difficulties associated with early selection, facilitate transfer between courses of study, offer a wider variety of such courses, and enable a more economic use to be made of expensive equipment like laboratories, gymnasia and playing fields.[7] Critics invoked the academic standards of existing grammar schools and the extensive opportunities for leadership available for less able children in secondary modern schools. Faced with two-stream grammar schools which became increasingly uneconomic in rural areas and mounting pressure from parents, local authorities began to adopt the comprehensive principle as much from considerations of expediency as of social justice. And so, whereas in 1956 only two per cent of the school population attended comprehensive schools[1], by 1965 it was said that there were only two types of school: comprehensive and apprehensive.

Apprehensive middle-class parents had long sought out schools in the private sector. Inefficient private schools were, under Part III of the 1944 Act, scheduled to be registered, but that was delayed until 1957. Then, when the axe fell, it was mainly on the inefficient private schools catering for primary children. The private secondary schools were relatively unaffected. The Minister of Education approved of this and told the Conservative Party Conference in October 1961 that children should start their education in similar schools. Some months later, in February 1962, he advised parents who could afford to pay fees to 'consider the long-term future of their children', in a society 'which would either be united socially or be still hampered by the "we" and the "they" complex that so bedevilled industrial relations'.[2]

Preparatory and public schools, on the other hand, built up the longest waiting lists in their history. Covenants, endowment policies and trusts enabled those who desired it to shift the economic burden of paying for their children to the Board of Inland Revenue: in 1960–1 for instance, sums of £400 a year saved some 50–60% in tax. Sometimes capital sums were transferred to these schools, sometimes employers gave educational benefits in cash and kind, sometimes 'charities' were created for the express purpose of paying fees.[3] The schools responded to this surge of applications. Preparatory schools became trusts and limited companies—only 38% were privately owned in 1964 as opposed to 72% in 1939—while public schools, helped by the Federation of British Industries, built better laboratories.

IV

This demand for scientific man-power had been seriously underestimated by two early post-war plans. The Percy Report (1945) envisaged an annual output of 1,500 engineers from technical colleges up to 1955,[4] and the Barlow Report (1946) envisaged the doubling of the output of university trained scientists in ten years.[1] In fact the technical colleges were producing 4,000 engineers by 1955, whilst the universities doubled their output in two, not ten, years.

The overlap between the two types of institution had prompted some members of the Percy Committee to recommend in 1946 that selected technical colleges should be empowered to award degrees, a suggestion opposed by all the universities. Four years later, in 1950, the National Advisory Council on Education for Industry and Commerce recommended that increased financial assistance should be given to the 60 technical colleges providing courses in higher technological education; that new courses, closely associated with industry should be developed in them, and that a Royal College of Technologists should be established to encourage the development of advanced courses at 'first award' and 'post-graduate' levels, by giving suitable awards ('associate-ship' and 'membership') to encourage students to take these courses. This Royal College was neither to teach nor examine, merely to approve and sponsor.[2] These recommendations were accepted by the government in September 1951.[3]

The strain of accommodating over-large enrolments in technical colleges was monitored by the ten regional advisory councils for further education established as a result of the Percy Report. Strange expedients were reported. As one H.M.I. remarked:

> Disused and ancient structures are common. Premises in one place have literally fallen down. In another, the technical institute is established in the railway station offices, and is getting ever nearer to the railway itself. There is now a class in one of the waiting rooms.[4]

For in spite of the increase in grants for capital improvements and maintenance from 60 to 75% to those colleges offering courses in advanced technology, they could not keep up with the quickened pace of technical tertiary training.

The Anglo-American Council on Productivity added their voice to the chorus, stressing that more work study (or 'industrial engineering'), management education and expanded apprenticeship schemes were needed.[1] 'Sandwich courses' (periods of full-time study alternating with work), now became increasingly popular at the higher standards.[2]

When brought to the notice of the Select Committee on Estimates, this caused a stir.[3] Not only were the examples of the U.S.A. and the U.S.S.R. cited, but the needs of the emergent nations of the Commonwealth began to clash with those of native British industries.[4] So the Parliamentary and Scientific Committee recommended that twenty of the large colleges should be empowered to award technological degrees under a co-ordinating council. A full-scale debate took place in the House of Commons on 1 July 1955.

It needed, however, the Advisory Council on Scientific Policy (established in 1947) and its Zuckerman report, issued in September 1955[5] to elicit the famous white paper *Technical Education* in February 1956.[6] This outlined an 'alternative and much broader road' than that afforded by the universities. Advanced course enrolments were to be raised from 9,500 to 15,000 and part-time day-release courses from 355,000 to 710,000. To sustain this, the sluice gates of finance were dramatically raised: £70,000,000, with a further £15,000,000 for equipment, was promised for the period 1956 to 1961. Both local authorities and industry hastened to implement this five-year plan: local authorities by making maintenance grants at university rates available for technical colleges; industry (prompted by B.A.C.I.E.) by making more use of sandwich courses.[7]

Colleges were reclassified as: local (offering varying amounts of work up to the Ordinary National Certificate level); area (offering varying amounts of work up to Higher National Certificate); regional (offering a substantial amount of advanced work in sandwich and full-time courses); or colleges of advanced technology (to concentrate exclusively on advanced work). Of these four, by far the greatest shortage was of the first type.[8]

The colleges of advanced technology were to work for a new graduate-equivalent award—the Diploma in Technology—devised by a National Council under Lord Hives, assisted by two boards of studies. This award was subsequently supplemented by the creation of a post-graduate qualification: Membership of the College of Technologists. Both the Dip. Tech. and the M.C.T. were recognised by the universities.

v

The universities themselves had been caught up in the planning of education. By 1955 two-thirds (as opposed to one-quarter in 1920) of their income[1] was coming directly from the University Grants Committee, which had, nine years earlier, acquired expanded terms of reference enabling it to prepare and execute 'such plans for the development of the universities as may from time to time be required in order to ensure that they are fully adequate to national needs'.

The first indication of the U.G.C.'s new power was given in 1946. Asked by a group in North Staffordshire to finance a university college specialising in the social sciences (including the history of technology), physical chemistry (including mathematics), physics and biology, the U.G.C. demurred, and referred the scheme back to be recast as a four-year curriculum based on a 'Foundation Year' common to the whole student body.[2] The U.G.C. grant list was also extended to include two private university colleges at Hull and Leicester—both subsequently chartered in 1954 and 1957, as were Nottingham (1948), Southampton (1952) and Exeter (1955).

The technique whereby the U.G.C. ensured that the universities were 'fully adequate to national needs' was the quinquennial grant system, reintroduced in 1947. No one, least of all the universities, could complain that it was anxious to force applied science on them. Indeed its *Note on Technology in the University* (1950) was distinctly cautious. Such a caution, however, was dissipated when the Advisory Council on Scientific Policy recommended in 1955 that the annual output of graduate (or equivalent) scientists and engineers should be doubled to 20,000 by 1970. In January 1960 they were further authorised by the Chancellor of the Exchequer to explore the possibility of raising that figure to 170,000 by the early 1970s.

Since such numbers were so far beyond the capacity, existing or contemplated, of existing universities, a rash of projects for new ones erupted. Sussex early set the pace, followed by Norwich and York, Canterbury, Colchester, Coventry and Lancaster.[1] Even this was derided by Sir Geoffrey Crowther, as 'a policy for national decline'.[2]

Though they doubled in size since 1938 and were educating their 110,000 students (less than half those receiving full-time higher education), universities still could not cope with the numbers seeking admission. So a clearing-house was set up to operate in 1963, partly in the hope that it would serve as a crush barrier until other new universities got under way.

That a similar clearing-house had previously been established by the training colleges was but another indication of the increasing measure of common ground between them. For in 1960 the training colleges began to offer three-year courses too which in the Ministry's words were to 'foster an academic and social life in the colleges more akin to that of the universities'. Training college expansion was also officially described as 'roughly equal in terms of places to the provision of eight new universities'.[3]

More common ground was evident between the universities and the colleges of advanced technology, for the Dip. Tech. and the M.C.T. had been recognised by the universities as the respective equivalents of their own bachelors' and masters' degrees.[4] As direct grant institutions, the colleges of advanced technology secured constitutions which, amongst other things, made provision for staff members to serve on their governing bodies.

All three (universities, C.A.T.s and training colleges), were committed to five-year 'plans' for expansion but under different auspices. Whereas the universities were under the aegis of the U.G.C., the C.A.T.s were under the Ministry, and the training colleges under the Ministry, the local authority and the institutes of education. Moreover, since places at all three institutions were now aided (state scholarships being abolished), 'higher education' was becoming a clear-way instead of a series of turnpiked roads.

The nomenclature of the clear-way was, however, so debatable that the Minister of Education agreed on 7 November 1960 that an enquiry into its size and nature ought to be made. This was duly launched, a month later, by the Prime Minister announcing that Lord Robbins would chair a committee which would not only do this, but also offer suggestions (in the light of national needs and resources) as to the principles on which its long-term development should be based.

As everyone 'waited expectantly for Robbins' the Labour party took advantage of some of the evidence that had found its way into print and, in March 1963, called for a ten-year crash programme for expanding higher education to be inaugurated immediately under the Minister of Education and some four or five (growing ultimately to twelve) regional university grants commissions. From existing technical or teacher-training colleges, especially those in economically under-privileged areas, the Labour party report argued that another 45 new universities could be founded, thus bringing by 1983 the total number of universities in England and Wales to 70, at a minimum cost of £30 million a year.[1]

With statistical precision, some seven months later the Robbins Committee recommended two programmes: an emergency expansion to provide places for 328,000 young people by 1968 (an expansion of 50%) and a long term plan to increase them by 1980 to 560,000. Six new universities were to be created immediately, the colleges of advanced technology upgraded, teacher training colleges to be associated with schools of education for degree purposes, and five new Special Institutions for Scientific and Technological Research (SISTERS to the CATS) each with 4,000 students were to be created. The whole programme would mean that there would be 60 universities in 1980–1 as compared to 32 today, and they would provide 60% of the 558,000 places needed in higher education.[2]

VI

The imperative harvest which the Robbins Committee urged the government to reap means that the number of places in higher education by 1980 would have to increase by over 150%. Put in another way it would mean that the percentage of the working population undergoing full-time education would increase from 3·4 to 6·1%.[1]

As the latest and most ambitious exercise in social geodesy, Robbins pointed to the existence of a pool of ability, whose depth and specific gravity had been tentatively explored four years earlier by the Central Advisory Council under Sir Geoffrey Crowther. Whereas Robbins called attention to the need to encourage more girls to read applied science, Crowther considered that 'the richest vein of untapped human resources' lay 'in the middle, between the brightest quarter and the great mass of ordinary children' where 'the deficiencies, relatively to the need, are greatest of all'.[2]

Three forces were identified by the Crowther Committee as affecting the education of the 15–18 age range: the 'bulge', the 'trend', and the 'swing'. The 'bulge' meant that the number of the children aged 15 to 19 having slowly increased from 2,799,000 (in 1950) to 3,021,000 (in 1960) was likely to increase to 3,580,000 (in 1963), 3,396,000 (in 1968) and 3,974,000 (in 1985). The trend (or tendency to stay longer at school), has so far been more than proportionate to the size of the age group.[3] Amongst 17-year-olds the percentage was:

	1950	*1956*	*1959*	*1962*	*1963**	*1980**	*1985**
Boys	7·29	9·41	11·51	13·47	14·05	25·18	28·40
Girls	5·95	8·03	9·16	10·53	10·80	18·00	20·08
Total	6·63	8·73	10·36	12·03	12·15	21·68	24·34

and for 16-year-olds:

	1950	*1956*	*1959*	*1962*	*1963**	*1980**	*1985**
Boys	14·46	18·26	21·59	23·66	25·29	40·69	45·32
Girls	13·60	17·04	19·69	21·14	22·58	34·09	37·58
Total	14·08	17·66	20·66	22·42	23·95	37·48	41·56

* Estimated

The 'swing' to science and mathematics is reflected in 'O' and 'A' level results. Passes in arts subjects at 'O' and 'A' levels between 1950 and 1960 increased by 63·2 and 82·90 (English literature), 84·6 and 95·3 (history) and 91·4 and 57·7% (French); but those in science subjects were of the order of 107·4 and 184·1 (physics) 180·7 and 128·5 (chemistry), 137·8 and 108% (mathematics) respectively.[1]

The Crowther Report, therefore, recommended that the school-leaving age should be raised to 16 by 1968; that, soon after, county colleges should be established for all children up to the age of 17 not already enjoying full-time education; that more sandwich courses should be given and more time allotted for all courses; and that the courses should cease to be a varied collection of plans for mere vocational training and become a coherent national system of practical education.

VII

The traditional horizons of the secondary school were severely limited by examinations which themselves survived from an era of competition for university places. On its reconstitution in 1948, the Secondary Schools Examinations Council stressed the importance of developing 'as rapidly and thoroughly as possible', a system of culmulative record cards and urged the periodic setting of 'objective tests of various kinds' by schools, 'to assist in guiding pupils towards suitable courses of study or types of employment'.[2] To prevent premature specialisation it also recommended that a new General Certificate of Education should be taken at Ordinary level by boys and girls of 16 and at Advanced level when they were 18.

After the new G.C.E. was launched in 1951 by the existing eight university boards, other examining bodies like the City and Guilds of London Institute, the East Midlands Educational Institution, the Union of Lancashire and Cheshire Institutes, the

Royal Society of Arts and the various associations of teachers in technical institutions, associated together to establish a ninth board to examine secondary technical schools and institutions of further education. This board began to operate as the Associated Examining Board in 1953.

So that the new secondary modern schools would enjoy freedom to experiment, the G.C.E. at ordinary level was restricted to boys and girls of 16. But, under pressure from grammar schools, this was relaxed in 1953. So secondary modern schools, realising that occupational changes were demanding more basic mathematics, English and science, leapt at the chance to prove and improve themselves. By 1959 a quarter of them had entered candidates for the G.C.E. 'O' level, and by 1960, a third.[1]

In the latter year a committee of the S.S.E.C. under R. Beloe, formerly the Chief Education Officer for Surrey, proposed that an examination in four or more subjects should be established for those not taking the G.C.E. This was to be run by some twenty regional units on which teachers were represented. After teachers and local authorities had been consulted, the S.S.E.C. endorsed the report, the Minister accepted it, and a research and development group was set up to consider its application. By 1962 schemes for teacher-controlled examinations were actively canvassed.[2] These examinations were planned to come into operation in 1965.

If the C.S.E. was to invest the exit channels of the secondary modern schools described by Sir John Newsom in *Half of our Future* (1963)[2] with some kind of glow, a veritable searchlight was turned on the entry channels by the reconstituted Central Advisory Council under Lady Plowden.[3] Her committee was helped by the increasingly important Curriculum Study Group. This body, formed under D. H. Morrell a year earlier, had begun to apply the operational research techniques found so profitable in the building of schools to what went on inside them. And the merging of the responsibilities for schools on one hand and universities and civil science on the other into the Department of Education and Science on 1 April 1964 indicated that further planning of education as an unending process from 5 to 21 was at last brought within administrative compass.

This administrative compass was strengthened five months later by the establishment of two new central bodies: the Schools Council for the Curriculum and Examinations and the Council for National Academic Awards. The former, superseding the S.S.E.C., was further empowered to review constantly curricula, teaching methods and examinations in primary and secondary schools. The latter, superseding both the National Councils for Technological Awards (established in 1955) and for Art Awards (established in 1961) acquired degree awarding powers in addition.[1] Indeed, the emphasis lay on bringing the examination jungle into some sort of recognisable order, so that the modern pilgrim could progress with as little bewilderment as possible.

Not all problems could be solved by examinations. In December 1964, five years after the Albermarle Report on the Youth Service (which recommended the initiation of a ten year programme to provide for all young people between 14 and 20 under a Youth Service Development Council), an assessment was ordered of the progress in enlisting help for corporate activities and raising the youth leader force to 1,300 by 1966.[2]

By themselves youth leaders could not solve problems posed by occupational adjustment and drift, much less occupational obsolescence. Here 'guidance' and 'counselling' based on objective type tests seemed most promising. And such types of test increasingly commended themselves to examiners, not only as instruments of assessment and prediction, but also as a part of the learning process itself.

VIII

An even greater educational dinosaur overshadowed the schools: the concept of apprenticeship. A survival of the day when servile labour was performed by human energy slaves, it absorbed no less than one-third of the school-leavers in 1959.[3]

Buttressed by trade union policy of confining employment to those who had served a five-year or seven-year period of apprenticeship and enforcing a ratio of apprentices to working men, apprenticeship had been eroded of much significance as the hierarchy of craftsmanship was toppled by electronic controls. Less and less did the prospect of 'fagging' their way through a craftsman's course appeal to intelligent boys. As the 'pool of ability' was progressively tapped by the technical colleges, apprenticeship became not so much an escalator as a cul-de-sac. Crafts themselves tended to become obsolete in an age of rapid technical change. By April 1963 only 28% of boys leaving school obtained apprenticeships, as against 34% of the years before.

Early critics like R. H. Tawney had blamed the class system:

'The organisation of education on lines of social class,' he wrote, 'the hereditary curse of the English educational system, has as one of its effects that those who determine educational policy have rarely themselves attended the schools most directly affected by it or sent their children to them, whilst those who attend such schools have hitherto had least to do with determining educational policy. It tends, therefore, to perpetuate itself.'[1]

After extensive inquiries in 1925–6,[2] and in 1945[3] a Central Youth Executive had been appointed, but progressive post-war 'creaming' of cheap adolescent labour meant that the 351,315 apprentices in Britain in 1951 were vastly different from their pre-war counterparts.

The raising of the school-leaving age to 15 and the sheer cost of training apprentices had also become too great for smaller firms. The West London group of the Engineering Industries Association had, in 1954, invited a firm of Engineering Consultants, Industrial Administration (R and A), to design a scheme on behalf of them all. Such group apprenticeship schemes spread in Greater London and the Midlands. The great increase in the number of students on day-release from 41,500 in 1937 to 417,007 in 1956, and 493,827 in 1961 showed how much more important formal training was becoming.

So the National Joint Advisory Council of the Ministry of Labour and National Service set up a sub-committee in 1956 to consider the whole problem of training young workers in industry. Following its report in 1957 an Industrial Training Council was created in 1958 to keep the recruitment and training of work-people under review.[1] More important was the agreement by representatives both of the trade unions and of industry that the inflexibility of apprenticeship rules should be mitigated. Here they were but echoing an earlier expressed opinion of the Anglo-American Productivity teams which 'wished to commend some of the American practices for consideration in this country'.[2] That commendation was reinforced by Professor Gertrude Williams who considered that 'the present system of recruiting and training young workers for skilled industry is . . . in all essential points . . . exactly the same as the method introduced more than 800 years ago for an entirely different economy'.[3]

So urgent was the problem that the government introduced an Industrial Training Bill on 14 November 1963. After an unopposed second reading it came into force on 12 March 1964, empowering the Ministry of Labour to set up training boards for various branches of industry. The first four boards (construction, engineering, wool textiles and iron and steel) were immediately constituted under a central training council.

Meanwhile a White Paper in 1961 had urged that boys and girls should be encouraged to stay at school until the age of 16 and then go directly to technical colleges (not to evening institutes), where a wide range of new courses for technicians and a two (instead of three) years O.N.C. course would be made available.[4]

In 1962 a national diploma in business studies was inaugurated based on the successful completion of a three-year sandwich (or equivalent full-time) course. For commercial studies were growing on the same pattern as technological ones, since the standard of this new award was 'approaching the standard of a university pass degree'.[5] This was part of the programme recommended by the Advisory Committee on Further Education for Commerce for increasing the number of students released in the day-time for intermediate commercial studies from 20,000 to 50,000 by 1964, as well as for expanding full-time courses in modern languages.[1]

IX

Business studies boomed in business too. Following the staff college practice during the war at Greenwich (Royal Navy), Camberley (Army), Bracknell and Andover (Royal Air Force), and Chesham (for all three), a number of independent staff colleges took shape, notably at Henley in 1947.

In these, traditional teaching methods, like the lecture, were abandoned in favour of various forms of group participation. Small 'syndicates' of from four to twelve students gathered to write reports, undertake case studies, play roles, and 'business games'. Such group participation, it was claimed, enabled eccentricities to be modified by means of 'group decision' techniques, developed decision-taking skills and gave practice in analysing problems. These techniques were also used by universities like Sheffield who operated 'sandwich courses' in management.[2]

These 'staff courses' were not only confined to the training of managers but filtered down to foremen and apprentices. A wide and extensive network of variants sprang up under the auspices of bodies like the British Iron and Steel Federation, whose college at Ashorne Hill trained some 615 managers from 68 companies during the period from 1956 to February 1962.[3]

As these industrial management courses siphoned off likely officials, the Trades Union Congress, as well as some 80 unions, set on foot an enquiry in 1957 which resulted four years later in the T.U.C. approving proposals for disbanding the National Council of Labour Colleges and the Workers' Educational Trade Union Committee. Trained officials became the rule rather than the exception as trade union administration became increasingly sophisticated.[1] So, on 1 January 1963, the Joint Trade Union Education Committee got under way.[2]

The establishment of two post graduate or post-'experience' business schools of high quality patterned on that at Harvard and costing up to £1,000,000 each was recommended in a report issued on 26 November 1963 by a committee under Lord Franks, who had been asked by the National Economic Development Council, the F.B.I. and the British Institute of Management to make the enquiry. These bodies also asked Lord Normanbrook in January 1964 to head a working party to consider the implications of the Franks recommendations, especially with regard to such schools being established at London and Manchester. Similar proposals had been made in October 1963 by the Robbins Committee.

x

An enhanced awareness of economic change in both sides of industry was increasingly diffused by the growth of television. After a major review of sound and broadcasting made by the Beveridge Committee between 1949 and 1951 it was held to be undesirable to leave television in the hands of a single authority. So an Independent Television Authority was established in 1954 as a public body for a period of ten years and began transmitting in 1955. The B.B.C. had restarted its television transmissions six years earlier, in 1949, and from then to 1962 the number of television licences jumped from 14,560 to 11,983,683; increasing by over a million a year after 1953. It looked likely that before long complete coverage of the whole country would be effected. The report of a second official committee under Sir Henry Pilkington appeared in 1962, as a result of which the B.B.C. was promised a second channel in 1964.

An amendment to the 1963 Television Act (which followed the Pilkington Report) empowered the I.T.A. to arrange for educational programmes to be supplied by bodies other than the programme companies. Cambridge University took advantage of this in October by starting a 'Dawn University' (at 7.15 a.m.) in conjunction with the I.T.A. and Anglia T.V., whilst Queen's University, Belfast, were working with Ulster Television to produce 'Midnight oil'.[1] The Labour party even suggested that a 'university of the air' working in conjunction with correspondence schools and area colleges should be established.

XI

The increasing intimacy of the state and science was symbolised by the reorganisation of the Scientific Civil Service in September 1945. Given pay and conditions of employment comparable to those prevailing in universities, the scientists in government service were 'managed' by scientists in that two years later an Advisory Council on Scientific Policy was appointed under the Lord President of the Council. One of its committees was specifically concerned with scientific manpower. A National Research and Development Corporation was set up in 1948, endowed with the royalties from service inventions during the war and materially helped the development of (amongst other things) computers.

All these changes led in 1956 to the D.S.I.R. being placed under a research council and its functions redefined. It was spending over £10 million a year of which £3¾ million were in grants and £6½ million in research establishments. These numbered fifteen and included among them the National Chemical and National Physical laboratories at Teddington, the National Engineering Laboratories at East Kilbride and the Warren Spring Laboratory and Water Pollution Laboratory at Stevenage. In addition it gave £1,650,000 of its money to the Co-operative Research Associations, which by now were obtaining £6½ millions from industry itself.

An Overseas Research Council was established in 1959. This with D.S.I.R., M.R.C., A.R.C. and Nature Conservancy, together with atomic energy establishments and space research, were placed under a newly created Ministry of Science in that year.[2]

Moreover, since the Colonial Office was being progressively liquidated with all the emotional overtones of its title, a Department of Technical Co-operation under the Minister of State was organised in July 1961. The dedication of the best professional minds in England to building up education in the colonial territories was thereby able to continue. Their activities involved the provision of facilities in British institutions for large numbers of Commonwealth students, some 36,000 in the year 1961 alone.[1]

To foster economic growth at home the Chancellor of the Exchequer established in 1962 a National Economic Development Council. This, even more than the Advisory Council on Scientific Policy (established in 1947), will affect educational planning. For as a nutrient of economic growth, education has engrossed an ever-increasing proportion of the gross national product. In 1900 that proportion was one per cent. It has risen from $1\frac{1}{2}$% in 1921 to $2\frac{3}{4}$% in 1938, $3\frac{1}{2}$% in 1955 and $4\frac{1}{2}$% in 1960.[2] To prime economic growth by scientific research a governmental committee under Sir Burke Trend recommended on 30 October 1963 that D.S.I.R. should be broken up into three new research councils: an autonomous Industrial Research and Development Authority; a Science Research Council, and a Natural Resources Research Council. It also recommended that the Ministry of Science be given augmented powers, resources and staff.[3] Since the Advisory Council on Scientific Policy had, on the same day, suggested a Natural Resources Council, and the Robbins Committee a Ministry of Arts and Science, it looked as if higher education was to receive priority over other forms, especially non-selective secondary.

This priority was emphasised by the Robbins Committee's assumption that the raising of the school leaving age could be delayed by a decade and even more by its recommendation that two ministries of education should be established: one for full-time higher education, the other for children at school and in part-time further education. Hence Sir Geoffrey Crowther's advice to the 1963 Campaign for Education—all to 16, half to 18, and one fifth to 21—acquired added importance.

Planning itself now needed planning.

XII

CONCLUSION: CO-ORDINATION & COSTING
1964–1969

I

The group of diners at Windsor have been followed by many others, all determining, in their various ways, the politics and practice of education over the last 400 years.[1] Within the system they have formed and reformed, from the Puritan *classis* of the sixteenth to the 'Heretics' of twentieth-century Cambridge, exerting no mean influence, as we know from fugitive autobiographical references by their members. Outside the system, pressure groups, like the Dissenting Deputies, the Central Society for Education, the National Education League, or the 1963 Campaign for Education have formed; sometimes concerned with particular schools—like the Society for Promoting Christian Knowledge, or with particular subjects—like the Royal Society of Arts, or the British Association—or with particular policies like the National Union of Teachers, or the Headmasters' Conference. If democracy is a state of legalised civil war, groups like these are the contending parties.

A mediating centre for these groups was established in 1964: the Schools Council.[2] Over the first five years of its existence it has become an operational body, mediating new ideas through some 200 teachers' groups. These discuss spreading knowledge of curriculum development work—from French and mathematics in primary schools to sixth form science and technology.

The Schools Council also closely monitors examinations, especially the C.S.E. and the G.C.E. The relationship between these two examinations has become one of its major preoccupations. For since the C.S.E. was first staged in 1965 the number of candidates has nearly tripled from 66,000 to 176,000. The value of the C.S.Es. of the 14 separate boards has to be improved by continuous comparability. The Schools Council's use of aptitude tests, inter-board crossmarking and cross-moderating exercises, and its assembly of a pilot bank of question items, are all part of a long range plan to develop inter-board co-operation.

II

Such inter-board co-operation becomes all the more imperative as schools become more comprehensive under the stimulus of Circular 10/65. Animated by an egalitarian-unitary concept of secondary education, this required local authorities to submit by 12 July 1966, plans for comprehensive education in their areas. These plans were to be for a three-year period from not later than September 1967, together with longer-term developments of the comprehensive idea. To help crystallise planning the circular offered five variant models to the original 11 to 18 unitary comprehensive school. These two-tier models varied between (i) a break for all at 13 or 14, (ii) with only a proportion of the age cohort going on to the senior school at 13, (iii) schools for those wishing to leave school at 15; others for those wishing to stay longer, (iv) sixth form colleges for pupils beyond the age of leaving a comprehensive school ending at 16 or (v) two-tier proper, i.e. a junior high school for 8/9 to 12/13 capped by a senior high for the 12/13 to 18. The intrusion of the age of 16 was due to the intention to raise the school leaving age to this by 1970—an intention postponed in 1968 owing to the deteriorating economic climate.[1]

The impact of the circular was profound. Parental opposition was mobilised. The protection of the law courts was invoked. Local elections were fought on the issue, as to whether the country could afford to 'botch up' schemes when the money for purpose-built schools was virtually unavailable.

Nevertheless by 1968, nearly half (73) of the 168 authorities had either implemented or had schemes approved for implementation, whilst another sixth (27) had schemes implemented or approved for part of their areas. Of the rest, a fifth (34) had submitted schemes, another third (57) had submitted or were reconsidering or preparing schemes. Indeed only five authorities—Bournemouth, Bury, Rutland, Westmorland and Worcester had formally declined to submit any scheme at all.[1]

On 22 December 1965, five months after circular 10/65, a labour Secretary of State for Education and Science appointed a commission to advise on the best way of integrating the public schools with the state system of education. This commission, under Sir John Newsome, was appointed after Circular 10/65 from the same minister had begun to propel local authorities along the road to comprehensive secondary schools.

Reporting in 1968 the Commission found that the schools were a 'divisive influence in society' and recommended that at suitable boarding schools, at least half the places should be made over to assisted pupils needing such education. To work out such schemes, school by school, the Commission suggested that a Boarding School Corporation should be established. The Commission did not entirely exclude proposals for 'catering for gifted children from an early age'. Moreover it recommended that 'a very small number' of public schools should become sixth form colleges, and that one or two might become 'academies', catering for special aptitude in music or the ballet.[2]

III

A worsening economic climate stimulated the unified deployment of resources in higher education as well. For in spite of the recommendation that there should be two ministers of education —one for schools and one for the universities—the government brought all education under one department of state, together with civil science, libraries, sport and the arts.

From its constitution on 1 April 1964, the Department of Education and Science has, for the first time, attempted to orchestrate all stages of national education. For not only has it inherited responsibility for primary and secondary education from the Ministry of Education, but tertiary (college and university) and quaternary (post-graduate) from the Ministry of Science.

Its position in the post-graduate sphere was strengthened by the

Science and Technology Act of 1965, which gave it responsibility for supporting the reorganised research councils and university-based scientific research. To the existing but reorganised four research councils (Agricultural Research, Medical Research, Natural Environment Research and Science Research) was added a fifth with an educational component: the Social Science Research Council (S.S.R.C.). As its name implies this helps a wide number of the social sciences. In addition it has an Educational Research Board and a Committee for the next Thirty Years.

Not only was the University Grants Committee placed under the Department of Education and Science, but its books and records, like those of the universities, were, from January 1968, made accessible for inspection by the Comptroller and Auditor General. His officers will visit every university over the next four years to ensure that money is being spent efficiently. Similar regard for efficiency and economy has led the collective body of all the university vice-chancellors to simplify entry procedures by establishing U.C.C.A. (the Universities Central Council for Admissions) in 1961, to constitute Organisation and Methods studies by groups of universities, to study the use-factor of laboratories and lecture rooms. As one of the vice-chancellors said in 1968 'there will have to be an increase of influence from the centre and a decrease of autarchy at the periphery'.[1]

Though the Robbins Report recommended that in a system of higher education the training colleges should be transferred to the administration of the universities, this was, in fact, rejected, though the colleges obtained their new names—colleges of education—as well as a new status—by being allowed to read for degrees of their local universities. They also obtained new governing bodies as a result of the Weaver Report.[2] The government also pressed ahead with their expansion, equalising schedules of residential accommodation as between them and the universities and other new institutions that now have come into view.

IV

Such new institutions were needed. The Robbins proposal that a Council for National Academic Awards (see p. 252) should be chartered to grant degrees for courses in all fields of study by all patterns was implemented in 1964.

Having lost the C.A.T.S.—which were upgraded to university status—C.N.A.A. looked to the regional colleges of technology. Here Mr Crosland on 27 April 1965, indicating the contours of what he called the 'public sector' of higher education, outlined the shape of institutions to come in the following year, when a White Paper proposed the incorporation of some sixty colleges of technology, building, art and commerce into 'polytechnics'.[1] These were to be institutions with 'closer and more direct links with industry, business and the professions' based on full-time, part-time and sandwich courses of high academic standards and a satisfactory corporate life. By 1968, 30 of these were designated— five in the Inner London Education Authority, one in East and one in North London and the remaining 23 in Birmingham, Brighton, Bristol, Coventry, Rugby, Glamorgan (Treforest), Hatfield (Herts.), Huddersfield, Kingston-on-Thames, Leeds, Leicester, Liverpool, North Lancashire, Manchester, Middlesbrough, Newcastle-upon-Tyne, Nottingham, Oxford, Plymouth, Portsmouth, Sheffield, Staffordshire, Sunderland and Wolverhampton.[2]

The increasing need to co-ordinate university growth with that of polytechnics, colleges of education and other elements in the further education system has prompted the U.G.C. and the Department of Education and Science to take steps to monitor it more effectively, so that overlapping is avoided. Numerous efforts in regional and area collaboration and co-operation in areas of common interest have followed.

Perhaps the greatest common voice in all institutions of higher education is heard from the National Union of Students which has, since 1966, called for a unitary policy in higher education. Their immediate concern has been for a voice in the councils not only of universities, but of other colleges in the higher educational system as well. A series of disturbances in several institutions in 1968 prompted the Committee of Vice-Chancellors and Principals to initiate a series of discussions with the N.U.S. out of which appeared on 7 October 1968 a policy endorsing 'varying degrees of participation of students in the decision-making progress'.

Here, one of the unforeseen stimulants has been the Latey Report,[1] which by recommending that the legal age of majority be lowered to 18, has indirectly endorsed students demands for increased participation.

But such massive expansion of higher education creates further problems in turn as David Reisman indicated:

Education succeeds in emancipating a large proportion of its graduates from provincial roots, only to tie them the more firmly to the big and subtly constricting orbits of corporate, academic, suburban and military organisations. With other graduates, higher education lowers its sights to avoid despair, and, hoping that some culture will rub off on the denizens in four years, often finds that these are only rubbed the wrong way and come out more anti-intellectual than when they went in, and better able to throw their weight around.[2]

Riesman's words had a prophetic ring by 1969 when students in his own country and Britain were in full rebellion against a system which to some of them seemed a soulless capacity-catching machine.

v

Student slogans only emphasise how American England has become. By 1900 75 American subsidiaries or Anglo-American enterprises were in operation in the United Kingdom mainly in engineering and chemical products, with combined capital holdings of nearly 100 million dollars. By 1940 there were 233 concerns with a value of 306 million dollars. By 1955 the amount invested had reached the total of 941 million dollars, and by 1959, 1,607 million. The spurt came after each world war, accelerated by shortages in the United Kingdom and the American desire to take shelter from tariffs.

One result of this was that American industrial research became available to British industry; almost a quarter of the

5,600 million dollars so spent was made directly available to the
United Kingdom, more than the whole of the British Industry
and the Co-operative Research Associations spent annually on
research. As one observer remarked:

In certain cases, too much reliance on the research and development
department of the American concern could well mean that the British
Company refrains from independent research, which in the long run
might have proved more profitable. Alternatively the withdrawal of
U.S. capital may deprive the U.K. of research facilities, which, left
to itself it might otherwise have built up. Then finally, too much
dependency on U.S. research and development knowledge may
result in the demand for pure scientists and technologists being
restrained, and hence in the stifling of initiative and development of
this country's industry in its own right.[1]

Since the very size of these American industrial complexes
depended on constant efficiency exercises like cost-benefit-
analysis, flow-charts and network-analysis: all these were seen
to be equally applicable to England's largest native industry,
education. So were techniques for maximising the efficiency of
the classroom, from programmed learning to team teaching.[2]
And as science education poses problems of size and expense,
English schools and colleges and universities have had to grow,
and, in growing, are finding it necessary to adopt American
type structures like two-tier systems, electives, counselling,
group dynamics, objective tests, and personality inventories.

America in short became an educational and scientific Mecca.

The emigration of British scientists to America was estimated
by the Royal Society to have trebled in ten years and to have
risen in quality as well. Among them were nine Fellows of the
Royal Society, whose departure 'caused difficulties in certain
important fields of scientific research in this country'.[3] As the
Provost of King's College, Cambridge, himself no scientist,
observed, 'Scientists cannot get the equipment, the funds, the
buildings to work in here. Cambridge has the most famous
laboratory in England, but its buildings are out of date.'[4] By

1967, a working group on migration under Dr F. E. Jones showed that the Brain Drain was increasing.[1]

VI

Just as the absconding Etonians of 1563 alarmed the government of Elizabeth I so the 'flight' from science alarmed that of Elizabeth II.

For by 1968 a 'flight' from science became visible to the Committee on Manpower Resources for Science and Technology. One of its groups forecast that the annual flow of science-based sixth-formers into higher education would shrink from 50,000 in 1964 to 31,500 in 1971, and that social science and arts/science students would swell from 54,500 to 76,000 and from 13,000 to 27,000 respectively over the same period.[2]

To arrest this, the group, under Dr F. S. Dainton, suggested that the sixth-form course should be broadened to include three or four main subjects (chosen from science, social studies, arts and their chosen specialism) with mathematics as a desirable addition.

These proposals strengthened the case for mitigating the impact of traditional sixth-form specialisation put forward by the Schools Council in one of its celebrated Working Paper No. 5 (May 1966) on 'Sixth Form Curriculum and Examinations'. This suggested that 'major' and 'minor' courses should be instituted for external examinations, and stimulated a dialogue with another new group—the university-inspired Standing Conference on University Entrance (S.C.U.E.). Out of this dialogue came the suggestion that instead of 'major' and 'minor' subjects, 'A' levels and 'electives' should be offered; 2 'A' levels being taken by the usual method but the 'electives'—up to 4—being based on internal syllabuses and examination with external moderation.

The increasing element of scientific method in modern society has called for the development of ever-more-generalised skills, and even further discredited the tradition of the amateur:

'There is no field of activity in the modern world in which the amateur, however benevolent, can retain his functions as a leader without risking the survival of those who depend upon him,' wrote Harold Laski, 'the gentleman's characteristics are a public danger where all matters where quantitative knowledge, unremitting effort, vivid imagination [and] organised planning are concerned.'[1]

Hitherto, amateur belle-lettrist traditions in higher education have been nourished by conventions of recruitment to, and employment in, the Civil Service. These conventions, recommended the Fulton Committee[2] in 1968, needed revising to afford scientists and other professionals a greater role in policy making and management. The Fulton Committee also recommended that a single grading system replace the present tiered, hierarchised structure.

A similar concern for the better education and employment of manpower had led to the appointment in 1965 of the Committee on Manpower Resources for Science and Technology. This also helped to define the education of those who will succeed the 'amateur'. Beginning with the Dainton recommendations (on the opposite page) for generalised sixth-form courses, it followed with the Swann recommendations for a generalised university course in science and technology. Stressing the importance of incorporating scientific method 'into the very framework of daily thought', one of the members of the Swann Committee said 'this can only be achieved by a new generation of school teachers for whom science is as potent a source of examples for illustration of ordinary affairs as English literature or as the classical authors.[3]

These problems are brought into sharp focus by the computer. Not only is it eroding the pyramid of servile crafts and the hitherto sacrosanct skills of brain and brawn that have determined much of our curriculum, but it is facilitating research and forward planning in education. Indeed the number of places in primary and secondary schools can now be predicted up to seven years ahead by a model designed by the Local Government Operational Research Unit. And, as Alisdair Fairley remarked:

It should not be impossible to use the experience gained with this model to build a national population model, which, taking account of the developing demands of employers, could forecast exactly how schools should aim to qualify their leavers.[1]

VII

Those not catered for by all this need libraries and television. The public libraries were strengthened in 1964 when their improvement was made the direct responsibility of the Secretary of State. The Act, embodying the report of the Roberts Committee[2] and of two subsequent working parties, made them the real cultural foci of the communities they served. It obliged them to acquire annually 250 volumes (of which 90 were to be non-fiction) per 1,000 inhabitants, at least 53 periodicals and at least 3 daily newspapers as the minimum basis of a proper lending and reference service. It also encouraged them to build up loan stocks of recorded music, prints or films.

Linked to The National Lending Library for Science and Technology (established in 1957), and the National Central Library (formed in 1930), as well as to each other by regional bureaux (set up in 1938), libraries could now offer to every inhabitant of the kingdom resources superior to most university libraries.

Not only do existing universities, colleges of education and polytechnics draw on these facilities, but, it is hoped so will the university of the air. The concept, first outlined in 1963, was explored in a White Paper in 1966,[3] and a planning committee was appointed in 1967 to launch it. As at present envisaged, it will begin operations in January 1971.

But we must avoid euphoria. As Sir Charles Snow reminded us:

.... Changes in education will not, by themselves, solve our problems: but without those changes we shall not even realise what the problems are.[4]

VIII

Indeed, the problem of providing 'an alternative form of education for those who had got incurably tired of school and for those whose schools had no sixth form' (as the Crowther

Report put it in 1959)[1] was focused by the announcement in February 1969 that a study of the cost effectiveness of colleges of further education was to be instituted. For these colleges had been growing rapidly since the Crowther Report had argued for 'a fresh start at 16 in a technical college or some quasi-adult institution'.[2]

Three other factors had led to the growth of colleges of further education since 1959. The first was the steady tramp of students to the 'Tech' to take 'A' levels. As monitored in 1966, these accounted for something like 42% of the whole 'A' level entry.[3]

The second was the Industrial Training Act of 1964, which set up some 21 training boards covering 11 million employees. One of these was concerned with engineering and covered three and a half million employees. It has made a big breakthrough, thanks to its annual levy income of £75 million a year by its modular approach to the various craft skills. These modules, five or more authorised units of skill for the six main groups of craft skills, have several advantages. They are admirably adapted for programmes or taped lectures, thereby eliciting active responses from students and providing immediate reinforcement and being available when and where the programme is needed.

The third was the action of the D.E.S. itself recognising the near adult-status of F.E. colleges by making provision in them for student unions. These, by emphasising relaxed, informal collegiate ways of life as opposed to the tensions engendered by school uniform and compulsory games, provided the 'Sixth Form Power' movement with an agenda, just as the 'Student Power' movement of their seniors provided them with a technique for carrying it out.

Argument, whether based on grounds of atmosphere, administrative convenience, or academic viability, intensified as the costly implications of a sixth form for every comprehensive school hove into the l.e.a. balance sheet. To cost was also added concern, concern for the hidden 'selection' which shrewd observers already detected in the all-in comprehensives covering the age range 11–18.[4]

269

NOTES

PAGE I

1 *The Schoolmaster.* The diners were Sir William Cecil (d. 1598), Secretary of State and Chancellor of Cambridge University; Sir William Petre (d. 1572), Secretary of State; Sir John Mason (d. 1664), Dean of Winchester and Chancellor of Oxford University; Nicholas Wotton (d. 1567); Sir Richard Sackville (d. 1566), M.P. for Sussex, Treasurer of the Exchequer; Sir Walter Mildmay (d. 1589), Chancellor of the Exchequer, later founder of Emmanuel College, Cambridge; Walter Haddon (d. 1572), Master of Requests and commissioner for the visitation of Cambridge and Eton; John Astley (d. 1695), Master of the jewel house and a Marian exile; together with Bernard Hampton, Clerk of the Council, Nicasius, and of course, Roger Ascham, Precentor of York.

2 C. H. Garrett, *The Marian Exiles* (1938), 43.

PAGE 2

1 V. J. K. Brook, *A Life of Archbishop Parker* (1962), 127–41.

2 As set forth in this and subsequent orders or injunctions and codified by the Canons of 1604, each teacher had to write out the subscription, add his signature, degree and the place where he intended to teach. From such books of subscription we can obtain a picture of the various schools in any particular area. See, for instance, the *Norwich Subscription Books* edited by an H.M.I., E. H. Carter (1937); Brian Simon, 'Leicestershire Schools 1625–1640', *British Journal of Educational Studies*, III (1954), 42 ff., P. Morgan, *Subscription Books of the Diocese of Worcester* (M.A. thesis, Birmingham, 1952) and W. E. Tate, 'The Episcopal Licensing of Schoolmasters', *Church Quarterly Review*, CLII, 426 ff.

3 Joel Hurstfield, *The Queen's Wards* (1958), 255.

PAGE 3

1 *Early English Text Society. Extra Series* VIII (1869), 1–17.

2 He subsequently emigrated to Holland with his followers, quarrelled with Harrison and returned to England three years later. He 'submitted' to the Bishop of Peterborough and became master of Stamford grammar school in 1581. He died in gaol 40 years later.

PAGE 4

1 A. O. Meyer, *England and the Catholic Church under Queen Elizabeth* (1915); Hubert Chadwick, *St Omers to Stonyhurst* (1962); A. C. F. Beales, *Education under Penalty* (1963).

2 Constantia Maxwell, *A History of Trinity College Dublin 1591–1892* (Dublin, 1946).

1 A. L. Rowse, *The England of Elizabeth* (1951), 498 calls him 'The Dean of educationalists'.

2 W. K. Jordan, *The Charities of London 1480–1660* (1960), 219. Elsewhere (p. 69) he points out that this was almost a fifth of their total gifts to charity. In spite of the criticism levelled against this and his other two books, *Philanthropy in England* (1959) and *The Charities of Rural England* (1961), that he has ignored the price-rise, it does provide a much needed corrective to the views of A. F. Leach, who in *The English Schools at the Reformation* (1896), *Early Yorkshire Schools* (1899–1903), *Early Education in Worcestershire* (1913), *Schools of Medieval England* (1915) and various articles in the *Victoria County History* tended to stress the medieval (and earlier) antiquity of grammar schools, for which he considered Tudor monarchs obtained unjustified credit. Leach himself has been generally criticised by Joan Simon in the *British Journal of Educational Studies* (1955), IV, i, 32–48 and particularly amended by W. E. Tate in *St Anthony's Hall Publication* No. 23 (York, 1963). Tate also criticises Jordan for his 'cavalier treatment of the chantry schools'. By and large, Jordan's interpretation is accepted in this chapter.

1 They included the Grocers' Company School at Stepney (1536), Christ's Hospital (1552), Merchant Taylors' (1560), Westminster (1560), Highgate (1568), St Olave's (1571) and Charterhouse (1611).

2 Jordan, *op. cit.*, 249. Elsewhere (*Philanthropy in England 1480–1660*, London, (1959), 289–90) he points out that £500 would build and endow a school of fair strength; £1,000 was quite sufficient for a school of notable resources.

3 Jordan, *op. cit.*, 67, 68.

4 W. K. Jordan, *The Charities of Rural England* (1961), 300, remarks, of Yorkshire, 'London aside, no county in England provided nearly so large a sum for this worthy and perhaps ultimately the most important of all the cultural institutions provided by private donors.'

1 See Lord Beveridge, *Voluntary Action* (1949), 187–213, for a history of its interpretation; W. K. Jordan, *Philanthropy in England 1480–1660* (1959), 154. P.R.O. *List and Indexes*, No. x (1899). It is significant that Oxford and Cambridge, and their colleges, together with Westminster, Eton and Winchester were exempted from the provisions of the Act.

2 H. C. Porter, *Reformation and Reaction in Tudor Cambridge* (1958), 108.

3 'He was so far carried away with an affection of that new devised discipline as that he thought all churches and congregations for government ecclesiastical, were to be measured and squared by the practice of Geneva.' Quoted by H. C. Porter, *op. cit.*, 88.

PAGE 8

1 William Haller, *The Rise of Puritanism* (New York, 1947), 51. 'After 1603,' as he remarks, 'with the successive checks administered to overt reform on the church, the number of men who devoted themselves to spiritual preaching grew in the next fifty years to be wellnigh legion.'
2 Millicent Burton Rea, *University Representation in England 1604–1690* (1954).

PAGE 9

1 Jocelyn Gibson, 'Cambridge: Nurse of a Nation', *Cambridge Journal*, IV (1951); and for the Puritan influence on grammar schools see S. E. Morison, *The Puritan Pronaos* (New York, 1936), 83–104.
2 F. R. Johnson and Sanford V. Larkey, 'Robert Recorde's Mathematical Teaching and the Anti-Aristotelian Movement', *The Huntington Library Bulletin*, No. 7 (April 1935), 59–87.
3 For Billingsley's Euclid and its source see *American Mathematical Monthly*, LVII (1950), 443–52. He was a Puritan, and probably because of this Queen Elizabeth intervened against him, most unconstitutionally, in the mayoral election in 1596.

PAGE 10

1 F. R. Johnson in *Journal of the History of Ideas*, III (1942), 94–109.
2 F. R. Johnson, *Astronomical Thought in Renaissance England* (Baltimore, The Johns Hopkins Press, 1937), 138 ff.
3 E. G. R. Taylor, *Early Tudor Geography* (1930), 79, calls him the 'technical instructor and adviser' of twelve and probably thirteen major Elizabethan voyagers, including Humphrey Gilbert. His circle included the Hakluyts and Thomas Harriot.
4 See Foster Watson, *The English Grammar Schools to 1660: Their Curriculum and Practice* (1908), and *The Beginnings of the Teaching of Modern Subjects in England* (1909); T. W. Baldwin, *William Shakespeare's Small Latine and Lesse Greek* (Urbana, 1944).

PAGE 11

1 H. M. Curtis, *Oxford and Cambridge in Transition 1558–1642* (1959), 234 ff.
2 *Ibid.*, 241.
3 F. R. Johnson, 'Gresham College: Precursor of the Royal Society', *Journal of the History of Ideas*, I (1940).

PAGE 12

1 For their repeal see T. K. Derry, 'The Repeal of the Apprenticeship Clause of the Statute of Apprentices', *Economic History Review*, III (1931–2), 67–87.

2 G. R. Elton, 'Informing for Profit', *Camb. Hist. Journal*, XI (1954), 149–67; G. Davies, *The Enforcement of English Apprenticeships 1563–1642* (Harvard, 1956); M. W. Beresford, 'The Common Informer, The Penal Statutes and Economic Regulations', *Econ. Hist. Rev.*, X (1957–8), 2nd Series, 221–37; S. T. Bindoff, 'The Making of the Statute of Artificers', *Elizabethan Government and Society: Essays Presented to Sir John Neale* (1961), 56; M. J. Havran, *The Catholics in Caroline England* (1962), 121–33.

3 S. & B. Webb, *English Local Government: English Poor Law History. Part I: The Old Poor Law* (1927), 65–99.

PAGE 13

1 G. M. Young, 'Shakespeare and the Termers', *Proceedings of the British Academy* (1947), 81–99.

PAGE 14

1 F. Smith Fussner, *The Historical Revolution 1580–1640* (1962).

PAGE 16

1 For translation and subsequent editions of his writings (which repay consideration as instancing his popularity), see R. W. Gibson's *Francis Bacon: a bibliography of his work and of Baconianism to the year 1750* (1950).

PAGE 17

1 J. O. Halliwell-Phillipps, *A Collection of letters illustrative of the progress of science in England from the reign of Queen Elizabeth to that of Charles the Second* (1841). Joseph Hall in his *Mundus Alter et Idem* had described a Utopian Academy in 1610.

2 Francis Yates, *A Study of Love's Labour's Lost* (1936).

3 E. M. Portal. 'The Academ Roial of King James I', *Proceedings of the British Academy* (1916), VI, 189–208.

4 G. H. Turnbull, 'Samuel Hartlib's connection with Sir Francis Kynaston's Musaeum Minervae', *Notes and Queries* (1952), CXCVII, 33–7.

PAGE 18

1 J. S. Brewer (ed.), T. Fuller, *Church History* (1845) V, 387.

2 From 1601 to 1640 merchants expended £46,253 on such lectureships as compared to £20,014 between 1580 and 1600. Jordan, *Philanthropy in England* (1959), 300, 312–13, 375.

3 M. H. Curtis, 'The Alienated Intellectuals of Early Stuart England', *Past and Present*, No. 23 (1962), 25–41, calculates that both universities by 1622 were producing 450 graduates a year and 200–250 non-graduates for a total of 10,500 places in churches, cathedrals, colleges and universities.

4 H. A. Parker, 'The Feoffees of Impropriations', *Publications of the Colonial Society of Massachusetts*, XI (1906–7), 263–77; E. W. Kirby, 'The lay feoffees', *Journal of Modern History*, XIV (1942), 1–25; I. M. Calder, 'A Seventeenth Century attempt to purify the Anglican church', *American Historical Review*, LIII (1948), 760–75.

PAGE 19

1 I. Calder, *The Activities of the Puritan Faction of the Church of England 1625–1633* (1957); C. Hill, *Economic Problems of the Church From Archbishop Whitgift to the Long Parliament* (1956), 245–74; Valerie Pearl, *London and the Outbreak of the Puritan Revolution* (Oxford, 1961), 163–8.

2 Foster Watson, *The Beginnings of the Teaching of Modern Subjects in England* (1909), 222 ff.

PAGE 20

1 H. R. Trevor-Roper, 'Three foreigners and the Philosophy of the English Revolution', *Encounter*, February 1960. It is worth noting that John Pell dedicated his *Idea of Mathematics* (1634) to Samuel Hartlib.

2 Foster Watson, 'The State of Education during the Commonwealth', *English Historical Review*, XV, 63–4; R. F. Young, *Comenius in England* (1932), *Comenius in England* (1941); G. H. Turnbull, 'Plans of Comenius for his Stay in England,' *Acta Comeniana*, II, i (Prague, 1958).

PAGE 21

1 'More of Bacon's works were published in 1640–1 than in all the fourteen years since his death.' Christopher Hill, 'The Emergence of Scientific Method,' *The Listener*, LXVII (1962), 985.

2 F. Bussby, 'An Ecclesiastical Seminarie and College General of Learning at Ripon,' *Journal of Ecclesiastical History* (1953), IV, 154–61.

3 M. Creighton, *Carlisle* (1889), 152.

PAGE 22

1 J. Thompson, *The University of Manchester* (1886), 512–16.

2 J. Rushworth, *Historical Collections* (1680), II, iv, 854.

3 G. H. Turnbull, *Dury, Hartlib and Comenius* (1947), 49.

4 H. M. Knox, 'William Petty's Advice to Samuel Hartlib', *British Journal of Educational Studies* (1952–3), I, 131–42.

5 G. H. Turnbull, *op. cit.*, 57–65.

6 C. R. Weld, *History of the Royal Society* (1848), I, 53.

NOTES

PAGE 23

1 John Dury, *A Seasonable Discourse* (1649).
2 *An Humble Motion to the Parliament of England Concerning the Advancement of Learning and Reformation in the Universities*, ed. A. K. Croston (Liverpool, 1953), 27.
3 William Dell, *The Right Reformation of Learning in Schools and Universities* (1650).
4 Emrys Evans, *The University of Wales* (1953).
5 G. H. Turnbull, 'Oliver Cromwell's College at Durham', *Research Review*, (1952), No. 3, 1–7.
6 T. Auden, *Memorials of Old Shropshire* (1906), 233–4.

PAGE 24

1 F. R. Barnett, *Theodore Haak 1605–1690* (The Hague, 1962); Sir H. Hartley (ed.), *Notes and Records of the Royal Society*, XV (1960).
2 Sir Henry Lyons, *The Royal Society 1660–1940* (1942), 8 and Dorothy Stimson, *Scientists and Amateurs* (1949), 46–50.

PAGE 25

1 He was probably the R. H. who 'continued' the *New Atlantis* in a description of a literary and scientific academy which is appended to Solomon's House. See Edmund Freeman, 'A Proposal for an English Academy in 1660', *Modern Language Review*, XIX (1924), 291–300.
2 J. I. Cope and H. W. Jones, *History of the Royal Society by Thomas Sprat* (1959), XXV, 329.

PAGE 27

1 G. R. Cragg, *Puritanism in the Period of the Great Persecution 1660–1688* (1957).

PAGE 28

1 S. E. Morison, *Harvard College in the Seventeenth Century* (1936), I, 249.
2 His *Review* (1704–12) was a forum of general opinion; his *Essay upon Projects* (1697) teems with suggestions on education, pensions, insane asylums and insurance; his *Giving Alms to Charity* (1700) argues that relief merely diverts from one channel to another; and his *Tour thro'* . . . *Great Britain* (1724–7) is a one-man social survey. True Nonconformists (the term now became common) did not suffer this without a struggle. They were encouraged by the case of William Bates in 1670, who was allowed to teach without a bishop's licence because he was appointed by the founder of the school. From this time on their own schools multiplied, freed from the restrictive tradition of foundation deeds.

PAGE 30

1 E. L. Giles, 'John Newton on Education', *Notes and Queries*, CLXXV (1938), 22–4.

PAGE 31

1 N. Hans, 'The Moscow School of Mathematics and Navigation', *The Slavonic and East European Review*, XXIX, 13 (1951), 532–6.
2 J. Arbuthnot, *Essay on the Usefulness of Mathematical Learning* (1709).
3 J. U. Nef, *Rise of the British Coal Industry* (1932), I, 29–30, 123–30.

PAGE 32

1 E. G. R. Taylor, *Mathematical Practitioners in Tudor and Stuart England*, 195.

PAGE 33

1 H. H. Cawthorne, *Journal of Adult Education*, III (1928), 155–66.
2 Bernard Fäy, *Revolution and Freemasonry 1680–1800* (Boston, 1935); F. H. Heinemann, 'John Toland and the Age of Enlightenment', *Review of English Studies*, XXX (1944), 125–46.

PAGE 34

1 Though twice deprived of his mastership (in 1714 and 1733) nobody had the courage to execute the sentence.
2 It remained on the great gate of Trinity until 1797.

PAGE 35

1 R. T. Gunther, *Early Science at Oxford*, III (1925), 292–322.
2 The cost 'did so exhaust the University mony, that no books were bought in severall years after it'.
3 His successor accused him of 'bad morals as ever an M.A. had'. He erected the statue of King Alfred on the gateway of University College, thus fathering a myth on the university which did it no credit.
4 For good contemporary accounts of both universities by three foreigners, see J. E. B. Mayor (ed.), *Cambridge under Queen Anne* (1911).
5 W. W. Rouse Ball, *A History of the Study of Mathematics at Cambridge* (1889), 161.

PAGE 36

1 C. H. Firth, *Modern Languages at Oxford 1724–1929* (1929).
2 J. Sprat, *History of the Royal Society* (1667), 374. A facsimile edition was edited by J. I. Cope and H. W. Jones and published by Routledge and Kegan Paul in 1959. See also Douglas McKie, 'The Origins and Foundation of the Royal Society of London', *Notes and Records of the Royal Society*, XV (1960), 33.

PAGE 37

1 Sprat, *op. cit.*, 374. See also G. R. Cragg, *From Puritanism to the Age of Reason* (1950).
2 Sprat, *op. cit.*, 377.
3 R. F. Jones, *The Seventeenth Century* (Stanford, 1951).
4 Sprat, *op. cit.*, 329.

PAGE 38

1 M. G. Mason, 'How John Locke wrote Some Thoughts Concerning Education', *International Journal of the History of Education* (Ghent, 1961), I, 244–90.
2 Dr Howard-Jones in *Journal of the History of Medicine* (New Haven, 1951), VI, 149–75, K. Dewhurst, *John Locke, Physician and Philosopher* (1963).
3 Bolingbroke, *Works IV*, 164.

PAGE 39

1 K. McLean, *John Locke and English Literature of the Eighteenth Century* (New Haven, 1936), 1.
2 *Essay concerning Human Understanding*, IV, xx, 5.
3 *Ibid.*, I, 15.

PAGE 40

1 Wase sent a questionnaire to the masters of the schools, or the Diocesan registrars, consulted the chantry returns in the Augmentation Office and corresponded with various individuals to obtain a clear picture of the condition of grammar schools. Much of the information he gathered was given to the Bodleian Library by Corpus Christi College in 1934. P. J. Wallis in 'The Wase School Collection', *Bodleian Library Record*, IV (1953), 78–104, thinks that there must have been 'at least 2000 grammar schools' in the seventeenth century. This is a more generous estimate than that of W. A. L. Vincent, *The State and School Education 1640–1660* (1950), who gives 857 in England and Wales.
2 In *Considerations concerning Free Schools* (1678).
3 Wallis, *op. cit.*

PAGE 41

1 L. W. Cowie, *Henry Newman, An American in London* (1956), 94.
2 A Society of informers actually existed who 'were much reviled, but have taken no advantage from their actions, all rewards having being appropriated to the poor.' S. B. Webb, *The History of Liquor Licensing in England* (1903). Ch. 3 and App. gives accounts of such societies.

3 See W. H. G. Armytage, *Heavens Below* (1961), 36, 59 for a fuller discussion of this.

4 As described in an anniversary sermon in 1706 by White Kennett, previously a great opponent of James II's toleration of Catholics and one of the most vigorous historically minded clerics of his day. In his parish of St Botolph's, Aldgate, he founded a school for 40 children. See G. V. Bennett, *White Kennett 1660–1728* (1957), 187. He became Bishop of Peterborough in 1718, a see subsequently occupied by other educationist bishops like William Connor Magee, Spenser Leeson and the present Bishop of London, Dr Stopford.

5 *Transactions of the Congregational Historical Society* (1927), x, 355. An alderman of Newcastle-on-Tyne said that 'charity schools were founded with a view to opposing and defeating the pernicious effects of the seminarie set up by papists in the reign of King James the Second, first began in this kingdom about 1688'. 'Life of Ambrose Barnes,' *Surtees Society* (1867), 454.

PAGE 42

1 E. Lipson, *Economic History* (1941), III, 430–3; Foster Watson, *The Beginnings of the Teaching of Modern Subjects in England* (1909), XLIV.

2 M. G. Mason, 'John Locke's Proposals on Work-house Schools', *Research Review*, IV (Durham, 1962), 8–16.

PAGE 43

1 Today (1963) it is one of the four residential secondary technical schools in the country, others being in Norfolk, Somerset and Wiltshire. Foley's father had twice voyaged to Sweden to learn the secrets of ironworking.

2 Rather less than half of these have survived to our own times as voluntary-aided, or voluntary-controlled schools.

PAGE 44

1 W. E. Tate, 'Church School Finance in the Reign of Queen Anne', *Church Quarterly Review*, CLIX (1958), 59–78.

2 *Fable of the Bees, or Private Vices Public Benefits* with a supplementary essay on *Charity and Charity Schools*, ed. F. B. Kaye (1924).

PAGE 45

1 C. E. Wright, 'Humphrey Wanley: Saxonist and Library Keeper', *Proceedings of the British Academy*, XLVI (1960), 99–129.

2 For his work see L. W. Cowie, *Henry Newman. An American in London* (1956), 73–103.

3 Dorothy Gardiner, *English Girlhood at School* (1929), 308.

4 L. W. Cowie, *op. cit.*, 83.

5 W. K. Lowther Clarke, *A History of the S.P.C.K.* (1959), 38.

PAGE 46

1 M. G. Jones, *The Charity School Movement in the XVIII Century* (1938), 109.
2 W. K. Lowther Clarke, *op. cit.*, 39–40.
3 D. Gardiner, *op. cit.*, 306.
4 W. O. Allen and E. McClure, *Two Hundred Years: The History of the Society for Promoting Christian Knowledge* (1898), 89–93.

PAGE 47

1 F. B. Kaye (ed.), *The Fable of the Bees* (1924), I, 285.
2 *Ibid.*, 271. Earl R. Miner, 'Dr Johnson, Mandeville and Publick Benefits', *Huntington Library Quarterly*, XXI (1958), 159–66.
3 *Ibid.*, II, 178.

PAGE 48

1 He inspired others who will be met in later pages of this book: T. H. Green, who with T. H. Grose, edited his works (1874), T. H. Huxley, who wrote his biography (1879), and L. A. Selby-Bigge who edited the *Treatise* (1888) and the *Inquiries* (1894). For the most suggestive study see Eugene Rotwein, *David Hume—Writings on Economics* (1955), and, for the fullest biography, E. C. Mossner (1954).
2 A. W. Coats, 'Changing Attitudes to Labour in the Mid-Eighteenth Century', *Economic History Review*, XI (1958–9), 35–51, presents a good case for the way in which the doctrine of beneficial luxury stimulated industry.
3 L. Hanson, *The Government and the Press 1695–1763* (1936).

PAGE 49

1 G. A. Cranfield, *The Development of the Provincial Newspaper 1700–1760* (1962), 106, 115, 185, 215, 271. Systematic examination of these advertisements would reveal the existence of many more private schools.

PAGE 50

1 B. L. Manning and Omerod Greenwood, *The Protestant Dissenting Deputies* (1952), 33. N. C. Hunt, *Two Early Political Associations: The Quakers and the Dissenting Deputies in the Age of Sir Robert Walpole* (1961).
2 Author of *Dioptrica Nova* (1692) which commends Locke *On human understanding* (1690), II, Ch. 9.
3 *Philosophical Transactions* (1728), XXXV, 402; R. Niklaus (ed.), *Denis Diderot, Lettres sur les aveugles* (Geneva, 1951), XXIV. D. G. Pritchard, *Education and the Handicapped 1760–1960* (1963) omits him.
4 R. L. Cru, *Diderot as a Disciple of English Thought* (New York, 1913), 155.

PAGE 51

1 *The Microscope made Easy* (1742), 309–10.

2 Isaac Watts, *Works*, v, 263.

3 *Ibid.*, v, 285.

4 A. D. McKillop, 'English Circulating Libraries 1725–50', *Library*, Series 4, XIV (1934), 477–85; H. M. Hamlyn, 'Eighteenth Century Circulating Libraries', *Library*, Series 5, 1 (1946–7), 197–222; F. Beckwith, 'The Eighteenth Century Proprietary Library in England', *Journal of Documentation*, II (1947), 81–98. Leo Lowenthal and M. Fiske, 'The Debate over Art and Popular Culture in Eighteenth–century England', in M. Komarovsky (ed.), *Common Frontiers of the Social Sciences* (Glencoe, 1957).

5 Shenstone found one in George's Coffee House in 1741; Shenstone, *Works*, III (1769), 12. The *Champion* of 10 August 1742 referred to 'a scandalous and low Custom that has lately prevail'd amongst those who keep *Coffee Houses*, of buying *one* of any new book so soon as it is publish'd, and lending it by Turns to such gentlemen to read as frequent their Coffee-House.'

6 The first Methodist chapel was opened in Bristol earlier in the year. In 1760, John Wesley, issuing another edition of his *Primitive Physic*, first published in 1747 and revised in 1755, wrote: 'In this course of time I have likewise had occasion to collect several other Remedies . . . and one, I must aver, from personal knowledge, grounded on a thousand experiments, to be far superior to all the other medicines I have known; I mean *Electricity*. I cannot but entreat all those who are well-wishers of mankind, to make full proof of this. Certainly it comes the nearest to a universal medicine, of any yet known in the world.'

PAGE 52

1 A. Wesley Hill, *John Wesley among the Physicians* (1958), 111–31, agrees with Sir George Newman that this stimulated the personal health movement.

2 R. D. Altick, *The English Common Reader: A Social History of the Mass Reading Public 1800–1900* (Chicago, 1957), 37.

3 Caroline Robbins, *The Eighteenth Century Commonwealthman* (Harvard, 1959), 221–70, 335–77.

4 'Modern scientific utilitarianism is the offspring of Baconism begot upon Puritanism.' R. F. Jones, *Ancients and Moderns, A Study of the Background of the Battle of the Books* (St Louis, Missouri, 1936), 92; R. K. Merton, 'Puritanism, Pietism and Science', *Sociological Review*, XXVIII (1936), 1–30. John Aikin claimed that the Dissenters had been the principal promoters of all plans of public improvement whether by the lectures of itinerant professors in natural philosophy, or by the establishment of public libraries', *Address to the Dissenters* (1790). This thesis is controverted by Lewis S. Feuer, *The Scientific Intellectual* (1963), 1–82.

5 J. W. Ashley-Smith, *The Birth of Modern Education. The Contribution of the Dissenting Academies 1660–1880* (1954), 134.

1 See, for instance, his *Essay on the First Principles of Government* and on the *Nature of Political, Civil and Religious Liberty* (1771), 4–5, and the essay by Carl L. Becker, *The Heavenly City of the Eighteenth Century Philosophers* (New Haven, 1952), 119–68.

2 E. Halévy, *The Genesis of Philosophical Radicalism* (1952). For Hartley's development of the idea of what we would now call conditioned reflexes see Sir W. Langdon-Browne, *Cambridge Medical History* (1946), 65–7.

3 *An Address to the Dissenters on Classical Literature* (1789). Cogan established a school at Walthamstow where amongst others, he had Benjamin Disraeli as a pupil; 'I don't like Disraeli,' he said, 'I could never get him to understand the subjunctive.' M. L. Clarke, *Greek Studies in England 1700–1830* (1945), 223–4.

4 H. McLachlan, *English Education Under the Test Acts* (1931).

5 H. McLachlan, *Warrington Academy* (1943).

1 D. Bogue and J. Bennett, *History of the Dissenters* (1810), III, 265.

2 This was why Priestley was such a keen advocate of the study of history. 'From this source only,' he wrote, 'can be derived all the future improvements in the science of government and [it] cures us of a narrow love of our country.'—*Lectures on History and General Policy, to which is prefixed an essay on a course of liberal education for Civil and Active Life* (1788), 33–4.

3 Priestley, *First Principles of Government* (1771), 54.

1 *Gentleman's Magazine*, 1791, I, 556.

2 H. J. J. Winter, 'Scientific notes from early minutes of the Peterborough Society', *Isis* (1939–40), XXXI, 51–9.

3 Stuart Piggott, *William Stukeley* (1950), XI, described him as 'almost a corporate sum of his contemporaries, with all their achievements, and their intellectual crochets concentrated and magnified in one man'.

4 F. W. Gibb, 'Chemistry in Industry', *Annals of Science*, VIII (1952), 275. This was not the first, for plans to found a 'Chamber of Arts' had been put forward in 1721–2.

5 A. T. Gage, *History of the Linnaean Society of London* (1938), 1–10. Martyn translated Tournefort's works, practised as an apothecary and lectured in London before becoming Professor of Botany at Cambridge in 1732.

PAGE 56

1 F. W. Gibbs, 'Peter Shaw and the Revival of Chemistry', *Annals of Science*, VII (1951), 234.
2 'Some Eighteenth-Century Chemical Societies', *Endeavour*, I (1942), 106.
3 W. K. Wimsatt and F. A. Pottle (ed.), *Boswell for the Defence 1769-1774* (1960), 68.
4 A. Armitage, 'A Naturalist's Vacation. The London Letters of J. C. Fabricius', *Annals of Science*, XIV (1958), 124.
5 G. Chandler, *Liverpool* (1957), 334.
6 W. H. Brindley, 'The Manchester Literary and Philosophic Society', *Journal of the Royal Institute of Chemistry*, LXXIX (1955), 63.

PAGE 57

1 Derek Hudson and K. W. Luckhurst, *The Royal Society of Arts* (1954).

PAGE 58

1 F. W. Gibbs, 'Robert Dossie and the Society of Arts', *Annals of Science*, VII (1952), 149.
2 F. W. Gibbs, 'William Lewis, M.B., F.R.S. (1708-1781)', *Annals of Science*, VIII (1952), 122 and 'A Notebook of William Lewis and Alexander Chisholm,' *op. cit.*, 202.
3 See, for instance, his papers at Chatsworth, Derbyshire, which contain accounts of a tour he made with Charles Blagdon, F.R.S.
4 W. K. Wimsatt and F. A. Pottle (ed.), *Boswell for the Defence 1769-1774* (1960), 74. He was born when Thomas Newcomen was salvaging the mining industry of Cornwall, Staffordshire and Newcastle by the steam pump, and died in the year in which William Murdock first utilised this new energy slave as a means of traction. F. W. Gibbs suggests in *Ambix*, VI (1960), 24-34 that Dr Johnson's first published work was a translation of part of Boerhaave's *Elements of Chemistry* in 1731.
5 Boswell, *Life of Johnson* (ed. Hill and Powell), II, 437, n. 2.

PAGE 59

1 L. P. Pugh, *From Farriery to Veterinary Medicine 1785-1795* (1962), 8-80.
2 For the spread of the steam engine on Tyneside see A. Raistrick, *Transactions of the Newcomen Society*, XVII (1936-7), 131; in the Durham Coalfield, E. Hughes, *Archaeologica Aeliana* (1949), 29; and on Merseyside, J. R. Harris in *Historic Society of Lancashire and Cheshire*, CVI (1955), 109. See also F. W. Gibbs, 'Itinerant Lecturers in Natural Philosophy', *Ambix*, VI (1960), 111-17.

1 Preface to an edition of Ferguson's lectures, which went to a phenomenal number of editions. Those on *Astronomy* went to twelve and *Select Subjects* to nine and were translated into German. They were reissued by C. F. Partington, a mechanics' institute lecturer, in 1825.

2 R. E. Schofield, 'Membership of the Lunar Society of Birmingham', *Annals of Science*, XII (1956), 118, and 'The Industrial Orientation of Science in the Lunar Society of Birmingham', *Isis*, XLVIII (1957), 408. Dr Schofield remarks: 'it is not unreasonable to claim [it] as an informal technological research organisation. Transport, roads, wheels, steam engines, geology, chemistry: all fell within the scope of their inquiries'. Eric Robinson, 'The Lunar Society and the Improvement of Scientific Instruments', *Annals of Science*, 296. Desmond King-Hele, *Erasmus Darwin* (1963).

3 A. and N. Clow, *The Chemical Revolution* (1952), 614.

PAGE 61

1 Eric Robinson, 'The Derby Philosophical Society', *Annals of Science*, IX (1953), 359–67; R. E. Wilson, *Two Hundred Precious Metal Years* (1960), 38, 72. Witt Bowden, *Industrial Society in England towards the end of the Eighteenth Century* (New York, 1925), gives information on other societies.

2 Few could be found to teach Latin and Greek at the salary provided, and since the stipend of a curate barely supported a single man, many curates offered themselves, and sought episcopal licences for non-residence. Particulars of clergy who combined cures with paid teaching can be found in D. McClatchey, *Oxfordshire Clergy 1777–1869. A Study of the Established Church and of the Role of its Clergy in Local Society* (1960), 136–8; J. Lawson, *The Endowed Grammar Schools of East Yorkshire* (1962), 21–6; and Nicholas Hans, *New Trends in Education in the Eighteenth Century* (1951), 211 ff. Hans has unearthed particulars of 243 classical private schools in the eighteenth century who sent people to Oxford and Cambridge, 54 masters of private academies and mathematical schools, 30 girls' schools, 19 writing masters and two co-educational schools.

PAGE 63

1 It is a moot point how much he owed to James Saxnay, his predecessor, the son of a Huguenot refugee. D. C. A. Agnew, *Protestant Exiles from France in the reign of Louis XV* (1866), 247. W. D. Templeman, 'The Life and Work of William Gilpin (1724–1804); Master of the Picturesque and Vicar of Bolding', *Illinois Studies in Language and Literature*, XXIV (Urbana, 1939).

2 C. Wordsworth, *Scholae Academicae* (1877), 76.

PAGE 64

1 R. T. Gunther, *Early Science at Oxford* (1937), xi, 173, 268, 277, 311.

PAGE 65

1 D. A. Winstanley, *Unreformed Cambridge* (1935), 318–30; B. R. Schneider, *Wordsworth's Cambridge Education* (1957), 125 comments: 'It was chiefly through Jebb's urging that the Society for Constitutional Information turned its attention away from petitions to Parliament by county freeholders and towards political education of the population as a whole.'

PAGE 66

1 *Letters* (ed. Lord Mahon, 1892), v, 511.
2 M. L. Clarke, *Greek Studies in England 1700–1830* (1945), 13–14.

PAGE 67

1 M. L. Clarke, *Classical Education in Britain 1800–1900* (1959); J. Lawson, 'An Early Disciple of Locke, John Clarke (1686–1734)', *Research Review* (Durham, 1962), 30–6. He was the uncle by marriage of Robert Raikes, the proprietor of the *Gloucester Journal*.

PAGE 69

1 Bernard Ward, *The Dawn of the Catholic Revival in England (1781–1803)* (1909), II, 69–175; A. C. F. Beales 'The Beginning of Catholic Elementary Education', *Dublin Review*, Oct. 1939, 284–389; H. O. Evenett, *The Catholic Schools of England* (1944); G. A. Beck (ed.), *The English Catholics 1850–1950* (1950); E. I. Watkin, *Catholicism in England. From the Reformation to 1950* (1957), 44.

PAGE 70

1 Also imprisoned during this period was Jeremiah Joy, a tutor (1763–1816) to the children of that scientific enthusiast, the Earl of Stanhope, and secretary of the Unitarian Society. He was a collaborator and friend of Lant Carpenter, another Unitarian and a former tutor at Hackney. Lant opened a boarding-school at Exeter in 1805 and another at Bristol in 1817. Here his pupils included James Heywood, R. N. Phillips and James Martineau. Joyce and Carpenter co-operated in the production of *Systematic Education (1815)*.
2 Some dissenting teachers went into business, or confined their educational work to lecture courses like Dr Warwick, a Unitarian minister in Rotherham who made notable discoveries in the art of fast dyeing. He started a business with his brother-in-law in 1801, and, at the same time began a series of Sunday afternoon lectures on physiology. On leaving the town he under-took similar lectures elsewhere, and went on to invent a microscope.
3 D. Bogue and J. Bennett, *History of the Dissenters from the Revolution in 1688 to 1808* (1812), IV, 308, wrote 'The establishment of a university to

which students of the seminaries of the various denominations may resort
to perfect their education has occupied the attention of dissenters'.
4 M. G. Jones, *Hannah More* (1952), 135.

PAGE 71

1 R. D. Altick, *The English Common Reader. A Social History of the Mass
Reading Public 1800–1900* (Chicago, 1957), 76. Naomi Royde-Smith, *The
State of Mind of Mrs Sherwood* (1946).

PAGE 72

1 Muriel Jaeger, *Before Victoria* (1956).

PAGE 74

1 They spread to Lancashire in 1784 as rescue agencies, undenominational
and managed by a committee on which both Church and Dissent sat. A. P.
Wadsworth, 'The First Manchester Sunday Schools', *Bulletin of the John
Rylands Library*, XXXIII (Manchester), 302. One offshoot of the parochial
Sunday school was established in 1816 in Glasgow by a young merchant
called David Stow, to rescue boys and girls from vagabondage. By 1837 it
had a thousand pupils. It was to serve as a model for Dr Kay, later Sir James
Kay Shuttleworth whom we shall meet in Chapter VI.

PAGE 76

1 Subsequent agitation for their removal led to the tax being reduced in 1836,
and abolished altogether in 1855.

PAGE 77

1 G. L. Phillips, *English Climbing Boys* (Boston, 1949). No less than 126 of
these para-educational societies were founded between 1790 and 1826.
Ford K. Brown, *Fathers of the Victorians* (1961), 334–6.

PAGE 78

1 D. H. Blelloch, 'A Historical Survey of Factory Inspection in Britain',
International Labour Review (1938).

PAGE 81

1 There is a story that in 1813 when the family was going round King's
College, Cambridge, accompanied by a tutor of the college, they mounted
the hundred stairs that led to the roof of the chapel as the organ played an
anthem of Handel's. Not unnaturally, the tutor with pardonable pride asked,
'is not the sound of the organ fine?' 'Yes,' replied Edgeworth, with his eyes
fixed on the roof vaulting, 'the iron was certainly added afterwards.' The

tutor walked patiently up and down the stone platform for three-quarters of an hour while Mr and Mrs Edgeworth examined the defects in the roof, and then turned to Maria and exclaimed, 'Mrs Edgeworth seems to have this taste for mechanics, too!' 'He spoke of it,' wrote Maria, 'as a kind of mania. So I nodded very gravely and added, "Yes, you will find us all tinctured with it, more or less"'; F. V. Barry (ed.), *Maria Edgeworth: Chosen Letters* (1931), 181. Recent biographies include those of Mrs Slade (1937), Isabel C. Clarke (1949) and E. Inglis-Jones (1959).

2 In the year of Waterloo, both *Practical Education* and *Letters for Literary Ladies* (a defence of female education), reached fourth editions. In 1848, the year before she died, she was being republished by William Chambers—of the *Encyclopaedia*—and achieving the real mass popularity that he could give.

PAGE 82

1 R. E. W. Maddison, 'Joseph Priestley and the Birmingham riots', *Notes and Records of the Royal Society*, XII (1956), 101. *The Records of King Edward's School, Birmingham*, v (Publications of the Dugdale Society, Oxford Uuiversity Press, 1963).

PAGE 83

1 Indeed, after five years, Thomas Wright Hill could say: 'I had the unspeakable pleasure to find that my boys could for a whole week conduct the school now larger than ever, without assistance from me. In a few years they will not only have the real power, but from age would be entitled to the public confidence.' Matthew was then 15, Edwin 14 and Rowland 12 years old.

PAGE 85

1 *Remarks on the tendency of certain clauses in A BILL now pending in Parliament to DEGRADE GRAMMAR SCHOOLS, with cursory strictures on the national importance of preserving inviolate the classical discipline prescribed by their founders* (1821). Reprinted in *The Works of Vicesimus Knox* (1824), v, 277–383. It is a sustained and spirited attack on the tradition of Bacon, Milton, Hartlib, Cowley and Locke, which Knox tries valiantly to reinterpret.

2 S. Butler, *Life and Letters of Samuel Butler* (1896), I, ii; D. S. Colman, *Sabrinae Corolla, The Classics at Shrewsbury School under Dr Butler and Dr Kennedy* (1950).

PAGE 87

1 James Mure, *John Anderson, Pioneer of Technical Education* (1950).

2 E. Ironmonger, 'The Royal Institution and the Teaching of Science', *Proceedings of the Royal Institution*, XXVII (1958), 139–58.

3 R. J. Cole, 'Friedrich Accum (1769–1839): A biographical study.' *Annals of Science*, VII (1951), 128.

1 In the National Portrait Gallery there is a painting 'Eminent Men of Science living in the years 1807–8', shown assembled at the Royal Institution. Most of them exploited technological discoveries during the war with France.

2 S. H. Steinberg, *Five Hundred Years of Printing* (1959), 199–201.

3 D. A. Winstanley, *Unreformed Cambridge* (1935), 147.

4 Hugh Thomas, *Sandhurst* (1961).

5 L. P. Pugh, *From Farriery to Veterinary Medicine 1785–1795* (1962).

1 W. H. Illingworth, *A History of the Education of the Blind* (1910); Vernon Barlow, 'The Centenary of Louis Braille', *Journal of the Royal Society of Arts* (1952), 707 ff. Napoleon was largely responsible for bringing trachoma to Europe with his soldiers after the Egyptian campaign.

1 In so far as true paternity is important (for the issue was shortly afterwards smothered in a shower of partisan pamphlets), it is perhaps worth remarking that it had been, in any case, proposed by F. Lanthen before the French National Convention on behalf of the committee of public instruction, as a system of using scholars 'whose intelligence had exhibited the most rapid advance' as assistant teachers.

2 The Madras system was introduced into the Charity School of St Botolph's, Aldgate in 1798 and the Kendal industrial schools the following year.

3 A rise in the birth-rate is now held to have been more responsible for the 100% increase in the population than G. T. Griffith (*Population Problems in the Age of Malthus*, 1926) once considered possible; J. T. Krause, 'Changes in English Fertility and Mortality 1781–1850', *Economic History Review*, 2nd series, XI (1958), 52–70; 'Some Neglected Factors in the English Industrial Revolution', *Journal of Economic History* (New York, 1959), 528–40.

4 Bell advocated a scheme of National Education in 1808 through schools run by the parochial clergy, *Sketch of a National Institution* (1808). Joseph Lancaster told the great naturalist Sir Joseph Banks that religious education in his scheme would be left to the clergy of the Established Church: Warren R. Dawson, *The Banks Letters* (1958), 520.

1 In part III of his *Elements of Tuition* (1815) Bell gave particular suggestions for the application of the Madras method to 'Schools for the Higher Order

of Children'. See also D. Salmon (ed.), *Lancaster's Improvements and Bell's Experiment* (1932); and Isabel McKenzie, *Social Activities of the English Friends* (New York, privately printed, 1935).

PAGE 92

1 R. W. Rich, *The Training of Teachers in England and Wales during the Nineteenth Century* (1935), 1-24.

PAGE 93

1 Such 'conspiracies' were common in Bentham's own lifetime. There were six at Winchester alone in 1770, 1774, 1778, 1793, 1808 and 1818, whilst at Eton Dr Keate, the headmaster from 1800 onwards, wielded his cane to such effect that he passed into legend as a flogger. The influence of Bentham over nineteenth-century administration is held by Dr O. MacDonagh, 'The Nineteenth Century Revolution in Government: A Reappraisal', *The Historical Journal* (1958), 1, 52-67, to have been exaggerated.

2 John Clive, *Scotch Reviewers: The Edinburgh Review 1802-1815* (1957), 21.

PAGE 94

1 Chester New, *The Life of Henry Brougham to 1830* (1961), 198-227. The 44 folio volumes, with digests and index of Lord Brougham's commission containing the origin, donor, property management and existing state of every charity in England and Wales, were issued between 1818 and 1842, and form an invaluable starting point for any scholars wishing to find out particulars of local benefactions for education.

2 John Stuart Mill made this distinction in his articles on 'Bentham' and 'Coleridge', in the *Edinburgh Review*, August 1838 and March 1840 respectively (see *Mill on Bentham and Coleridge*, ed. F. R. Leavis 1950).

3 E. L. Griggs (ed.), *Collected Letters* (1956), II, 589. An earlier version in *Unpublished Letters* (ed. E. L. Griggs) (1932, I, 318) gives 'a fire engine'.

4 A. D. Snyder, *Coleridge on Logic and Learning* (1929).

5 K. Coburn (ed.), *The Notebooks of Samuel Taylor Coleridge* (1957). In his poems he borrowed so freely from Erasmus Darwin, that as Miss Kathleen Coburn has said, 'one can find almost anything one is looking for'. *Notebooks*, 80, II, 130n. 137.

PAGE 95

1 Snyder, *op. cit.*

2 A. D. Snyder, 'Coleridge on Böhme', *P.M.L.A.* (1930), XLV, 617.

3 He aimed at perfecting them in 'the following studies' in order as follows:
   (1) Man as animal: including the complete knowledge of Anatomy, Chemistry, Mechanics and Optics.

(2) Man as an *Intellectual Being:* including the Ancient Metaphysics, the systems of Locke and Hartley—of the Scotch Philosophy and the new Kantian Systems.

(3) Man as a *Religious Being:* including an historic survey of all Religions. *Biographia Literaria* (1847), II, 361–3. As I. A. Richards, *Coleridge on Imagination* (1934), 61, indicates, his opposition to 'associationist' psychology anticipated much that was most fruitful in later psychology.

4 J. D. Campbell, *op. cit.,* 250–1.

5 *Biographia Literaria* (1817), I, 6; C. R. Sanders, *Coleridge and the Broad Church Movement* (Durham, N. Carolina, 1942).

PAGE 96

1 E. L. Griggs (ed.), *Collected Letters of Samuel Taylor Coleridge* (1959), IV, 842. He asked another friend in the following months for more instances 'in which the Legislature had directly, or by immediate consequence, interfered with what is ironically called *"Free Labour"?* (i.e. DARED to prohibit Soul Murder and Infanticide on the part of the Rich, and Self slaughter on that of the Poor)'.

He wrote circulars (three at least) from the Spring Garden Coffee House urging the protection of children.

2 John Colmer, *Coleridge, Critic of Society* (1959).

3 J. E. Gilbert, *Wordsworth's Contribution to Educational Thought* (Nottingham, M. Ed. thesis, 1961).

4 J. H. Rigg, *Modern Anglican Theology* (1857), 32.

PAGE 97

1 K. Smith, *The Malthusian Controversy* (1951); D. V. Glass, *Introduction to Malthus* (1953); H. A. Boner, *Hungry Generations* (1955); D. E. C. Eversley, *Social Theories of Fertility and the Malthusian Debate* (1959).

2 E. Halévy, *Thomas Hodgskin,* trans. A. J. Taylor (1956), 59–87. Dr Ure, the professor at Anderson's institution, from which the Glasgow mechanics seceded, wrote twelve years later in his *Philosophy of Manufactures* (1835) that 'the most perfect manufacture is that which dispenses entirely with manual labour.'

PAGE 98

1 Charles Newman, *The Evolution of Medical Education in the Nineteenth Century* (1957), 56–81; E. M. Brockbank, *The Foundation of Provincial Medical Education in Britain* (1936); O. R. McGregor, 'Social Research and Social Policy in the Nineteenth Century', *British Journal of Sociology,* VIII (1957), 146–57.

2 The Conservatoire des Arts et Métiers in Paris established free public instruction in the industrial arts at the request of Baron Dupin, who had been much impressed by Ure's classes at Glasgow in 1817. After another visit to England in 1824 Dupin returned even more impressed and by 1825 helped to establish such instruction in 59 French towns. He was a professor of mechanics at the Conservatoire des Arts et Métiers, an institution much admired by public figures like Benjamin Heywood (a founder of the Leeds Mechanics' Institute). See A. Audigane, 'Du mouvement intellectuel parmi les populations ouvriers', *Revue des Deux Mondes*, x (1851), 860–93; and M. Tylecote, *The Mechanics' Institutes of Lancashire and Yorkshire before 1851* (1957), 36–9. There were 1,750 mechanics' institutes and variants on them in England by 1884. They had dwindled to 30 by 1951. T. Kelly, *George Birkbeck* (1957), 271 n. 1; P. A. W. Collins, *Dickens and Adult Education* (1962).

PAGE 100

1 Frank Smith, *Life of Sir James Kay Shuttleworth* (1923), 251.

PAGE 101

1 J. F. C. Harrison, *Learning and Living 1790–1960* (1961), 115–16. J. D. Davies, *Phrenology, Fad and Science* (New Haven, 1955).

PAGE 102

1 T. Kelly (ed.), *A Schoolmaster's Notebook* (Chetham Society) VIII, 3rd Series, 1957; A. Black, 'The Owenites and the Halls of Science', *Co-operative Review*, XXIX (1955), 42–3. Other places were Coventry, Bradford, Leeds, Yarmouth, Macclesfield and Radcliffe Bridge.

2 F. Podmore, *Life of Robert Owen* (1923), 497–574.

3 Even the novels of Walter Scott were banned from the mechanics' library at Sheffield in 1823, and when the Mechanics' Institute was formed in 1832 the promoters assured the townsmen that there was 'no danger that the increase of knowledge will cause those who possess it to show want of respect to their superiors or to disobey their masters . . . the best and most orderly servants have invariably been these that received the best education'. The intellectual seduction by socialists of the secretary of the Mechanics' Institute was followed by his expulsion in 1839 for admitting 'subversive' books to the library. The secretary's response was to take a leading part in the establishment of the Hall of Science, where, amongst others, G. J. Holyoake, the great Co-operative pioneer, ran a Pestalozzian school. G. C. Moore Smith, *The Sheffield People's College* (1912); J. Taylor, 'A Nineteenth Century Experiment', *Adult Education*, XI (1938), 151–62.

PAGE 103

1 H. Hale Bellot, *University College London* (1926); F. J. C. Hearnshaw, *A Centenary History of King's College London* (1928).

PAGE 104

1 E. A. Hughes, 'The Bishops and Reform 1831–2', *English Historical Review*, IV (1941), 459–89; C. E. Whiting, *The University of Durham* (1932).

2 He was much impressed by Lorenz Oken's convention of an annual conference of scientists in Germany because it 'exalted science in general estimation'. His observations, published in the *Edinburgh Journal of Science* in 1831 stimulated the editor to suggest that a similar 'Society of British Cultivators of Science' should meet annually in England. From this grew the British Association. O. J. R. Howarth, *The British Association for the Advancement of Science—a Retrospect 1831–1931* (1931).

3 One of its early graduates, Edward Bradley (perhaps better known as Cuthbert Bede), wrote *The Adventures of Mr Verdant Green, an Oxford Freshman* (1853), from which many people obtained quite unjustified opinions of two ancient foundations.

4 T. S. Ashton, *Economic and Social Investigations in Manchester* (1934); E. Fiddes, *Chapters in the History of Owen's College and of Manchester University* (1937).

5 One of its pupils was Joseph Chamberlain; F. W. Felkin, *From Gower Street to Frognal* (1897).

PAGE 105

1 Unfortunately, neither foundation took firm root. The Collegiate School was leased to a tenant whose rent barely covered the interest on the debt incurred in building it, while Wesley College failed as a boarding school and also as an embryo university college. Eighty years later both were amalgamated with the old Sheffield Grammar School to form King Edward VII School.

2 *Quarterly Journal of Education*, IX (1835), 254.

3 He wrote in 1834; S. Butler (ed.), *Life and Letters of Samuel Butler* (1896), II, 96. The editor was his grandson, the author of *Erewhon*.

PAGE 106

1 See for example, 'Schools for the Middle Classes and Commercial Schools of the Church of England', *Educational Magazine*, November 1838.

2 W. E. Gladstone described this in 1861 as 'a perfect mastery of the machinery of philanthropic agitation'; K. E. Kirk, *The Story of the Woodard Schools* (1937), 37.

3 It cost a quarter of a million pounds and was only finished in 1911.

4 Apart from the three mentioned above there were fourteen others: at Abbots Bromley (1874 for girls); Bloxham (taken over from private ownership in 1896); Bognor (taken over from private ownership in 1855); Denstone (1873 for boys); Duncombe Park (1925 for girls, a virtual off-shoot

of Harrogate); Ellesmere (1884 for boys); Harrogate (1912 for girls); Heatherton Park, near Taunton (1922 for girls); Llanfairfechan (1887 and 1922 for girls); Penzance (1889 for girls, taken over from a private owner); Scarborough (1903 for girls); Taunton (bought as a boys' school in 1850); Worksop (1895 for boys). Two ventures floundered: a day grammar school at Dewsbury (1884–99) and a military and engineering school at Leyton (1850–7).

5 H. J. Burgess, *Enterprise in Education* (1958), 69, who comments exuberantly 'Here was the first approach to selective secondary education as the crown of success in the primary stage'.

PAGE 107

1 James Yates, *Notes on Dr Arnold's Principles of Church Reform* (1833). Yates, a secretary of the British Association for the Advancement of Science, had also proposed a wider distribution of educational opportunities in his *Thoughts on the Organisation of Academic Education in England* (1826).

2 *Postscript to Principles of Church Government* (1833), 27.

3 *Principles of Church Reform* (1833). A good edition, edited by M. J. Jackson and J. Rogan was published in 1962.

4 A. P. Stanley, *The Life and Correspondence of Thomas Arnold DD* (6th edn, 1846), 219–20. Arnold felt that the *Penny Magazine* 'should take a more decided tone on matters of religion'. He also objected to its 'ramble scramble character'. So he sent it some 'Christianising' articles. He also resigned from the Senate of the University of London for the same reasons.

PAGE 108

1 Stanley, *op. cit.*, 38, C K. Gloyn, *The Church in the Social Order. A Study of Anglican Social Theory from Coleridge to Maurice* (Pacific University, 1942); O. J. Brose, *Church and Parliament. The Reshaping of the Church of England 1828–1860* (1959).

2 R. J. Campbell, *Life of Arnold* (1927), 203; A. P. Stanley (ed.), *Miscellaneous Works* (1845), 492.

3 Stanley's *Life and Letters* (1844) ran to twelve editions by 1881. It was translated into German by K. Heintz and published at Potsdam in 1847. After Hughes' *Tom Brown's Schooldays* (1857), came biographies by Emma J. Worboise (1859), E. M. Rollo (1859), A. Zinzow (1869), Rose E. Selfe (1869), and J. G. Fitch (1897). An American study by Joshua Bates (1835), a Swedish study by L. Stenback (1851), a German by J. Wuttig (1884), and a Russian by V. Gringmut (1873) show the fascination he held for foreign observers. In this century no less than eight have appeared. J. J. Findlay (1914), Lytton Strachey in *Eminent Victorians* (1918), Arnold Whitridge (1928), R. J. Campbell (1927), N. Wymer (1953), Frances J. Woodward (1954), G. F. Lamb (1959)

and T. W. Bamford (1960). The last, based on much new material, points out that Arnold was bored by lower forms, opposed the entry of local Rugby children and flogged, once at least, mercilessly.

4 Stanley, *op. cit.*, 144.

1 Arnold had learned German and introduced it at Rugby in 1833. He admired Niebuhr, the great German historian. Now Francis Lieber, tutor to Niebuhr's children, was one of the most enthusiastic disciples of Turnvater Jahn, the great German gymnast, and not only accompanied Jahn on a number of his excursions, but spent four months in prison when Jahn was arrested in 1819. After serving with Niebuhr's family from 1822 to 1823, Lieber came to England, where he supported himself by giving private lessons in German. He certainly made an impression on Arnold, who later wrote: 'I was very much pleased with the pamphlet of Dr Lieber about Education, and thought him the more worthy of having had so much intercourse with Niebuhr.' And Arnold certainly seems to have absorbed the gymnastic doctrine. For three years after he was appointed headmaster of Rugby he told the Archbishop of Dublin: 'I have got a gallows at last, and am quite happy; it is like getting a new twenty horse power in my capacities for work. I could laugh like Democritus himself at the notion of my being thought a dangerous person when I hang happily upon my gallows, or make it serve as a target to spear at.' Spearing, in fact, was one of his favourite exercises. 'I used to spear daily,' he told someone else in the same year, 'as the Lydians used to play in the famine, that I may at least steal some portion of the day from thought.'

2 Stanley, *op. cit.*, 472.

3 He said again: 'The Church as it now stands, no human power can save; my fear is, that, if we do not mind, we shall come to the American fashion, and have no provision made for the teaching of Christianity at all.' Campbell, *op. cit.*, 199.

4 As Miss Woodward remarks (*The Doctor's Disciples*, 1954, 32), 'he set them on the road to the City of God but furnished them with no precise itinerary'. Some of them, like A. H. Clough, lost their way. Others, like those who made a cult of athletics, took the wrong turning. And yet others, like C. H. Pearson, saw precipices ahead. Pearson's *National Life and Character. A Forecast* (1873) exhibited great pessimism.

1 For a corrective to much sentimental writing about conditions see R. M. Hartwell, 'The Rising Standard of Living in England', *Economic History Review*, XIII (1960), 397.

PAGE III

1 The language in which these vouchers were written affords a direct commentary on the type of teacher who often wrote them: 'this is to sertify that 1838 thomas Cordingley as atend martha insep school tow hours per day January 6.' M. W. Thomas, *The Early Factory Legislation* (Leigh-on-Sea, 1948), 169.

2 Quoted by G. Ward, 'Education of Factory Child Workers 1833-1850', *Economic History*, III (1935), 119.

PAGE 112

1 Some idea of the change can be gleaned from the figures of those attending schools in eastern England and Yorkshire (as given by Saunders) and northern England and Lancashire (as given by Horner):

Saunders	1843	1846	Horner	1843	1846
National schools	1,547	4,434		596	4,355
Dissenting schools	243	2,272		179	3,231
Factory schools	3,367	3,038		3,155	3,746
	4,159	6,037		2,689	3,908
	9,316	15,781		6,619	15,240

2 One of a group of able Catholics educated at the new Jesuit college of Stonyhurst in Lancashire and at Trinity College Dublin (where religious tests had been relaxed in 1793). J. J. Auchmuty, *Sir Thomas Wyse 1791-1862* (1939), 145-74; R. P. J. Batterberry, in a biography of the same title published at Dublin also in 1939, says that Wyse was influenced by A. R. Blake, a Treasury Remembrancer at Dublin Castle.

3 Wyse's friend, James Simpson founded a similar school in Edinburgh, and J. A. Roebuck, M.P., another at Bath, for which he lost his seat.

4 His work bore fruit when secular colleges were founded not only in Cork but in Galway and Belfast as well. These colleges were also an answer to the agitation for a repeal of the union with Great Britain; T. W. Moody and J. C. Beckett, *Queen's Belfast 1845-1949* (1959). Opened in 1849 with a government grant of £100,000 and sustained by an endowment of £21,000 a year, these colleges were condemned by High Churchmen as 'a gigantic scheme of godless education' and by Catholics as 'dangerous to the faith and morals of the people'; indeed, the Catholics were so determined to have nothing to do with them that they founded their own university in Dublin in 1854 and chose John Henry Newman as rector. Fergal McGrath, *Newman's University, Idea and Reality* (1933); Dwight Culler, *The Imperial Intellect* (New Haven, 1955).

PAGE 113

1 He saw that 'Educational Reform will be the *third great* Reform, the crowning capital of the column of National Regeneration . . . the natural sequence to Church Reform as Church Reform has been to Parliamentary'. J. J. Auchmuty, *Sir Thomas Wyse 1791–1862* (Dublin, 1939), 150.

2 James Murphy, *The Religious Problem in English Education. The Crucial Experiment* (1959), 146–201.

PAGE 114

1 H. M. Pollard, *Pioneers in Popular Education* (1956) described the spread of Pestalozzian ideas in England.

2 R. W. Rich, *The Training of Teachers* (1933), 64.

PAGE 115

1 B. C. Roberts, *Victorian Origins of the British Welfare State* (New Haven, 1960), 152–202, 222–44; Nancy Ball, *Her Majesty's Inspectorate 1839–1849* (1963).

PAGE 116

1 Arvel B. Erickson, *The Public Career of Sir James Graham* (1952), 210–18; J. T. Ward, 'A lost opportunity in British Education, 1843', *Researches and Studies* (Leeds, 1959), xx; *The Factory Movement 1830–1855* (1962).

2 Other societies which ran schools were, in order of foundation: The Home and Colonial School Society (1836); The Wesleyan Education Committee (1840); The London Ragged School Union (1844); The Catholic Poor School Committee (1847); The Church Education Society (1853); The London Committee of British Jews and the various diocesan boards of the Church. Standing outside this framework were the Congregational Board of Education (1843) and Voluntary School Association.

3 'The Catholic Poor Schools Committee', *The Month*, IX, Sept.–Dec. 1876; G. A. Beck (ed.), *The English Catholics 1850–1950* (1950), ch. 13; M. H. Allies, *Life of T. W. Allies* (1907).

4 J. A. Jackson, 'The Irish in Britain', *The Sociological Review* (Keele, 1962), 5–16. In the 1851 census 519,959 Irish were living in England where they comprised 2·9% of the population, and by 1861 there were 610,634, comprising 3%.

5 A. P. Stanley, *The Life and Correspondence of Thomas Arnold DD* (1846), 311.

PAGE 117

1 C. C. Gillispie, *Genesis and Geology* (Cambridge, Mass. 1951).

PAGE 118

1 See C. E. Mallett, *History of the University of Oxford* (1924); D. A. Winstanley, *Early Victorian Cambridge* (1940); Lewis Campbell, *On the Nationalisation of the Old English Universities* (1901), 72–95 and A. I. Tillyard, *A History of University Reform* (1913).

2 The phrase is from D. Hudson and K. W. Luckhurst, *The Royal Society of Arts 1754–1954* (1954), 188.

3 D. Vervynker et E. Dubois, *Histoire des Expositions industrielles depuis 1788 jusqu'à nos jours* (Paris, 1867); 'International Exhibitions and Technical Instruction', *American Journal of Education*, XXI (1871), 29–32; Regnier, *Revue et examen des Expositions nationales et internationales en France et à l'étranger depuis 1798 jusqu'à 1878*, (Paris, 1878).

4 Frank Smith, *A History of English Elementary Education 1760–1902* (1931), 219–25.

PAGE 119

1 J. Bright, J. E. T. Rogers, *Speeches of R. Cobden* (1903), 597. He was greatly influenced by George Combe, with the result that as his biographer says (J. Morley, *Life of Cobden* (1881), I, 94): 'In this intrepid faith in the perfectibility of man and society, Cobden is the only eminent practical statesman that this country has ever possessed.'

2 *Lectures on the Results of the Great Exhibition of 1851* (1852), I, 197. Roger Fulford, *The Prince Consort* (1949), 203–25.

PAGE 120

1 S. E. Maltby, *Manchester and the Movement for National Elementary Education 1800–1870* (1918).

2 G. C. T. Bartley, a former examiner in the Department and later a Conservative M.P. has left a good account of its history in *Schools for the People, the History, Development and Present Working of Each Description of English School for the Industrial and Poorer Classes* (1871), 121–74. See also D. S. L. Cardwell, *The Organisation of Science in England* (1957) and K. J. Fielding, 'Charles Dickens and the Department of Practical Art', *Modern Language Review*, XLVIII (1953), 270–7.

PAGE 121

1 F. E. Foden, 'Popular Science Examinations of the Nineteenth Century', *Journal of the Royal Institute of Chemistry* (1963), 6–9.

2 E. Hughes, 'Civil Service Reform 1853–5', *Public Administration*, XXXII (1954), 27; 'Sir Charles Trevelyan and Civil Service Reform 1853–5', *English Historical Review*, LXIV (1949), 53–88, 206.

PAGE 122

1 See his *Examination of the Province of the State: Or the Outlines of a Practical System for the Extension of National Education* (1847); J. Booth, *Open Letter to Members of the Society of Arts* (1857), 17–35, and D. S. L. Cardwell, *The Organisation of Science in England* (1957), 65.

PAGE 123

1 A. H. D. Acland, *Memoirs and Letters of the Right Honorable Sir Thomas Dyke Acland* (1902), 88, which points out that the idea originated with G. F. Mathison. W. S. Fowler, 'The Origin of the General Certificate', *British Journal of Educational Studies*, VII (1959), 140; John Roach, 'Middle-Class Education and Examination', *ibid.* (1962), 176.

PAGE 124

1 See his address in *Transactions of the National Association for the Promotion of Social Science* (1857), 183–94.

2 The Parliamentary grant had risen from £100,000 in 1846 to £160,000 in 1852, but from now on it increased at a very rapid rate; £260,000 (1853), £263,000 (1854), £396,921 (1855), £451,213 (1856), £541,233 (1857), £663,435 (1858) and £836,920 (1859). The Commission found that there were 58,975 schools in the country with 2,535,462 children. Of these just over 40% were public elementary schools (24,563 containing 1,675,158 children), the rest were private. Of these public schools, all (with the exception of 560 endowed schools containing 35,000 children), enjoyed a state subsidy. Four-fifths of them were connected with the Church of England, 1,131 were British and Colonial, 743 Roman Catholic, 445 Wesleyan and 388 Congregational. In terms of children this meant that 1,250,000 were being educated by the Church, 150,000 by the British and Colonial Societies, 85,000 by the Catholics, 60,000 by the Wesleyan Methodists and 33,000 by the Congregationalists. The Church's predominance even extended to evening schools (1,500 of the 2,000 reported containing 54,000 of the total of 80,000 scholars), and the Sunday schools (with two-thirds of the 33,526 schools and rather less than half of the 2,388,397 children in them).

PAGE 125

1 *Report of the Committee of Council for 1865*, 291.

PAGE 126

1 Asher Tropp, in the *School Teacher* (1957), 80 n. 6, argues that Lowe was the secularist, but Lowe's contemporaries, like the Rev. Francis Close, thought R. R. W. Lingen, the permanent secretary, was the real villain. 'How far is your friend Lingen at the bottom of this,' asked Kay-Shuttleworth,

'He is a secularist and he said the present system worked too well' (Frank Smith, *Life of James Kay-Shuttleworth* (1923), 265). G. S. R. Kitson Clark in *The Making of Victorian England* (1962), 174, suggests that the Newcastle Commission itself was 'probably steered by men in some ways hostile to the system'. See also J. Sullivan, *Educational Work and Thought of R. Lowe* (University of London M.A., 1951). Yet the teaching which the Revised Code was subsequently accused of encouraging had been ridiculed eight years earlier by Charles Dickens in *Hard Times* (1854). Dickens himself later ridiculed the Rousseau-Pestalozzi-Froebel tradition in Mr Barlow, 'an instructive monomaniac' (John Mannering, *Dickens on Education* (Toronto, 1959), 173).

2 R. Lowe, *Middle Class Education, Endowment or Free Trade* (1868), 3, 4.

3 C. A. Mallet, *History of the University of Oxford*, III (1927), 298–332; D. A. Winstanley, *Early Victorian Cambridge* (1950), 148–338.

PAGE 129

1 'In bringing about the appointment of this Commission, Arnold appeared to have played no small part'. W. F. Connell, *The Educational Thought and Influence of Matthew Arnold* (1951), 255.

2 Previously his essay on *Liberty* (1859) and *Representative Government* (1861) had become the text books of Victorian Liberals. See M. St J. Packe, *The Life of John Stuart Mill* (1954). Between 1878 and 1885 Sidney Webb gained no less than forty-one certificates by examination: Janet Beveridge, *An Epic of Clare Market* (1960), 4.

PAGE 132

1 O. R. McGregor, 'The Social Position of Women in England 1850–1914; A Bibliography', *British Journal of Sociology*, VI (1955), 48–60.

2 *Education: Intellectual Moral, Physical* (1861), ed. F. A. Cavenagh (1932), E. Compayré, *Herbert Spencer and Scientific Education*, trans. M. E. Finlay, (1908). For his impact on America see R. Hofstadter, *Social Darwinism and American Thought* (1955), 31–50.

PAGE 133

1 It must be admitted that Spencer was certainly no advertisement for his own philosophy. He himself looked for health so much that his American disciple, Professor Youmans, said that he 'disciplined himself to amusement'. After prolonged literary labours, he had a nervous break-down, and to prevent its recurrence he walked, fished, climbed mountains, skated, rowed and played both rackets and billiards. 'The maxim on which I have acted,' he told his public, 'and the maxim which I have often commended to my friends is—Be a boy as long as you can.' There was almost a ritual adopted

when he was opposed in an argument, for he would finger his pulse and say: 'I must not talk any more.' Nor could he sleep. Year after year he dosed himself with morphia, arguing that opium was a good thing and that his dreams were always rational and pleasant. See his life by D. Duncan (1908) and studies by A. D. White (1897), H. Macpherson (1900), J. A. Thomson (1906) and H. S. R. Eliot (1917).

2 B. D. Corbett, *Annals of the Corinthian Football Club* (1908); F. Wall, *Fifty Years of Football* (1937), H. B. T. Wakelam, *Rugby Football* (1936); P. C. McIntosh, *Physical Education in England since 1800* (1952), 36; J. G. Dixon, P. C. McIntosh, A. D. Munrow, R. E. Willets, *Landmarks in the History of Physical Education* (1957), 185.

3 E. C. Mack and W. H. G. Armytage, *Thomas Hughes* (1952); David Newsome, *Godliness and Good Learning* (1961), 198 ff.

4 *Charles Kingsley: Letters and Memoirs by his Wife* (1881), II, 88. By 1872 he was anxious to appoint professors of Physical Hygiene at Oxford and Cambridge and 'make every young landowner and student of holy orders attend their lectures', *ibid.* II, 292.

PAGE 134

1 G. R. Parkin, *Life and Letters of Edward Thring* (1898).

2 R. J. Mackenzie, *Almond of Loretto* (1905).

PAGE 135

1 A Wesleyan Chapel team formed Aston Villa (1874), St Luke's Church, Blakenhall formed Wolverhampton Wanderers (1877), St Domingo's Sunday school formed Everton (1878) and St Andrew's Sunday school, West Kensington formed Fulham (1880). 'Old boys' of the grammar schools caught the fever. In 1874 the old boys of Blackburn grammar school formed what became the Rovers, whilst ten years later the old boys of Wyggeston school formed Leicester City. The Sunderland and District Teachers A.F.C., formed in 1879, dropped the indications of its professional origin two years later. Later the board school boys were to follow suit. Queen's Park Rangers took shape in 1886 from the Droop Street board school and the Boys' Brigade of St Jude's Church.

2 P. Appleman, W. A. Madden and Michael Wolff (ed.), *Entering an Age of Crisis* (Bloomington, 1959).

3 H. Carter, *The English Temperance Movement, A Study in Objectives* (1933).

4 Temple's contribution was to lead to strong opposition to his consecration as Bishop of Exeter in 1869.

PAGE 137

1 W. F. Connell, *The Educational Thought and Influence of Matthew Arnold* (1950); G. Müller-Schwefe, *Das persönliche Menschenbild Matthew Arnolds*

in der dichterischen Gestaltung (Tübingen, 1955). G. Harrison, 'Matthew Arnold and the Training of Teachers', *Educational Review* (1956), IX, 19–28; W. Robbins, *The Ethical Idealism of Matthew Arnold* (1959), 176–81, synthesises critical opinions on Arnold's religious writings. Two recent studies of his theological position have been microfilmed by University Microfilms, Ann Arbor: D. J. De Laura (Ph.D., Wisconsin, 1960), and C. K. Lenosian (Ph.D., Boston, 1960). D. G. James, *Matthew Arnold and the Decline of English Romanticism* (1961); A. H. Roper, 'The Moral Landscape of Arnold's Poetry,' *P.M.L.A.* (1962), LXXVII, 289–96, and R. H. Super (ed.), *Matthew Arnold: Democratic Education* (Ann Arbor, 1962.).

2 Matthew Arnold, *The Popular Education of France, with notices of that of Holland and Switzerland* (1861), XXIX–XXX. J. H. Raleigh, *Matthew Arnold and American Culture* (Los Angeles, 1961).

PAGE 138

1 The Factory Inspectors did actually take over the administration of the act in 1871. A. H. Robson, *The Education of Children Engaged in Industry in England 1833–1876* (1931); M. W. Thomas, *Young People in Industry 1850–1945* (1945).

PAGE 139

1 *Culture and Anarchy*, ed. J. Dover Wilson (1932), 211.

PAGE 140

1 G. A. N. Lowndes, *The Silent Social Revolution* (1937), 5, 46.

PAGE 141

1 G. R. Parkin, *Life and Letters of Edward Thring* (1898), I, 169, 171. He continued, 'For my part I desire to separate my lot entirely from the fashionable schools, and to cast it in, come weal come woe, with earnest working men and smaller schools.

2 *Op. cit.*, 181.

PAGE 143

1 Francis Adams, *History of the Elementary School Contest in England* (1882), 192–320, together with reports of the National Education League. W. O. Lester Smith, *To Whom do the Schools Belong?* (1943).

PAGE 144

1 John Morley, *The Struggle for National Education* (1873).

PAGE 146

1 Lyulph Stanley, himself an agnostic, had an elder brother who was a Mohammedan, and a younger brother who was chaplain to the Pope.

His brusque caustic directness, abounding energy and complete absence of personal ambition made him a great stimulus to efficiency on the board. Graham Wallas, *Men and Ideas* (1940), 81–5; H. B. Philpot, *London and School. The Story of the School Board 1870–1904* (1904). A number of studies of northern school boards exist, like J. H. Bingham, *The Sheffield School Board* (1949).

2 G. M. Young, *Victorian England: Portrait of an Age* (1960), 117.

PAGE 147

1 Written in 1889, according to the ingenious W. S. Baring-Gould, *Sherlock Holmes* (1962), 259.

PAGE 148

1 The Anglican Church was greatly strengthened by the creation of six new dioceses; St Albans (1875), Truro (1876), Liverpool, Newcastle, Wakefield and Southwell (1878).

2 F. Adams, *History of the Elementary School Contest in England* (1882), 319.

PAGE 149

1 J. McCabe, *Life and Letters of G. J. Holyoake* (1908), II, 177.

PAGE 153

1 T. S. and M. B. Simey, *Charles Booth, Social Scientist* (1961); J. D. Chambers, *The Workshop of the World, British Economic History from 1820–1880* (1961), argues (223) that the progress made by factory and education acts enlarged rather than reduced the hard core of poverty by lessening children's contribution to the family income.

PAGE 155

1 G. P. McEntee, *The Social Catholic Movement in Great Britain* (New York, 1927), 45; C. H. D. Howard, 'The Parnell Manifesto of 21st November, 1885 and the Schools Question', *English Historical Review* (1947), 42–51, and V. A. McClelland *Cardinal Manning* (1962), 84–6.

PAGE 156

1 Asher Tropp, *The School Teachers* (1957), 103–17.

PAGE 157

1 *Nineteenth Century*, XLV (1899), 1023. Between 1851 and 1881 the total population grew from 17,927,600 to 25,974,400, the number of male teachers rose from 28,000 to 51,500 while ministers of religion rose from 30,100 to 43,900. For a wider discussion of the growth of professionalism see H. J. Perkin, 'Middle Class Education and Employment in the Nineteenth Century: A Critical Note', *Economic History Review*, XIV (1961), 128.

PAGE 159

1 *Mind*, II (1877), 877 ff.; G. S. Brett, *A History of Psychology* (1921), III, 297 ff.;
Gardner Murphy, *A Historical Introduction to Modern Psychology* (1949), 389 ff.;
J. Anthrop. Inst. XXL (1891), 32 ff. In 1871 Huxley started a course in Biology
for teachers, 'with a view of converting them into scientific missionaries
to convert the Christian heathens of these islands to the true faith'. Twelve
years earlier he had devised a scheme whereby South Kensington could
become an institute, co-operating with provincial colleges to train teachers;
a scheme he elaborated in 1892. C. Bibby, *T. H. Huxley* (1959), 140–2.
2 C. H. Lake, Headmaster of Oxford House School for Boys in Chelsea
was the founder and secretary to the Education Society in 1875, at which
papers were read and discussed and model lessons were given and criticised.
Dr Sophie Bryant was headmistress of the Camden High School for Girls.
3 The Contagious Diseases Act of 1864 allowed the compulsory examination
in certain towns of any woman suspected by the police of being a prostitute
and, if found diseased, authorised her detention in hospital. In 1865 medical
police were to examine prostitutes periodically.

PAGE 160

1 For a good bibliography of this movement see O. R. McGregor, 'The
Social Position of Women in England 1850–1914: A Bibliography', *The
British Journal of Sociology*, VI (1958), 48–60; W. C. R. Hicks, *Lady Barn House
and the work of W. H. Herford* (1936).

PAGE 161

1 T. Kelly, *Outside the Walls* (1950), 26; *A History of Adult Education in Great
Britain* (1962), 219–27.

PAGE 163

1 R. R. W. Lingen was succeeded by Sandford in 1870. Sandford held office
till 1884 and was in turn succeeded by Patrick Cumin, who had been
private secretary to W. E. Forster during the critical years 1868 to 1870.
Cumin was in turn succeeded in 1890 by Sir George Kekewich, who held
office till 1902. See *Bulletin of the John Rylands Library*, XXX (1947), 271–7;
XXXI (1948), 110–19.
2 In addition to the good short account in the *Report of the Board of Education
for 1922–3* there are a number of biographical studies in John Leese's
Personalities and Power in English Education (1950), 45–147.

PAGE 164

1 Jowett's introduction of the study of the German philosopher Hegel to
Oxford did much to influence the growth of idealist philosophy, with its

emphasis on the emancipating power of the state. Sir Geoffrey Faber, *Jowett, a portrait with background* (1957), 181–3.

PAGE 166

1 George Haines, 'German Influence upon Scientific Instruction in England 1867–87', *Victorian Studies* I, 230 (Bloomington, Indiana), 1958. *German Influence upon English Education and Science 1800–66*, New London, Connecticut, 1957.

2 *Nature*, II (1870), 25.

3 8th Report, 45.

4 H. B. Charlton, *Portrait of a University* (1951), 54: 'It was largely through Roscoe . . . that experimental science became the motive force by which the British idea of a university was revolutionized.'

PAGE 167

1 A. Wood, *The Cavendish Laboratory* (1946). Laboratories followed thick and fast. The Clarendon (Oxford) and Jodrell (Kew) were two of many established in these years. A biology laboratory was built for T. H. Huxley at South Kensington. The younger generation, represented by E. Ray Lankester, who became director of the Marine Biological Station at Plymouth in 1887, carried on this strong German tradition. A former student at Heidelberg and Bonn, he was instrumental in establishing the first state department to finance scientific work: the Department of Scientific and Industrial Research, which began operating in 1916, at the height, need one say it, of a war with Germany. D. S. L. Cardwell, *The Organisation of Science in England* (1957) argues that it was the production of scientists in England which created an appetite for them in industry. H. J. Habbakuk, *American and British Technology in the Nineteenth Century* (1962), 216, holds that there is not much force in the argument that the English entrepreneur in this period was hampered by the absence of the scientific skills required by the new technological developments.

PAGE 168

1 V. H. H. Green, *Oxford Common Room* (1957), points out (248) that Pattison wished to merge Merton and Corpus Christi colleges for the study of science: Diderik Roll-Hansen, *The Academy 1869–1879, Victorian Intellectuals in Revolt* (Copenhagen, 1957), 77–9.

PAGE 169

1 Matthew Arnold, *Higher Schools and Universities in Germany* (1874).

2 The soul, according to Herbart, was not endowed with faculties, but was an arena for presentations from without. He stressed the importance of

presentation in teaching by four steps—clearness (isolating the concept), association (connecting it with related concepts), system (arranging these in a system of relationships) and method (perfecting the relationships). His ideas were popularised in this country by John Adams (1897) and F. H. Hayward (1902, 1903, and 1907) as well as by the Felkins. His demonstration school at Königsberg, which lasted from 1809 to 1833, coupled with his desire to apply quantitative methods to education, influenced the movement towards educational measurement.

3 A. H. D. Acland and H. Llewellyn Smith (ed.), *Studies in Secondary Education* (1892).

PAGE 170

1 T. H. Green, *Principles of Political Obligation* (1886). He figures as Mr Gray in Mrs Humphry Ward's *Robert Elsmere*.

PAGE 174

1 Edited by Bernard Shaw, it sold some 46,000 copies in a very short space of time. See Louis Simon, *Shaw on Education* (New York, 1956).

2 E. R. Pease, *The History of the Fabian Society* (1916); M. Cole (ed.), *The Webbs and Their Work* (1949). E. J. T. Brennan, *The Influence of Sidney and Beatrice Webb on English Education* (M. A. Sheffield, 1959); T. S. Simey, 'The Webbs' contribution to Sociology', *British Journal of Sociology*, XII (1961); A. V. Judges, 'The Educational Influence of the Webbs', *British Journal of Educational Studies* (1961), 33–88.

PAGE 175

1 Beatrice Webb, *Our Partnership*, ed. Barbara Drake and M. I. Cole (1948), 76–102; Brennan, *op. cit.*, 92. A. M. McBriar, *Fabian Socialism and English Politics 1884–1914* (1962), 212, considers it 'altogether more probable that Webb was not a prime initiator' of the idea that education should be administered by the new county authorities, 'but that he was gradually convinced of the need for it by the Royal Commission on Secondary Education of 1894–5, by his practical experience of the difficulties of divided control, and by the arguments of the Education officials at Whitehall.'

PAGE 176

1 I have to thank Sir Richard Acland for permission to quote this and subsequent extracts from the unpublished diaries of his grandfather.

PAGE 180

1 Lyulph Stanley, 'Reopening the Education Settlement of 1870', *Nineteenth Century*, XXXVIII (1895), 915–30.

2 B. M. Allen, *William Garnett* (1933), 66.

PAGE 181

1 *Our Partnership* (1948), 133.

PAGE 183

1 B. M. Allen, *Sir Robert Morant* (1934), 125-6.

PAGE 185

1 For an exhaustive account see E. J. R. Eaglesham, *From School Board to Local Authority* (1956); and 'Planning the Education Bill of 1902', *British Journal of Educational Studies*, IX (1960), 3-24; John Graves, *Policy and Progress in Secondary Education 1902-42* (1943).

PAGE 186

1 Julian Amery, *Life of Joseph Chamberlain*, IV (1951), 479. It is perhaps significant that Bernard Shaw stood (unsuccessfully) for the L.C.C. as an advocate of rate aid for voluntary schools, arguing that their improvement was essential. St John Ervine, *Bernard Shaw* (1956), 369-71.
2 *Report of the Committee of Council* 1895-6.

PAGE 187

1 Olive L. Banks, 'Morant and the Secondary School Regulations of 1904', *British Journal of Educational Studies*, III (1954), 33-41. Her *Parity and Prestige in English Secondary Education* (1955) also includes a good bibliography.
2 Lynda Grier, *Achievement in Education* (1952), 92-114. Sadler helped nine counties, six urban and three rural authorities to draft proposals to the board to remodel their secondary schools. They included Sheffield, Birkenhead, Huddersfield, Liverpool, Newcastle-upon-Tyne, Exeter, Hampshire, Derbyshire and Sussex. For a more intimate picture see Michael Sadler, *Michael Ernest Sadler* (1949); and for a corrective to these D. N. Chester, 'Robert Morant and Michael Sadler', *Public Administration*, XXVIII (1950), 109-16.

PAGE 188

1 To provide them with a perspective, Foster Watson wrote his still valuable book, *The Beginnings of the Teaching of Modern Subjects in England* (1909).

PAGE 189

1 Its members were Sir John Lubbock, Sir Henry Roscoe, J. Percival, G. F. Browne, R. C. C. Mowbray and Henry Oakely. A. W. Chapman, *The Story of a Modern University* (1955), 44-67.
2 Section A, *British Association* (1891), Cardiff.

PAGE 190

1 T. M. Lockyer, *Life and Work of Sir Norman Lockyer* (1928), 184–93; see also Joseph Chamberlain in *The Times*, 6 November 1902.

PAGE 191

1 J. F. Lockwood, 'Haldane and Education', *Public Administration* (1957), xxv, 234. Dudley Sommer, *Haldane of Cloan* (1960), 95–109.

PAGE 192

1 J. A. Petch, *Fifty Years of Examining. The Joint Matriculation Board 1903–1953* (1953). Seven such boards were in existence by 1911.
2 W. Pitcht, *Toynbee Hall and the Settlement Movement* (1914); J. A. R. Pimlott, *Toynbee Hall* (1935).

PAGE 193

1 T. H. Huxley, *Social Diseases and Worse Remedies: Letters to 'The Times' on Mr Booth's Scheme* (1891).
2 Fredrick Marquis, a former pupil of the Ardwick Higher Grade School, went on to Manchester University to read science. He worked in the Ancoats settlement there. In succession he taught mathematics at Burnley Grammar School, then went on to be assistant secretary of the Co-operative Holidays Association. *Memoirs of the Rt Hon. the Earl of Woolton* (1959), 1–38.
3 She illustrates the Conservative nature of the movement. Grand-daughter of Dr Thomas Arnold of Rugby, she was also the founder of the National Anti-Suffrage League (1908) and looked to a joint council of Women Social Workers and M.P.s to bring the feminine point of view in front of Parliament.

PAGE 194

1 Mary Stocks, *The Workers' Educational Association: The First Fifty Years* (1953).
2 See also its journal, the *Highway*, first issued in 1908. One of those thrown up by the W.E.A. was A. P. Wadsworth, late editor of the *Manchester Guardian*.

PAGE 195

1 Its American founder, Bishop J. H. Vincent, had written for the *Contemporary Review* of 1887 of which Paton was a consulting editor, an article entitled 'Chautauqua a popular university.' For recent histories see those by J. L Hurlbut, *The Story of Chautauqua* (New York, 1921); V. and R. Ormond Case, *We called it Culture* (New York, 1948).

2 *The Story of Ruskin College Oxford* (1952).

3 *Special Reports on Education Subjects* (H.M.S.O., 1902), II, 419–32.

PAGE 196

1 Lionel W. Fox, *The English Prison and Borstal Systems* (1952), 332.

2 R. H. Heindel, *The American Impact on Great Britain* (Philadelphia, 1940), 273–98.

PAGE 197

1 Published in 1904 it was followed by A. Edmund Spencer, *Random Notes on the Mosely Education Commission*. Extracts of it were reprinted in *Annual Report of the Department of Interior for 1905* (Washington, 1907), 11–39.

2 *The Problem of Agricultural Education in America and England* (1910).

PAGE 199

1 H. G. Wells, *The Story of a Great Schoolmaster* (1924), 74.

2 *Sanderson of Oundle* (1923), 137.

3 Cecil Reddie, *Abbotsholme* (1900); B. M. Ward, *Reddie of Abbotsholme* (1934).

4 J. H. Badley, *Bedales. A Pioneer School* (1923). He points out that E. J. Swift's book *Mankind in the Making* (1908) outlines the 'laboratory' or 'project' method before Miss Parkhurst took it up.

PAGE 200

1 Demolins so much admired the individualism generated in British schools that he published *À quoi tient la supériorité des Anglo-Saxons?* (1897) which was subsequently translated into English and the subject of much comment. For the colourful life of Alexander Devine, the founder of Clayesmore, see Frank Whitbourne, *Lex* (1937).

2 Cyril Norwood and A. H. Hope, *The Higher Education of Boys in England* (1909), 155–97.

3 C. F. G. Masterman, *The Condition of England* (1909), 83. Lord Hugh le Cecil confessed in *The Times*, 7 January 1907, that churchmen were 'keenly afraid of some form of decay of the religious habit'.

4 W. Warren Wagner, *H. G. Wells and the World State* (New Haven, 1961).

PAGE 201

1 For a detailed history see Benjamin Sacks, *The Religious Issues in the State Schools of England and Wales 1902–1914* (Albuquerque, 1961). Birrell did, however, succeed in settling the vexed question of the Irish universities by establishing in 1908 the Queen's University of Belfast as well as the National University of Ireland. The latter comprising a new University College in Dublin, and the two previous Queen's University Colleges at Cork and Galway, gave the majority of the Irish what they wanted.

2 B. J. Rowntree, *Poverty. A Study of Town Life* (1901), 86; Major-General Maurice, *Contemporary Review*, LXXXIII, 52.

3 Cd. 2175, 91.

PAGE 202

1 F. le Gros Clark, *Social History of the School Meals Service* (National Council of Social Service, 1948).

2 S. and V. Leff, *The School Health Service* (1959), 43; Mary Fels, *The Life of Joseph Fels* (New York, 1940), 164-9; Margaret McMillan, *The Life of Rachel McMillan* (1927), 109-17 and Albert Mansbridge, *Margaret McMillan* (1932), 61-72, and other biographies by W. D'A. Cresswell (1948), and G. A. N. Lowndes (1960).

3 Sir George Newman, *The Building of a Nation's Health* (1939), 183-220, for a good account of the school medical service.

PAGE 203

1 Albert Mansbridge, *Life of Margaret McMillan*, 70. For the correspondence see *The Times*, 10 January, 22, 23, 24, 25 and 27 March, 10, 19, 20, 22, 25 and 26 April and 16 May 1911; J. Leese, *Personalities and Power in English Education* (1950), 251-7. E. L. Edmonds, *The School Inspector* (1962), 144-50.

PAGE 204

1 Men like Graham Balfour, Director of Education for Staffordshire from 1903 to 1926. A cousin of Robert Louis Stevenson, and author of a standard work on the educational system of England and Wales that is still valuable, he was described by Sir Charles Grant Robertson as the most notable director of education in Great Britain. For to him education was a 'second religion' and under him Staffordshire was the first to organise day-school gardens (1904) and rural county libraries (1916).

2 L. A. Selby-Bigge, *The Board of Education* (1934), 212. Selby-Bigge's successors, men like Sir Aubrey Symonds (1925-31), Sir Henry Pelham (1931-7) and Sir Maurice Holmes (1937-45), carried on the tradition. The last-named was the son of Edmond Holmes, who was an enthusiastic admirer of Bernard Shaw on whom he was something of an authority.

3 *Ibid.*, 212.

4 Cmd 9230, Ch. 8, sect. 17.

5 Soon afterwards committees on the Place of Natural Science (1918), Modern Languages (1918), Classics (1921) and English (1921) in the curriculum reported, whose conclusions the board tried to synthesise in circular 1294 of 1922.

6 Cd 6004 (1911). In 27 aided secondary schools in Lancashire, for example, containing 3,200 pupils, 26 different examinations were taken in a single year. Each pupil might take five, six or seven external examinations in the course of his or her school life.

7 Circular 1034 of March 1918, but the Spens Report (1938) remarked: 'it has been widely felt that the examination is affecting, and often adversely, not only courses of study and methods of instruction, but also the physical health and mental outlook of children in ways which were certainly never contemplated by those who framed the original regulations.' (p. 256) 'We believe,' it went on, 'that this criticism contains much substance.' It considered its discontinuance as a matriculation operation as 'imperatively necessary,' wished to discourage specialisation and advocated a simple test in the use and understanding of the English language as a necessary qualification for obtaining a school certificate. (pp. 260–4)

PAGE 205

1 See his *Distribution of Educational Abilities* (1917), *Mental and Scholastic Tests* (1921), *Handbook of Tests* (1923) and *The Young Delinquent* (1924). In the latter year he became Professor of Education in the University of London, which he relinquished in 1931 to become Professor of Psychology.

PAGE 207

1 Kenneth Lindsay, *Social Progress and Educational Waste, Being a Study of the 'Free Place' and Scholarship System* (1926).
2 *Ibid.*, 5.

PAGE 208

1 He was the author of *Secondary Education for All* (1924) and his ideas can be seen in various stages of the Hadow Report.

PAGE 209

1 See, for instance, his *Modern School Buildings* (1902) and article in *Year Book of Education for 1933*, 329, 11 November 1941.
2 C. G. Stillman and R. Castle Cleary, *The Modern School* (1949), 17.

PAGE 210

1 Lord Rowallan (ed.), *Scouting for Boys* (1960), 290.

PAGE 211

1 Leslie Paul, *Angry Young Man* (1950); Evans, *Woodcraft and World Service* (1930).
2 Oliver Coburn, *Youth Hostel Story* (1950).

PAGE 212

1 A. E. Morgan, *The Needs of Youth* (1939).
2 J. MacAlister Brew, *Youth and Youth Groups* (1957), 115–44.

L

PAGE 213

1 The Royal Navy's Dockyard schools set a pattern for the services in 1843 at Portsmouth, Devonport, Chatham, Sheerness and Rosyth, followed by the Army in 1857. The firm of Mather and Platt in Manchester set the pattern for industry in 1871. *The Report of the Royal Commission on Labour* (1894, c. 7421) considered them instruments for improving adaptability and three years later the Webbs (*Industrial Democracy*, 1897, II, 769) wished to make them compulsory.

2 *Report on the Attendance, Compulsory or Otherwise at Continuation Schools* (under A. H. D. Acland), Cmd 4757 and 4758 (1909). It was for this committee that R. H. Tawney conducted an enquiry to show that new developments in industry were increasing the blind-alley occupations of boys and girls. Its recommendation was echoed by an *Interdepartmental Committee on Partial Exemption from School Attendance* (1909) and the minority *Report of the Royal Commission on the Poor Laws* (1910).

3 *Juvenile Education in Relation to Employment after the War*, Cd 8374 (1916), Cd 8512 and 8577 (1917).

4 P. I. Kitchin, *From Learning to Earning* (1944).

5 There were 72 in 1926 and by 1939 there were 42,000 students in continuation schools. *Balfour Committee on Industry and Trade* in its third volume, *Factors in Industrial and Commercial Efficiency* (1927), pointed out that the growing complexity of industrial trade processes had removed trade training from the workshop to the school. Its *Final Report* (1929), 218 observed 'before British industries taken as a whole can hope to reap from scientific research the full advantage which it appears to yield to some of their most formidable trade rivals, nothing less than a revolution is needed in their general outlook on science'.

6 H. Morris, *The Village College* (1924); H. C. Dent, *The Countryman's College* (1943).

PAGE 214

1 V. A. Bell, *Junior Instruction Centres and their Future; A Report to the Carnegie United Kingdom Trust* (1934), 77; W. Howarth, *The New Junior Instruction Centre* (1936).

PAGE 215

1 F. J. Gillman, *The Workers and Education* (1916); A. J. Allaway, *The Educational Centres Movement* (1961).

2 T. Kelly, *A History of Adult Education in Great Britain* (1962).

3 J. W. Robertson Scott, *The Story of the Women's Institute Movement* (Idbury, 1925); Inez Jenkins, *History of the Women's Institute Movement in England and Wales* (1933).

PAGE 216

1 John Morgan, 'The National Council of Social Service', in H. A. Mess, *Voluntary Social Services* (1948), 80–105.
2 R. D. Waller, *Design for Democracy* (1956).
3 J. C. W. Reith, *Into the Wind* (1949).
4 C. V. Bailey, *The Listening School* (1957).
5 Andrew Buchanan, *The Film in Education* (1951), *Annual Abstracts of Statistics 1935–1946*, 72. *The Distribution and Exhibition of Cinematograph Films* (H.M.S.O. 7837, 1949). H. E. Browning and A. A. Sorrell, 'Cinemas and Cinema going in Great Britain', *Journal of the Royal Statistical Society*, CXVII (1954), 133–65.

PAGE 217

1 The influence here was that of Frank Pullinger who, as chief inspector of the technological branch from 1908, issued circular 776 of 1911.
2 W. P. Donald, J. B. Johnson, J. E. Pickles and Percival Sharp, *Education in Relation to Industry* (1912).

PAGE 218

1 F. E. Foden in *The Vocational Aspect*, III (1951), and E. R. Cradock, *ibid.*, XIII (1961).

PAGE 219

1 P. F. R. Venables, *Technical Education* (1955), 23–68.
2 This problem was posed, but not resolved, ten years earlier by a Royal Commission on Taxation in which the minority had declared themselves in favour of block grants (Cd 8515). See tables in A. T. Peacock and Jack Wiseman, *The Growth of Public Expenditure in the United Kingdom* (Princeton, 1961), 92.

PAGE 220

1 In two circulars (1185 of 1920 and 1190 of 1921).
2 A national demonstration against the economies was held on 4 March 1922 and 'Education Defence Committees' were formed in many areas. Teachers, to their great credit, offered and accepted a five per cent salary cut.
3 The Geddes proposals, which were intended to save £36 millions, involved the raising of the school-admission age to six, the reduction of the number, salaries and superannuation of teachers, of provision for school meals, medical inspection, special schools, free places to secondary schools, state scholarships and training grants. Fees were to be increased and so was the size of classes.

4 It reappeared, successfully this time in 1959, as a comprehensive grant to local authorities.

PAGE 221

1 David Ogg, *Herbert Fisher 1865–1940* (1947), 62.

2 H. V. Wiseman, 'The University Grants Committee', *Public Administration*, XXXIV (1956), XXV (1957), 185–6. Its first secretary was that very fine historian, G. M. Young.

PAGE 222

1 Sir Harry Melville, *The Department of Scientific and Industrial Research* (1962), 20–7.

PAGE 223

1 Eric Ashby, *Community of Universities* (1963) 61–91.

2 Asher Tropp, *The School Teachers* (1957), 246.

PAGE 224

1 E. V. Hollis, *Philanthropic Foundations and Higher Education* (Columbia, 1938); W. S. Rich and N. R. Deardoff, *American Foundations and their Fields* (1955). See the Reports of the Carnegie United Kingdom Trust from 1915 onwards.

2 Its four predecessors were a trust for the betterment of his own town of Dunfermline, another for the Universities of Scotland in 1901, the Carnegie Hero Fund Trust in 1908 and the Carnegie Corporation of New York in 1911. The income from 7·4 per cent of the Corporation's assets (some $135 million), may be used in certain areas of the British Commonwealth.

3 Beginning with Staffordshire in 1915 by 1921 there were 22 county schemes in existence in England and Wales and a further 17 in Scotland.

PAGE 225

1 This should be compared to the decline of the U.G.C. non-recurrent grants from £393,000 (for 1919–20) to £272,750 (for 1921–2), then to £48,285 (for 1922–3) and finally £19,000 (for 1923–4), their value is enhanced.

2 A. Flexner, *Universities American, English, German* (1930), 312.

PAGE 226

1 W. H. G. Armytage, 'Rockefeller Money and British Universities', *Universities Quarterly*, XI (1957), 254–61; R H. Bremner, *American Philanthropy* (1960).

2 H. R. Hamley, *Proceedings of the Child Guidance Inter-Clinic Conference of Great Britain* (1937); D. N. Hardcastle, 'The Child Guidance Clinic in America', *British Journal of Medical Psychology*, XIII (1933), pt. 4; G. S. Stevenson and S. Smith, *Child Guidance Clinics* (1934).

3 The Dalton plan was much discussed at the British Association meeting in 1920 and publicised by Belle Rennie, A. J. Lynch, C. W. Kimmins and others.

C. M. Fleming, *Research and the Basic Curriculum* (1946), 14. See R. D. Bramwell, *Elementary School Work 1900-1925* (1941), 4; W. H. Burston 'The Influence of John Dewey in English Official Reports', *International Review of Education*, VII (1961), 311-25; M. H. Thomas, *John Dewey; A Centennial Bibliography* (Chicago, 1962).

PAGE 227

1 Holmes had been impressed by these activities in a school at Sompting near Worthing. E. Sharwood Smith gave a good assessment of his work in *Report of the 22nd Conference of New Ideals in Education* (1936).

2 See, for further details, Edmond Holmes in Board of Education pamphlet No. 24; Josephine Ransome, *School of Tomorrow* (1919), E. Young, *The New Era in Education* (1920); Alice Woods, *Educational Experiments in England* (1920); Sir John Adams, *Modern Development in Educational Practice* (1927); William Boyd (ed.), *Towards a New Education* (1930); and W. J. McCallister, *The Growth of Freedom in Education* (1931), 403-65.

3 Edmond Holmes, *In Quest of an Ideal* (1920), 15 and 41. Holmes's later interest in the Albigensians and Cathari, his pantheism, and his ethical idealism resembled a kind of modern Buddhism. His son M. G. Holmes became deputy secretary of the Board of Education in 1931.

4 E. T. Bazeley, *Homer Lane and the Little Commonwealth* (1928).

5 See his *Schoolmaster's Harvest* (1954). Norman MacMunn, author of *A Path to Freedom in School* (1914), influenced his own account in *An Adventure in Education* (1917).

PAGE 228

1 Adolf Ferrière (1879-1960) was the son of a psychotherapist who in 1899 had founded the International Bureau of New Schools and in 1912 began to teach at the Institut J. J. Rousseau. His book *The Activity School* (1929) gives a good account of the movement.

2 William Boyd, 'The Basic Faith of the New Education Fellowship', in *Year Book of Education* (1957), 193-208. A superb account of the transatlantic background is given by Lawrence A. Cremin, *The Transformation of the School: Progressivism in American Education 1876-1957* (New York, 1961), 179-273.

3 Gerard Holmes, *The Idiot Teacher* (1952). E. F. O'Neill had addressed the New Ideals Group before going to Prestolee.

4 David Lampe, *Pyke, The Unknown Genius* (1959).

5 Susan Isaacs later became, from 1933 to 1943, head of the Department of Child Development at the London Institute of Education.

6 S. R. Slavson's techniques were so like those of J. L. Moreno that the latter remarked in *Who Shall Survive* (New York), 1953, lxi, 'he liked my concepts, and began to use them without quotation'.

PAGE 229

1 A. S. Neill, *Summerhill, A Radical Approach to Child Rearing*, 1960, xiv.
2 See, in addition to notes above, Bertrand Russell, *On Education* (1926) and *Education and the Social Order* (1938); T. Blewitt, *The Modern Schools Handbook* (1934); Joseph Wicksteed, *The Challenge of Childhood* (1936); Victor Bonham-Carter, *Dartington Hall, The History of An Experiment* (1958); and H. A. T. Child, *The Independent Progressive School* (1962).

PAGE 230

1 J. H. Badley, *Memories and Reflections* (1955), 183.
2 *Education 1935* (H.M.S.O. 1936), 4.
3 S. Freud, *Collected Papers* (1925), III, 149–295.

PAGE 231

1 Joshua Bierer, *Therapeutic Social Clubs* (1949); David Wills, *The Hawkspur Experiment* (1941); *The Barns Experiment* (1944).
2 E. C. Mack, *Public Schools and British Opinion since 1860* (New York, 1941), 285–9; Selina Gray (ed.), *Gray of Bradfield, A Memoir* (1931).
3 A. C. Benson, *The Schoolmaster* (1907), 55.

PAGE 232

1 E. Driver, *A Pathway to Dalcroze Eurhythmics* (1951).
2 Frank Fletcher, *After Many Days: A Schoolmaster's Memories* (1937).
3 See, for instance, S. P. B. Mais and Edmond Holmes in *The Fortnightly Review*, 1915, but especially Alec Waugh, *The Loom of Youth* (1917), the 'instigator of the unparalleled attack on the schools that followed the war' (Mack, *op. cit.*, 332).

PAGE 233

1 *The World of William Clissold* (1926), III, 704–7.
2 See his *Schoolmasters' Harvest* (1954).
3 During the war Gordonstoun was taken over by the Army and later Hahn's methods attracted the attention of the Admiralty and the War Office. A. Arnold Brown, *Unfolding Character* (1962).
4 T. C. Worsley, *Barbarians and Philistines: Democracy and Public School* (1940), 231 ff.
5 Lees Smith in *Hansard*, March 1940. One must remember that Bishop Creighton once called the public school 'a cross between a barracks and a workhouse', C. A. Arlington, *A Schoolmaster's Apology* (1914), 37. See also R. H. Tawney, 'The Problem of the Public Schools', *Political Quarterly*, April–June 1943, reprinted with alterations and additions by the W.E.A.
6 *The Spectator*, 9 February 1940, 175.

NOTES

PAGE 234

1 One story went that a school-teacher after describing, in rather unnecessary
detail, the story of the crucifixion, noticed that one little girl was near to
tears. Touched, the teacher patted the child, to comfort her. The child looked
up and said: 'Please miss, them men was proper bastards.'

PAGE 235

1 H. C. Dent, *Education in Transition* (1944), R. M. Titmuss, *Problems
of Social Policy, History of the Second World War*, U.K. Civil Series No. 1,
(1950), 500 ff.; Philip Whitaker, 'The Roman Catholics and the Education
Act of 1944', *Political Studies*, IV (1956), 186–90, Marjorie Cruikshank,
Church and State in English Education, 1870 to the Present Day (1963).

PAGE 237

1 K. R. Popper, *The Open Society and its Enemies* (1945), II, 210.
2 C. H. Waddington, *The Scientific Attitude* (1941), 54 and J. D. Bernal,
The Freedom of Necessity (1949). This was opposed by other scientists like
Michael Polanyi, A. G. Tansley and J. R. Baker, who formed a Society for
Freedom in Science in 1940. See 'The Course of the Controversy on
Freedom in Science', *Nature*, CLVIII (1946), 574–6. Waddington added to
the second edition of his book (118 ff.) material on war-time operational
research teams. His views can also be found in 'Science and Government',
The Political Quarterly, XIII (1942), 4 ff., and 'The Relation between Science
and Ethics', *Nature*, CXLVIII (1901), 270–4.
3 C. S. Lewis had just previously registered on the public mind with his
Screwtape Letters (1942).

PAGE 238

1 T. S. Eliot, *Notes towards the Definition of Culture* (1948), 101, 102, 109.
2 Sir Walter Moberly, *The Crisis in the University* (1949), 71.
3 T. S. Eliot, *op. cit.*, 37.
4 Karl Mannheim became Professor of Education in the University of London
in 1945. Before this he was a lecturer in sociology at the London School of
Economics. His *Ideology and Utopia* (1936), *Man and Society in an Age of
Reconstruction* (1940), and *Diagnosis of our Time* (1943), were overtures to the
foundation of an *International Library of Sociology and Social Reconstruction*
of which he was first editor.

PAGE 239

1 *Education and Social Change* (1940) and *Freedom in the Educative Society* (1947).
2 By 1960 the Ministry could report, 'It is now possible to say with certainty
that the "battle of the bulge has been won", and of the 2,600,000 places

provided half are in primary schools and half in secondary schools', *Report for 1959* (1961), 72.

PAGE 240

1 *Manchester Guardian*, 27 November 1961 and 26 February 1962, 14; Elizabeth Layton, *Building by Local Authorities* (1961).
2 See the report of Bishop Beck, Chairman of the Catholic Education Council in *Catholic Education*, December 1959, and Tudor David, *Church and School* (1961), 7–8.

PAGE 241

1 The Minister expressed his confidence on 19 May 1962 that day training colleges would become prominent features of the educational system.
2 *The Demand and Supply of Teachers 1960–1980* (H.M.S.O. 1962). This does not include any forecasts for the 80,000 teachers in universities (13,000), institutions for further education (20,000), training colleges (3,000) independent schools (31,000), direct grant schools (7,000) or other institutions.
3 An omission thought to be due to the stand taken by the Labour party at its 1942 Conference when it urged the development of a new type of school providing a variety of courses suitable to children of all types.
4 Political and Economic Planning XXIII, No. 396 (1956), 75; H. C. Dent, *Secondary Modern Schools* (1958).
5 D. V. Glass, 'Education and Social Change in Modern England', in M. Ginsberg (ed.), *Law and Opinion in the Twentieth Century* (1959). Undoubtedly, it was one of the causes for the formation of Associations for the Advancement of State Education in 1960; another being the publication of the government White Paper on Local Finance, 1957, which introduced block grants.
6 A. J. P. Taylor in *The Twentieth Century* (Oct. 1957), 294.

PAGE 242

1 Extensive research into the adequacy of selection methods was made by a committee of the British Psychological Society as reported in P. E. Vernon, *Secondary School Selection: A British Psychological Enquiry* (1957); A. Yates and D. A. Pidgeon, *Admission to Grammar Schools* (1957); Michael Young in *The Rise of the Meritocracy 1870–2033* (1958); *Year Book of Education* (1956), Sect. iv, Ch. 2, J. E. Floud (ed.); A. H. Halsey and F. M. Martin, *Social Class and Educational Opportunity* (1957).
2 See the L.C.C. inspectors' study of *London Comprehensive Schools* (1961). As defined by the Minister of Education on 4 March 1954 a comprehensive school was intended to provide all the facilities needed for secondary education in a given area without being organised in clearly defined sides.
3 A notable early champion of these was J. H. Whitehouse.

4 See the various development plans issued by these local authorities for full details. Also Reese Edwards, *The Secondary Technical School* (1960), and William Taylor, *The Secondary Modern School* (1963).

5 Stewart C. Mason, *The Leicestershire Experiment* (1957 and 1960).

6 A variant of the Croydon idea, though stemming from entirely different needs, is St Donat's in North Wales which opened in September 1962, and takes boys from 15 to 18.

7 High-lights of the controversy can be followed from Shena D. Simon, *Three Schools or One* (1948); *A Policy for Comprehensive Schools* (the Labour party, 1951); R. Pedley and others, *Comprehensive Education Today, an Interim Survey* (1955); Brian Simon, *The Common Secondary School* (1955) and *Inside the Comprehensive School* (1960); T. W. Miller, *Values in the Comprehensive School* (1961) .

PAGE 243

1

	January 1950		January 1960	
	Schools	Pupils	Schools	Pupils
All ages	6,357	954,962	1,281	267,350
Modern	3,227	1,095,247	3,837	1,637,879
Bilateral	31	13,467	57	38,359
Multi-lateral	4	3,524		
Comprehensive	10	7,988	130	128,835
Grammar	1,192	503,008	1,268	672,881
Technical	301	72,449	251	101,913

The extent of this experiment is shown by the above table indicating the various distribution of pupils between 1950 and 1960.

2 In 1861 there were 860,000 pupils in private schools (*Newcastle Commission*), in 1931 there were 400,000 (*Departmental Committee on Private Schools*), and in 1961, 495,600 (*Education in 1961*). Between 1950 and 1961 the percentage of children attending private and independent schools declined.

3 R. M. Titmuss, *Income Distribution and Social Change* (1962).

4 *Scientific Manpower, Report of the Committee appointed by the Lord President of the Council* (Chairman Sir Alan Barlow), H.M.S.O. 1946, Cmd 6824.

PAGE 244

1 *Higher Technological Education* (1946).

2 *The Future Development of Higher Technological Education—Report of the National Advisory Council on Education for Industry and Commerce* (1950). Strong support for a technical university was given by, amongst others, Lord Cherwell. See *The Case for a Technical University* (1950).

3 *Higher Technological Education. Statement of Government Policy for the Development of Higher Technological Education in Great Britain* (Cmd 8357, Sept. 1951).
4 *Education in 1951* (1952), 17.

PAGE 245

1 Anglo-American Council on Productivity pamphlets, *Training for Operatives, Training of Supervisors, Education for Management* and *Universities and Industry*. The number of successful candidates for the City and Guilds, the Ordinary National and the Higher National Certificates rose from 38,963, 9,739 and 4,421 in 1949, to 49,902, 12,443 and 6,940 respectively in 1954.
2 The pioneers in this were the Royal Technical College, Glasgow, in about 1880, followed by the Sunderland Technical College in 1903 and the Northampton Polytechnic in 1905. P. F. R. Venables, *Technical Education* (1955), 86. Following the report of the Advisory Council on Scientific Policy high-lighting the shortage of engineers, such courses increased from 70 (1954) to 100 (1955) to 154 (1956).
3 For the Select Committee's Report see *H. of C. Papers, Session 1952–3*, No. 273 and for the Ministry's reply see No. 295.
4 The increase of students is shown by the following table:

	1951–2	1952–3	1953–4
Full-time	54,017	56,000	59,000
Part-time	333,830	353,000	372,000
Evening	1,031,097	1,829,000	1,860,000

5 *Report on the Recruitment of Scientists and Engineers in the Engineering Industry* (1955).
6 *Technical Education* (Cmd 9703, 1956).
7 *Education in 1956*, 30.
8 Circular 305 (1956).

PAGE 246

1 John Vaizey, *The Finance of Education* (1958).
2 W. B. Gallie, *A New University: A. D. Lindsay and the Keele Experiment* (1960), 52.

PAGE 247

1 As James Dundonald wrote, 'Overnight the idea of a university hit a large number of local authorities. There, it seemed, was the money; there, certainly were others already in the swim.' *Letters to a Vice-Chancellor* (1962), 20. Such a queue of interested parties presented themselves as likely candidates for universities that *Punch* ran a feature on them. The Mormons were reported as being interested in promoting a university in Lancashire.

2 Sir Geoffrey Crowther, 'The Future of Britain's Universities', *Education Today*, XI (1961) 2, 13–19, 23 (1961).

3 *Education in 1960* (1961), 72, 75.

4 Among the 6,026 full-time and 3,332 sandwich and 25,291 part-time students at the C.A.T.S. in 1960 there were 4,600 degree and Dip. Tech. students.

PAGE 248

1 *The Years of Crisis, Report of the Labour Party's Study Group on Higher Education* (1963).

2 *Higher Education Report of the Committee appointed by the Prime Minister under the Chairmanship of Lord Robbins 1961–63*, Cmnd 2154 (H.M.S.O. 1963).

PAGE 249

1 *Ibid.*, Appendix 1. 79 considered that this reserve of ability 'on present trends' was 'most unlikely to be mobilised within the next twenty years'.

2 *Crowther Report*, 472, 51.

3 At first the Ministry of Education was disturbed by the number of early leavers who partly because of the social assumptions of the home, partly because of a 'desire to assert their independence and grown up status', went to work. More than a third of the leavers 'at least' were influenced by such feelings but by 1957 the Report of the Ministry (p. 17) called attention to this new trend. The figures quoted are from *Statistics of Education* (H.M.S.O. 1963), 11 and 17.

PAGE 250

1 See *Statistics of Education 1961, Part 2* (*1962*), 12–13, for fuller figures. This was the first time these were presented separately from the Ministry Annual Report.

2 *Examinations in Secondary Schools* (1947), 4.

PAGE 251

1 *The General Certificate of Education and Sixth Form Studies* (*Third Report of the S.S.E.C.*) (1960).

2 *Secondary School Examinations other than the G.C.E.* (1960); *The Certificate of Secondary Education* (1961).

3 *Half our Future. A Report of the Central Advisory Council for Education* (England). H.M.S.O. (1963)

PAGE 252

1 For the names of the first members see *The Times*, 3 July 1964, 17.

2 *The Youth Service in England and Wales* (1960).

3 *Ministry of Labour Gazette*, LXVIII (June 1960), 236.

PAGE 253

1 R. H. Tawney, *Juvenile Employment and Education*, Sidney Ball Lecture, 2 May 1934 (Oxford, 1934).
2 Ministry of Labour, *Report of an Enquiry into Apprenticeship and Training for the Skilled Occupations of G.B. and Northern Ireland 1925–1926*, VII, General Report (1928).
3 *Report on Recruitment and Training of Juveniles for Industry* (The Ince Committee, H.M.S.O. 1945).

PAGE 254

1 *Report of the Carr Committee on the Recruitment and Training of Young Workers in Industry* (H.M.S.O. 1958).
2 *Training of Operatives*, Anglo-American Council on Productivity (1951).
3 Gertrude Williams, *Recruitment to Skilled Trades* (1957), 117; Kate Liepmann, *Apprenticeship, An Enquiry into its Adequacy under Modern Conditions* (1960), P. F. R. Venables and W. J. Williams, *The Smaller Firm and Technical Education* (1961), point out that 47·5% of employees belong to 4·7% of all manufacturing industries.
4 Circular 1/59, 13 April. *Technical Education—The Next Step* (1959); *Better Opportunities in Technical Education* (Cmd 1254, Jan. 1961).
5 *Education in 1961* (1962), 34.

PAGE 255

1 *Report of the Advisory Committee on Further Education for Commerce* (1959); *The McMeeking Report*.
2 M. Argyle and Trevor Smith, *Training Managers* (Acton Society Trust, 1962), 14–22.
3 *British Iron and Steel Federation Management College Ashorne Hill* (N.d.), 66.

PAGE 256

1 H. A. Clegg, A. J. Killick and Rex Adams, *Trade Union Officers* (1961), 228, found that only six per cent of full-time officers and three per cent of full-time secretaries had no further education since leaving school.
2 G. Woodcock (ed.), *Report of Proceedings at the 93rd Annual Congress* (1961), 176–81.

PAGE 257

1 For the background see Burton Paula, *British Broadcasting in Transition* (1961).
2 D. N. Chester (ed.), *The Organisation of British Central Government 1914–1956* (1957); F. M. G. Willson, 'The Organisation of British Central Government 1955–1961', *Public Administration*, XL (1962), 159–206.

NOTES

1 Duncan Crow, *Commonwealth Education, Britain's Contribution* (H.M.S.O., 1961), 77.
2 *Some Economic Aspects of Educational Development in Europe* (International Universities Bureau, Paris, 1961), 9. See also the prelude to the 1963 Campaign, *Investment for National Survival. The Report of an Independent Committee under the chairmanship of Sir Charles Morris on the expenditure needed for future educational development* (N.U.T., 1962).
3 *The Committee of Enquiry into the Organisation of Civil Science.* Cmnd 2171 (H.M.S.O., 1963).

1 E. B. South, 'Some Psychological Aspects of Committee Work', *Journal of Applied Psychology*, XI (1927), 346–68, 437–69; G. Homans, *The Human Group* (1951); W. R. Bion, 'Experiences in Groups', *Human Relations*, I, 314, 20; II, 13–22, 295–303; III, 3–14, 395–402; IV, 221–7 (1948–51); J.Klein, *The Study of Groups* (1956); W. J. H. Sprott, *Human Groups* (1958); Hugh Thomas (ed.), *The Establishment* (1959), 9–13.
2 *Schools Council: the First Three Years*, London; H.M.S.O., 1968.

1 The decision to raise the school leaving age to 16 was postponed in 1968 to 1972/3.

1 *Education and Science in 1967: Being a Report of the Department of Education and Science*, Cmnd. 3564, H.M.S.O., 1968, pp. 33–4.
2 *Public Schools Commission First Report, Volume 1 Report*, London; H.M.S.O., 1968.

1 Sir Eric Ashby, *Hands Off the Universities?* The Foundation oration delivered at Birkbeck College, 1968, p. 14. His history of the Committee of Vice-Chancellors and Principals *Community of Universities,* Cambridge University Press, 1963, is a useful introduction to its reorganisation four years later into five 'divisions'.
2 *The Government of Colleges of Education*, H.M.S.O., 1966 (The Weaver Report).

1 *Plan for Polytechnics and Other Colleges: Higher Education in the Further Education System*, Cmnd. 3006, London; H.M.S.O., 1966.
2 Eric E. Robinson, *The New Polytechnics*, London; Cornmarket, 1968.

PAGE 264

1 *Report of the Committee on the Age of Majority* (Chairman: Hon. Mr Justice Latey) Cmnd. 3342, H.M.S.O., 1967.
2 David Riesman, *Constraint and Variety in American Education* (Lincoln, Nebraska, 1956), 52.

PAGE 265

1 J. H. Dunning, *American Investment in British Manufacturing Industry* (1958), 310; James MacMillan & Bernard Harris, *The American Take-over of Britain* (1968).
2 For more detail see W. H. G. Armytage, *The Rise of the Technocrats* (1965), pp. 238–260 and 286–302, and *The American Influence on English Education* (1967), pp. 97–106.
3 Sir Gordon Sutherland, *Emigration of Scientists from the United Kingdom* (1963).
4 *The Times*, 19 February 1963.

PAGE 266

1 *The Brain Drain: Report of the Working Group on Migration*, Cmnd. 3417, H.M.S.O., 1967.
2 *Report of the Enquiry into the Flow of Candidates in Science and Technology into Higher Education*, Cmnd. 3541, H.M.S.O., 1968. The growth of sixth forms and the expansion of certain fields of univerities between 1954 and 1964 has also been monitored. Between these two dates the number of passes at 'A' level in Economics increased by 465% from 1,263 to 7,138, whereas those in Latin by only 24%—from 4,628 to 5,772. Mathematics, desired as a basic component of all 'A' level studies by Dainton, increased by 169% from 13,017 to 34,991. See *Statistics of Education Part three,* H.M.S.O., 1966 p. 10, for more revealing detail.

PAGE 267

1 H. J. Laski, *The Danger of Being a Gentleman and other Essays* (1939), 22.
2 *Report of a Committee on the Civil Service*, Cmnd. 3638, H.M.S.O., 1968 (The Fulton Committee).
3 Committee on Manpower Resources for Science and Technology, *The Flow into Employment of Scientists, Engineers and Technologists. Report of the Working Group on Manpower for Scienctific Growth*, Cmnd. 3780, H.M.S.O., 1968, p. 106.

PAGE 268

1 Alisdair Fairley, 'National Universities', *The Listener*, Vol. 80, No. 2064, p. 519. Concomitantly this has accelerated the rise of predictive groups and extrapolatory fantasies for which see W. H. G. Armytage, *Yesterday's*

NOTES

Tomorrows (1968) and Michael Young (ed.) *Forecasting and the Social Sciences* (1968).

2 *The Structure of the Public Library Service in England and Wales,* Cmnd. 660, H.M.S.O., 1959.

3 See *A University of the Air,* Cmnd. 2922, H.M.S.O., 1966.
The deployment of mass media in the primary and secondary schools has of course been accelerated by the establishment of B.B.C. local radio stations in the large towns since 1967. These offer opportunities for children themselves to participate in programmes.

4 See F. R. Leavis, *Two Cultures, The Significance of C.P. Snow with an Essay on Sir Charles Snow's Rede Lecture by Michael Yudkin* (1962), 45; and C.P. Snow's reply in *The Times Literary Supplement,* 25 October 1963, 829–44.

PAGE 269

1 *15 to 18: Report of the Central Advisory Council for Education in England* (The Crowther Report), H.M.S.O., 1959, p. 412.

2 *ibid,* p. 412. With striking prescience it continued: 'the custom of being treated as an adult in the conventions of speech and administration may be the best way of eliciting genuine mature behaviour in place of the rebelliousness which so easily springs up as resentment at any fancied affront to their still insecure sense of adult dignity'.

3 *Where,* June 1966.

4 Brian Macarthur 'Sixth Form or College', *The Times,* 24 May 1969, 8. For the development of the junior college idea in England see W. H. G. Armytage 'Secondary Education' in B. Crick, *Essays in Reform: A Centenary Tribute.* (1967), 142–4. In all this the needs of the part-time student should not be forgotten. When the Crowther committee reported, one in eleven students climbed the National Certificate ladder from bottom to top and only one in thirty did so in the standard time (p. 367). Later Lady Ethel Venables suggested that 'colleges in the future will have still larger numbers of students with a greater spread of ability and interest, and with ambitions and attitudes to work and study still fluid. To achieve the least frustration a permissive and open situation coupled with a guidance programme based on objective assessments will be needed. It will be surprising therefore if the local colleges in Britain do not come to resemble in some respects state colleges in America where the desirability of universal education to the age of eighteen is commonly accepted' (*The Young Worker at College: A Study of a Local Tech.,* London, Faber & Faber, 1967, p. 227). This seems to endorse the argument for providing American style junior colleges, from which students can 'go out prepared for activities that satisfy them instead of being branded as failures. They cross the finishing line before growing weary of the race.' Burton R. Clark quoted in 'The "Cooling-Out" Function in Higher Education', *American Journal of Sociology,* LXV (1960), pp. 569–576. See

323

also his study *The Open Door College: A Case Study*, London (1960) in which he predicted (p. 7) that the junior college 'will assume a larger place in American education during the next half century'. For, as the educational escalator becomes more efficient, there is a need to guide, mollify and accommodate those incapable of travelling along the highways of opportunity. This incapability breeds frustration and recalcitrance: qualities described by a distinguished sociologist as 'a symptom of dissociation between culturally prescribed aspirations and socially structured avenues for realising those aspirations.' (Robert K. Merton, 'Social Structure and Anomie' in *Social Theory and Social Structure* (new ed. Glencoe, III, Free Press, 1957, p. 134)).

INDEX

Associations—*continued*
Higher Education of Working Men, to promote the, 193
Historical, 188
Ladies Sanitary, 131
Mathematical, 188
Modern Languages, 188
Organisation of Academical Study, 168
Organising Secretaries for Technical and Secondary Education, 173
Preparatory Schools, 199
Private Schools, 157
Promotion of the Employment of Women, for the, 130
Science Masters, 188
Astbury, W. T., 226
astronomy, 17, 25, 67
Athenaeums, 99
athletics, 233
attendance, 110–11, 148, 153
Aubrey, John, 40
Aurelian Society, 55
aviation, 64, 87, 190
Ayrton, W. E., 165

Babbage, Charles, 84
Bablake School, Coventry, 32
backwardness, 206
Bacon, Sir Francis, 13, 14, 15–16, 20, 21, 23, 24, 25
Bacon, Sir Nicholas, 13
Baden-Powell, Col. R. S., 210–11
Badley, J. H., 199, 229–30
Bain, Alexander, 158
Baker, Henry, 50–1, 57
Balfour, A. J., 181, 186; Graham, 308
Ball, Hannah, 74
balloons, 64, 87
Banks, Sir Joseph, 56, 287
Baptists, 53, 75
Barbauld, Mrs, 83
Barbier, C., 89
Barlow Report (1946), 244–7
Barlow, William, 11
Barnard Castle, 123
Barnard, Sir Thomas, 89, 90, 92
Barnett, Canon S. A., 193
Barrington School, 92
Bateman-Champain, J. V., 89
Bath, 59, 62

Bath and West of England Agricultural Society, 59, 122
Bathurst, Dr, 22, 24
Battersea Training College, 114
Baxter Richard, 23
Beale, Miss D., 130
Beale, S., 83
Beard, Charles, 195
Beaumont, 128, 165
Bedales, 199, 229–30
Beddoes, Thomas, 64, 87
Bede, Cuthbert, 291
Bedford, 6, 28
Bedford College for Women, 180
Bedford Modern School, 128
Bees, Fable of the, 48
Belfast, Queen's University of, 294, 307
Bell, Dr Andrew, 90, 92
Bellers, John, 42
Beloe Report (1960), 251
Belsham, Thomas, 70
Benson, A. C., 231
Bentham, Jeremy, 63, 84, 92–3, 110
Bentley, Richard, 34
Berlin, University of, 166
Bernal, J. D., 237
Bernard, Sir Thomas, 89, 92
Bernouilli, N., 55
Beveridge Committee on Television, 256
Beveridge, W. H. (later Lord), 193
Bibliotheca Technologica, 34
Billingsley, Henry, 8, 9, 10
biology, 246, 302
Birkbeck, Dr George, 59, 97, 99, 103
Birley, H., 143
Birmingham, 49, 60, 69, 74, 82–5, 99, 102, 109, 127, 138, 143, 144, 164, 166, 168, 242
Education Committee, 242
Grammar School, 104–5
League, 138, 143, 144
Lunar Society, 60
school board, 145
University, 164, 166, 168, 191
Birrell, A., 201, 307
birth rate, 110, 239, 248, 287
bishops, influence of, 20–1, 28–9, 66, 91, 152, 193, 234
Bishop's Stortford College, 104
Blackheath Proprietory School, 105
Rugby F.C., 134

Doddridge, Philip, 52, 55, 260
Donkin, B., 98
Donnelly, J. F. D., 120, 121, 161-2, 177
Dorchester Company, 19
Dossie, Robert, 57
Douai, 4, 68
Downside, 68
drainage, 55
Drake, Sir Francis, 19
drama in school, 86, 215
Dress Reform Society, 131
Drury, H. J. T., 85
Dryden, John, 67
'Dual System, The', 143-5, 185-7, 235
Dublin, Trinity College, 4; University
    College, 307
'Dunces' Certificates', 104, 150
Durham, Bishop of, 66, 92
    University of, 22, 23, 25
Dury, John, 20, 22, 24
Dymock, Cressy, 22

Eames, John, 37, 134
early leavers, 319
East India Company, 87-8
East Lancashire Union, 99
East Midlands Education Union, 217,
    251
École des Ponts et Chaussées, 88
    Polytechnique, 87
    des Roches, 199
economics, 176
Economist, The, 142, 156, 258
Edgeworth, Maria, 80-2, 83, 84
Edgeworth, Prof. F. Y., 159
Edgeworth, Richard Lovell, 60, 73, 80,
    87
Edinburgh Review, 84, 93-4
Edinburgh School of Arts, 98
Edinburgh, University of, 53, 60, 103,
    225
Education
    Acts (see Acts)
    adaptability and, 310
    anticipated experience, 54
    character building, 79
    civil liberty and, 54
    compulsory age of (10) 150, (11)
        177, 182, 186, (12) 186, (13)
        186, (15) 208, 213, 239, 253, (16)
        249-50, 251, 254, 258
    crime, 41

degrees in, 157
economic growth and, 33, 225, 258
experiments in, 19, 25, 37-8, 62-3,
    82-5, 86, 90, 198-200, 215, 228,
    231-4
factories and, 77, 78, 79, 111
formal education, English mistrust
    of, 267
happiness, 54, 93
health, 38, 77, 78, 112, 131-5
individualising role of, 195
ingredient of economic growth, 3,
    15-16, 21, 29-34, 42-3, 52-3, 55-
    56, 57-61, 82-4, 88, 98, 120-1,
    138, 162, 164, 168-9, 196-7, 217-
    219, 243-6, 255-6, 258
institutes of, 223, 247, 302
intelligence, 101
lag with society, 267
low esteem of, 221
'member for', 113
minister of, 112, 179, 238
moralising force, 59, 78, 81, 90,
    136-7, 259
prophylactic against crime, 41
quaternary, 262
'rebellion', 2-4, 39-40, 69-70, 75,
    93, 98, 99, 108, 182, 269
redemptive potential of, 100-1, 114,
    238
sifter for élite, 174, 183
social class, 54, 242, 253
social mobility, 165, 172, 175, 205
social sedation, 69, 99, 194, 260
socialism, 192, 195, 200
sociological determinants, 39, 43, 54,
    58, 69-70, 140, 141, 207, 242, 253
state and, 54, 88, 96, 111-12, 136-7,
    138
study of, 156-8, 187, 198, 262
theology of, 194, 308
Education Department Whitehall, 119,
    122, 141, 162-3, 171, 182
Education Defence Committees, 311;
    Society, 158
Educational measurement, 100-1, 158,
    228-9, 235-6, 304; Settlements
    Association, 215
    Technology, 216
Education Muddle and the Way Out
    (1901), 185
Edwards, Passmore, 193

Herbart, J. F., 169, 303–4
Hereford, 6
Herefordshire County Council, 240
Hertz, Heinrich, 168
Heylin, Peter, 19
Heywood, Benjamin, 102, 290
Heywood, James, 117, 284
Hicks, W. M., 168, 189
Higgins, William, 64
High Wycombe, 88
higher elementary (or grade) schools,
    146, 151, 154, 165, 175, 183, 187,
    306
    local examination, 169
Hill, Herbert, 109
Hill, Rowland, 82–5
Hill, Thomas Wright, 82–5, 286
Historical Association, 188
historicism, 237
history, 3, 36, 52–3, 94, 125, 126, 150,
    176, 185, 237, 250, 267, 321
history of science, 160, 215
Hives, Lord, 245
Hoare, Sir Samuel, 203
Hobbes, Thomas, 40, 47–8
Hoby, Sir Thomas, 13
Hodgskin, Thomas, 97, 98
Hodgson, James, 30
Hofmann, A. W. von, 120, 121, 166
Hogg, Quintin, 136
Holland, 53, 54, 60, 63, 112, 114
Holmer, Andrew, 12
Holmes, E. G. A., 203, 227, 308, 313;
    Sir Maurice, 308, 313, 314
Home Office, 195, 196
Homer, 67
Hook, Dr W. F., 115
Hooke, Robert, 25
Hopkins, Sir F. G.,
Horner, Leonard, 98, 103, 110, 112,
    114
H.O.R.S.A. Huts, 239
Horsley, Samuel, 75
Houghton, John, 32, 56
How, Bishop Walsham, 134
Howard, Henry, 35
Howson, 227
Hoxton Academy, 53
Huddersfield, 99, 102
Hues, Robert, 17
Hughes, Thomas, 109, 133
Huguenots, 287

Hull, 67
    Proprietary School, 105
    University, 246
Hullah, J. P., 115
Humanism, 230, 238
Hume, D., 48
Hume, Joseph, 84
Hungerford, 28
Hunt, Leigh, 67
Hunter, John, 56
Huntingford, James, 59
Hutton, Charles, 61
Huxley, Aldous, 109; Julian, 109, 237;
    T. H., 84, 121, 136, 137, 146, 158–
    159, 161–3, 164, 170, 171, 279,
    302, 303, 306
Hyde, R. R., 193
hydraulic engines, 59
hygienic standards, 177–8, 209

immigrants, 116–17
Independent Television Authority,
    256–7
India, 73, 88–9
Indian Civil Service, 121
industrial
    classes, 138
    college, 42, 145, 218, 266
    education, 254, 310
    exhibitions, 57, 59, 93
        (1851) 118, 132, 163, 168, 190
        (1867) 138, 163
    Health Board, 206
    management, 255–6
    opposition to education, 162
    Training Act (see apprenticeship),
        254, 269
    Welfare Society, 193
Inns of Court, 13–14
Inspectors, 2, 12, 42, 78, 79, 83, 150–1,
    163, 277
    of Chemistry, 58
    County, 176, 203
    Factory, 79, 111–12, 114, 124
    influence of, 112, 150–1, 187, 251
    Medical, 147, 179
    School, 115, 124, 125, 127, 129,
        141
    South Kensington, 177
Institute of Education, 223
    of the Blessed Virgin Mary, 117
Institution of Civil Engineers, 98

UNIVERSITY OF OXFORD
DEPARTMENT OF EDUCATIONAL STUDIES
15, NORHAM GARDENS, OXFORD. OX2 6PY